D1074663

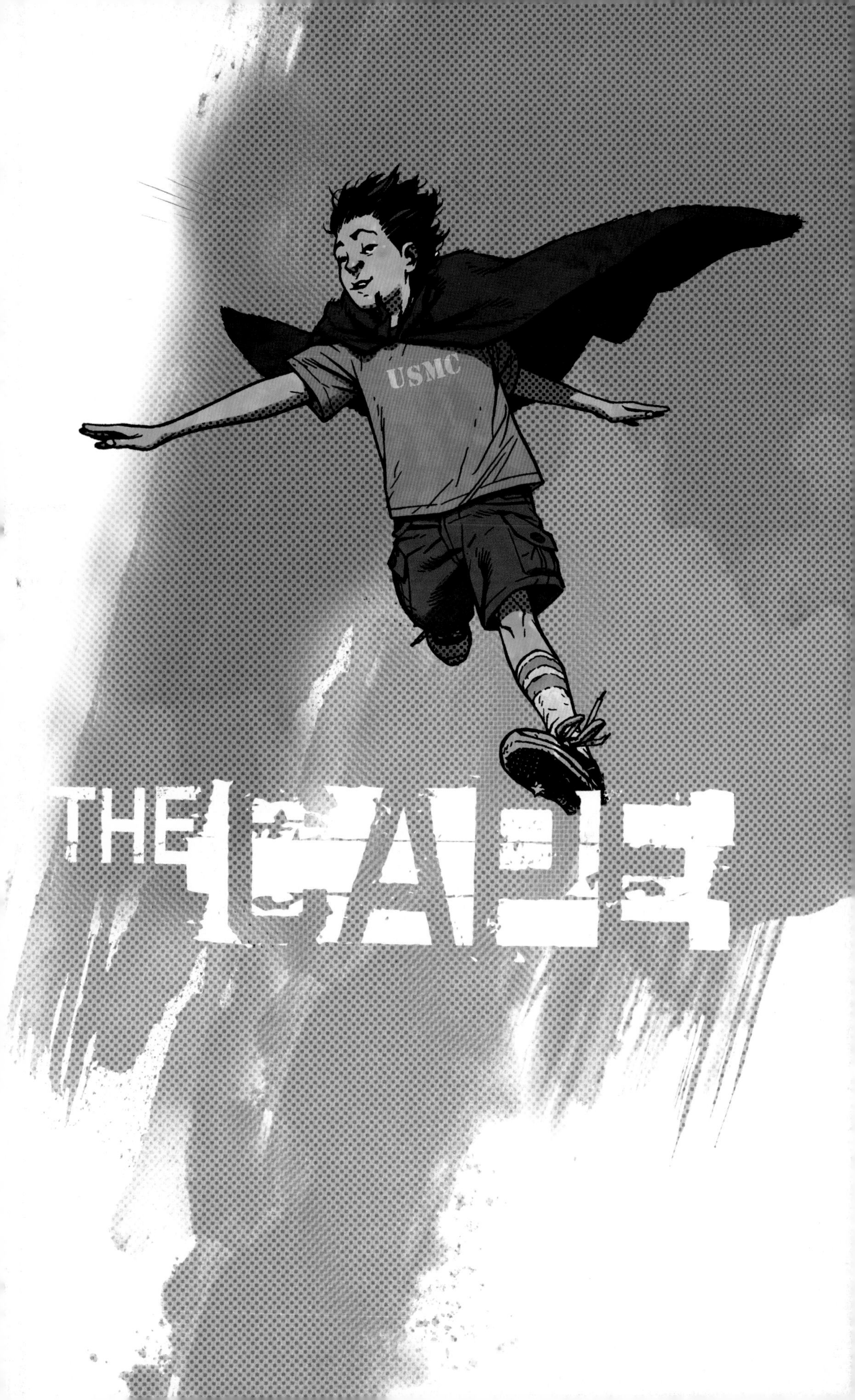
USMC
THE CAPE

WRITTEN BY **Jason Ciaramella**

BASED ON THE SHORT STORY "THE CAPE" BY **Joe Hill**

ART BY **Zach Howard**

COLORS BY **Nelson Daniel**

LETTERS BY **Shawn Lee** AND **Robbie Robbins**

SERIES EDITS BY **Chris Ryall**

CREATIVE CONSULTANT **Joe Hill**

COVER BY **Zach Howard**

COVER COLOR BY **Nelson Daniel**

COLLECTION EDITS BY **Justin Eisinger**

AND **Alonzo Simon**

COLLECTION DESIGN BY **Robbie Robbins**

Special thanks to Mickey Choate and Nick Runge.

The Cape created by Joe Hill.

IDW founded by Ted Adams, Alex Garner, Kris Oprisko, and Robbie Robbins | International Rights Representative, Christine Meyer: christine@gfloystudio.com

ISBN: 978-1-61377-196-9

15 14 13 12 1 2 3 4

IDW

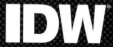

Ted Adams, CEO & Publisher
Greg Goldstein, President & COO
Robbie Robbins, EVP/Sr. Graphic Artist
Chris Ryall, Chief Creative Officer/Editor-in-Chief
Matthew Ruzicka, CPA, Chief Financial Officer
Alan Payne, VP of Sales

Become our fan on Facebook **facebook.com/idwpublishing**
Follow us on Twitter **@idwpublishing**
Check us out on YouTube **youtube.com/idwpublishing**
www.IDWPUBLISHING.com

Originally published as THE CAPE ONE SHOT and THE CAPE Issues #1–4.

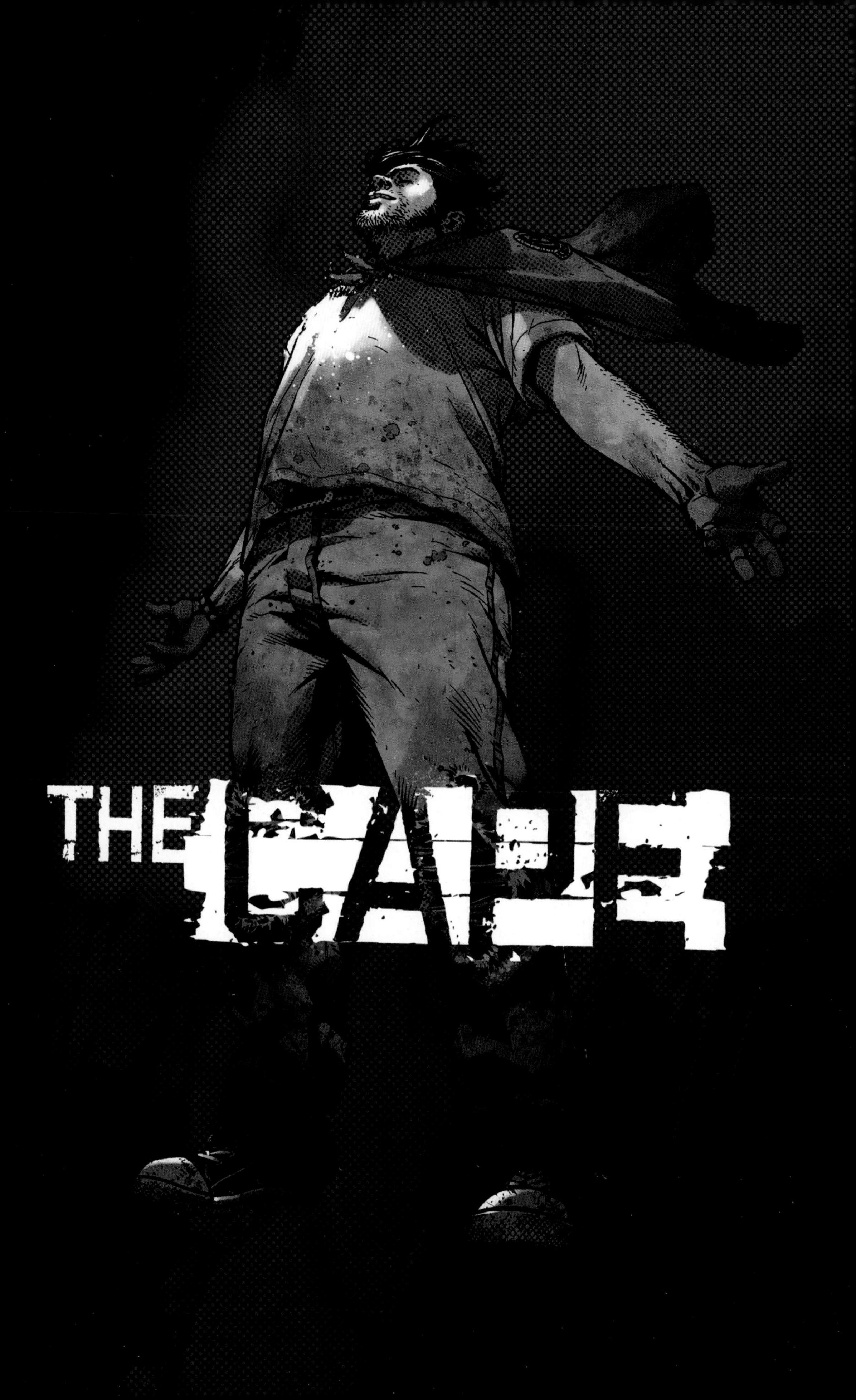
THE CAPE

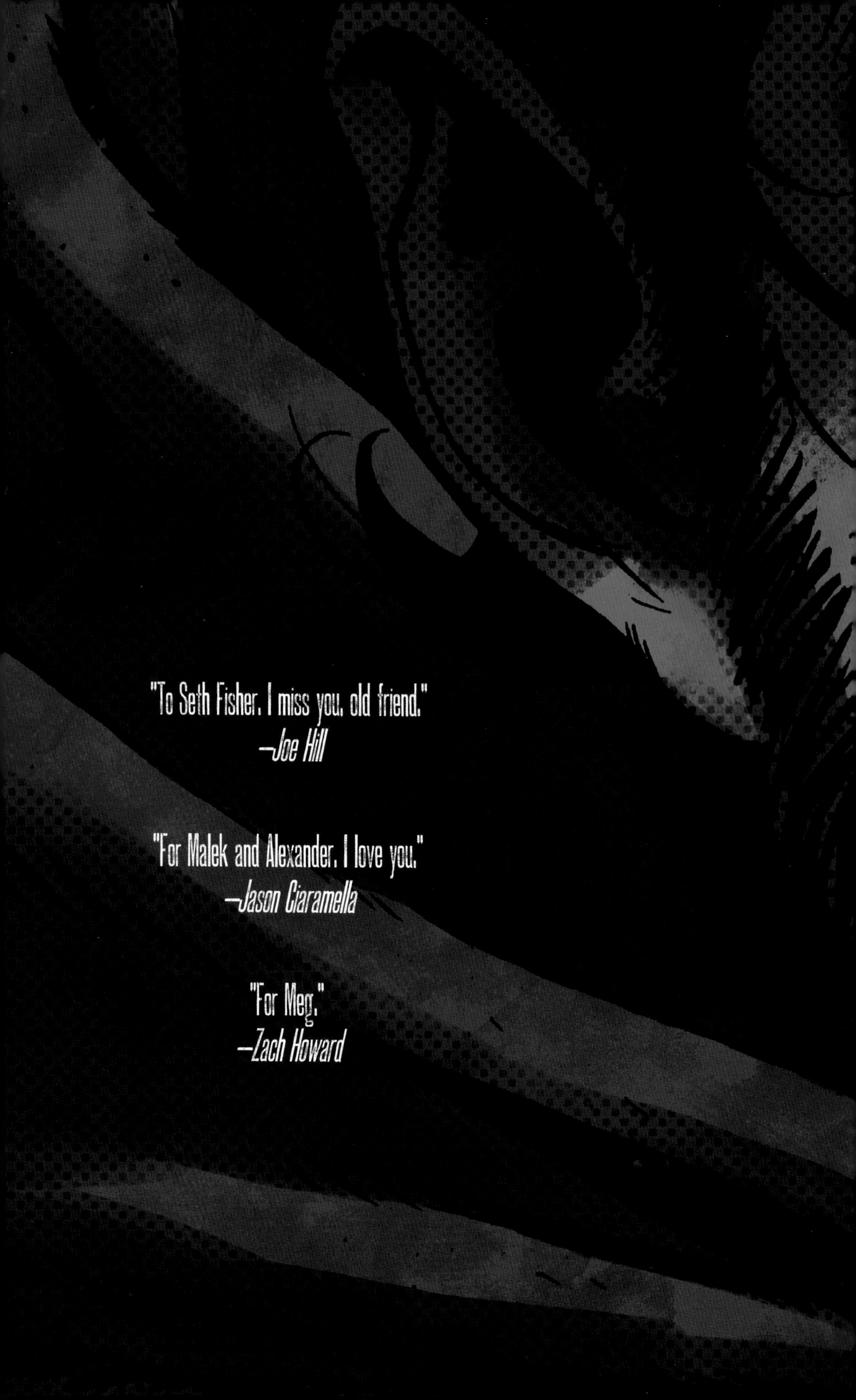

"To Seth Fisher. I miss you, old friend."
—*Joe Hill*

"For Malek and Alexander. I love you."
—*Jason Ciaramella*

"For Meg."
—*Zach Howard*

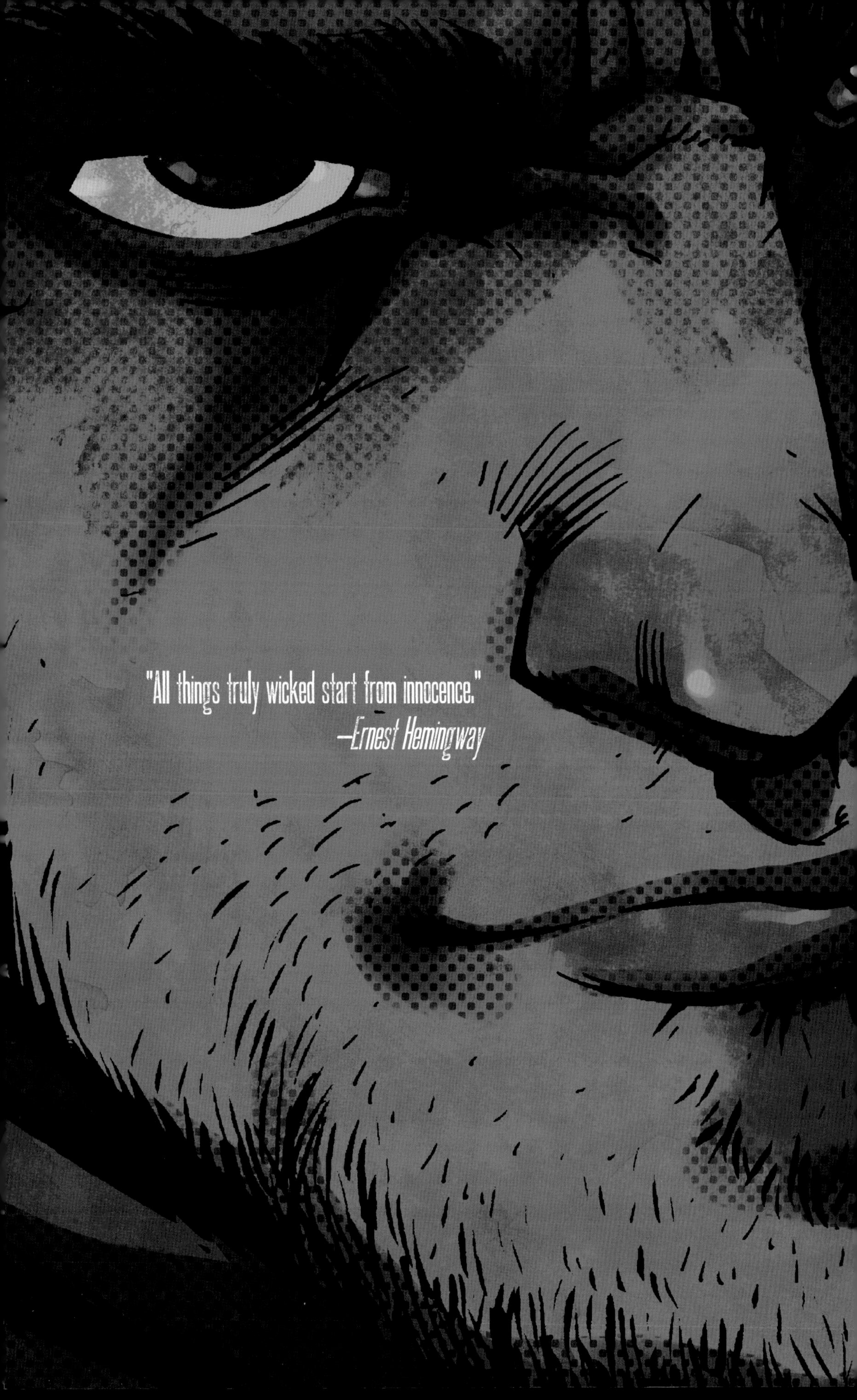
"All things truly wicked start from innocence."
—Ernest Hemingway

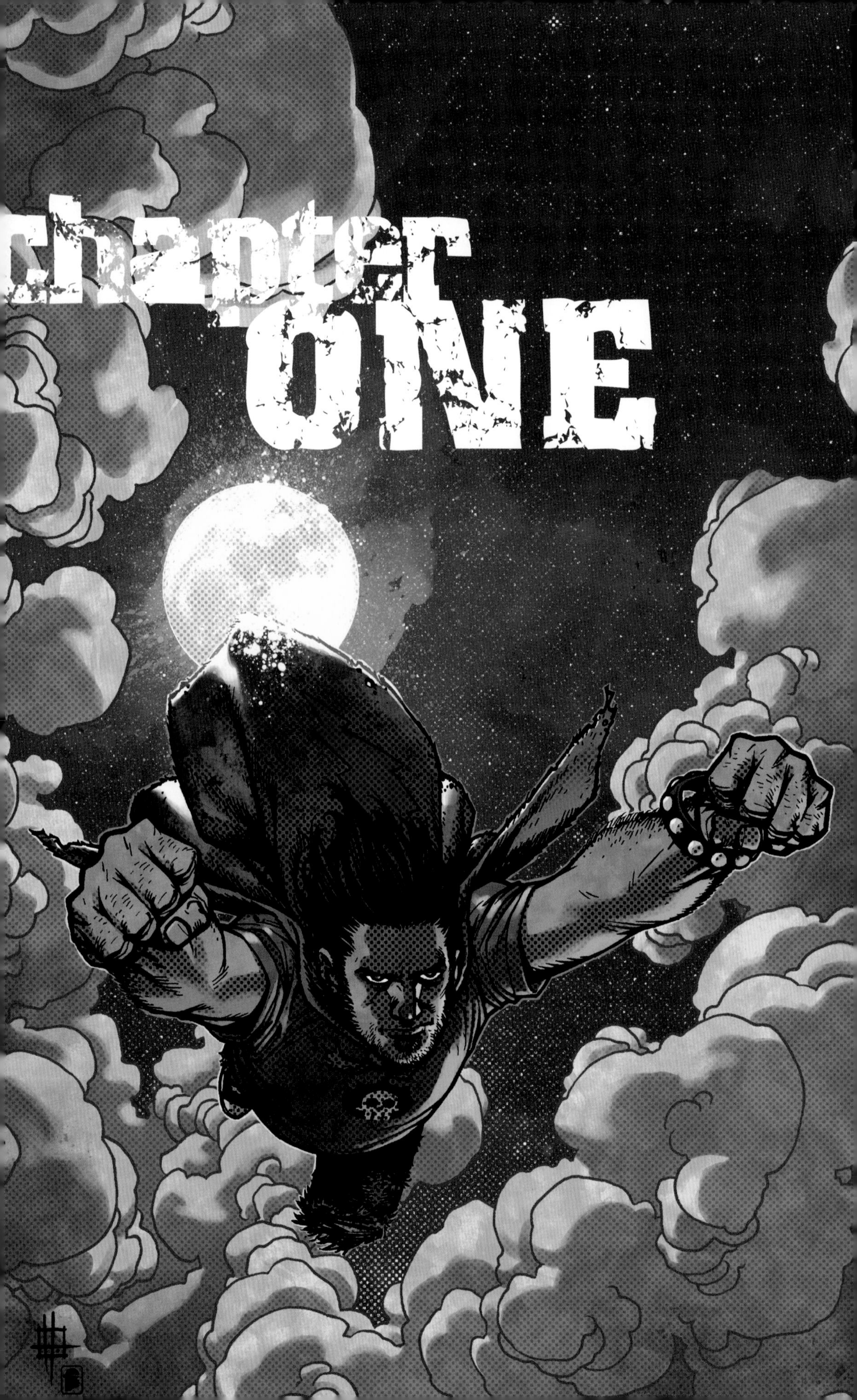
chapter
ONE

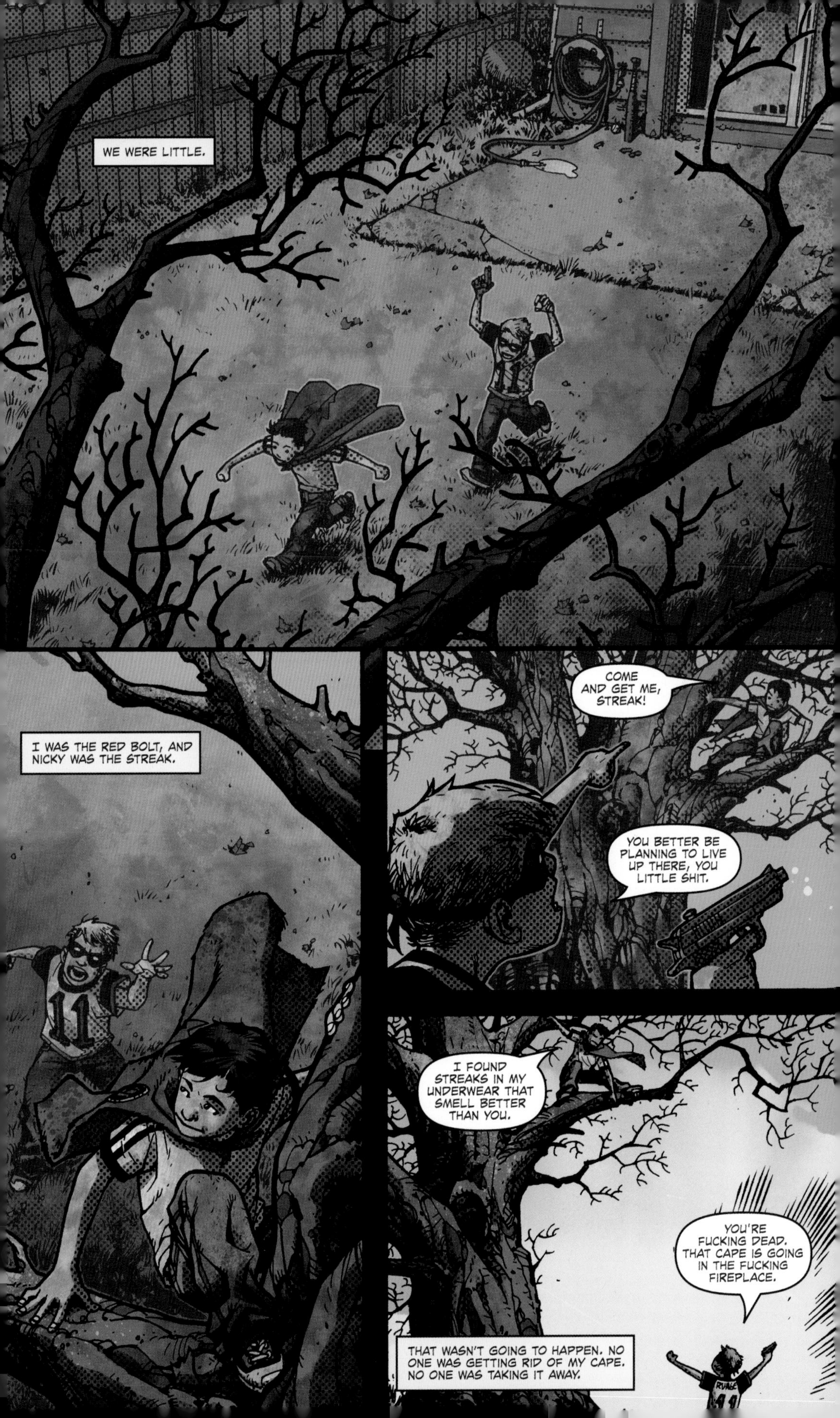
WE WERE LITTLE.
I WAS THE RED BOLT, AND NICKY WAS THE STREAK.
COME AND GET ME, STREAK!
YOU BETTER BE PLANNING TO LIVE UP THERE, YOU LITTLE SHIT.
I FOUND STREAKS IN MY UNDERWEAR THAT SMELL BETTER THAN YOU.
YOU'RE FUCKING DEAD. THAT CAPE IS GOING IN THE FUCKING FIREPLACE.
THAT WASN'T GOING TO HAPPEN. NO ONE WAS GETTING RID OF MY CAPE. NO ONE WAS TAKING IT AWAY.

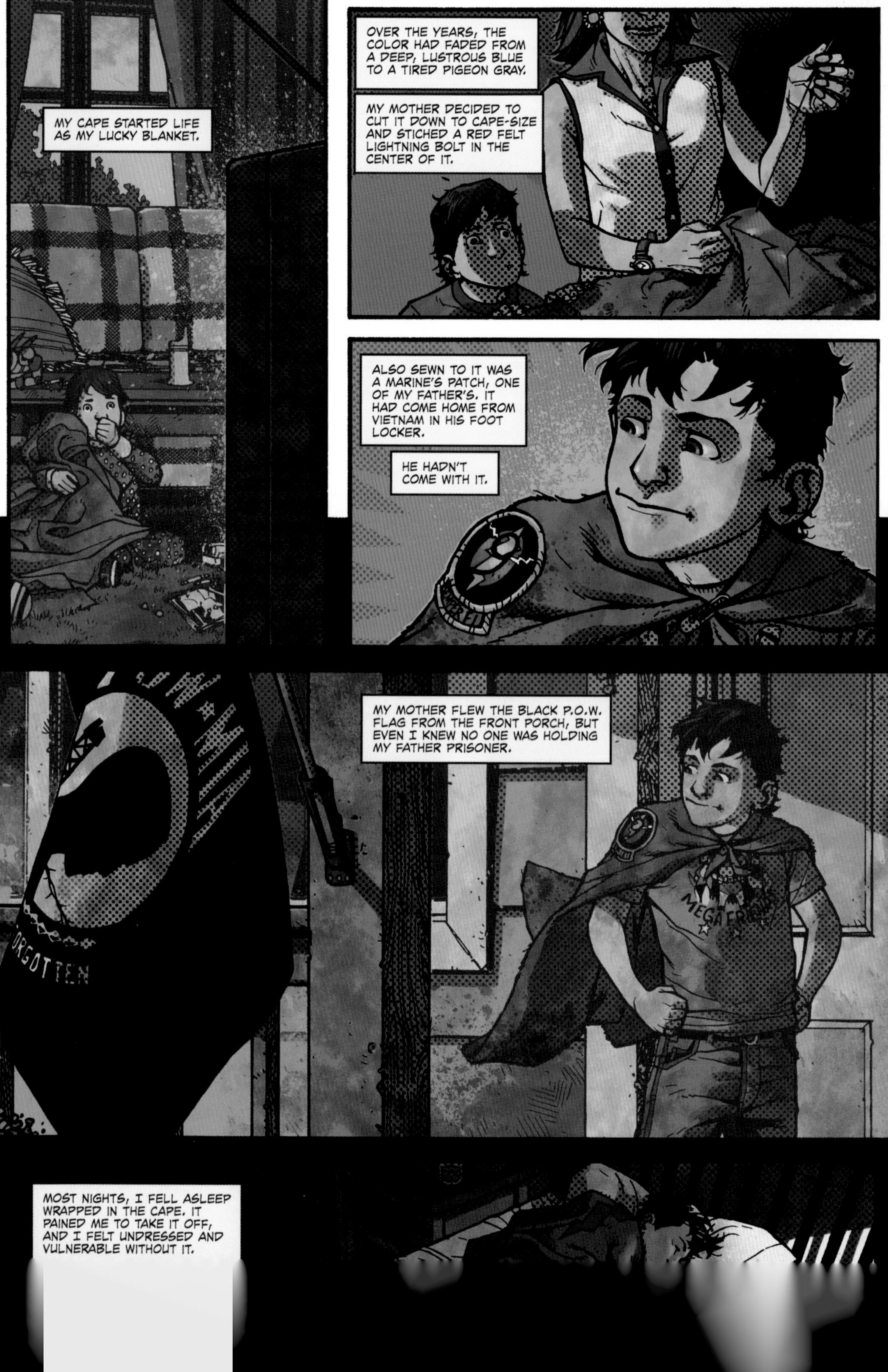
MY CAPE STARTED LIFE AS MY LUCKY BLANKET.
OVER THE YEARS, THE COLOR HAD FADED FROM A DEEP, LUSTROUS BLUE TO A TIRED PIGEON GRAY.
MY MOTHER DECIDED TO CUT IT DOWN TO CAPE-SIZE AND STICHED A RED FELT LIGHTNING BOLT IN THE CENTER OF IT.
ALSO SEWN TO IT WAS A MARINE'S PATCH, ONE OF MY FATHER'S. IT HAD COME HOME FROM VIETNAM IN HIS FOOT LOCKER.
HE HADN'T COME WITH IT.
MY MOTHER FLEW THE BLACK P.O.W. FLAG FROM THE FRONT PORCH, BUT EVEN I KNEW NO ONE WAS HOLDING MY FATHER PRISONER.
MOST NIGHTS, I FELL ASLEEP WRAPPED IN THE CAPE. IT PAINED ME TO TAKE IT OFF, AND I FELT UNDRESSED AND VULNERABLE WITHOUT IT.

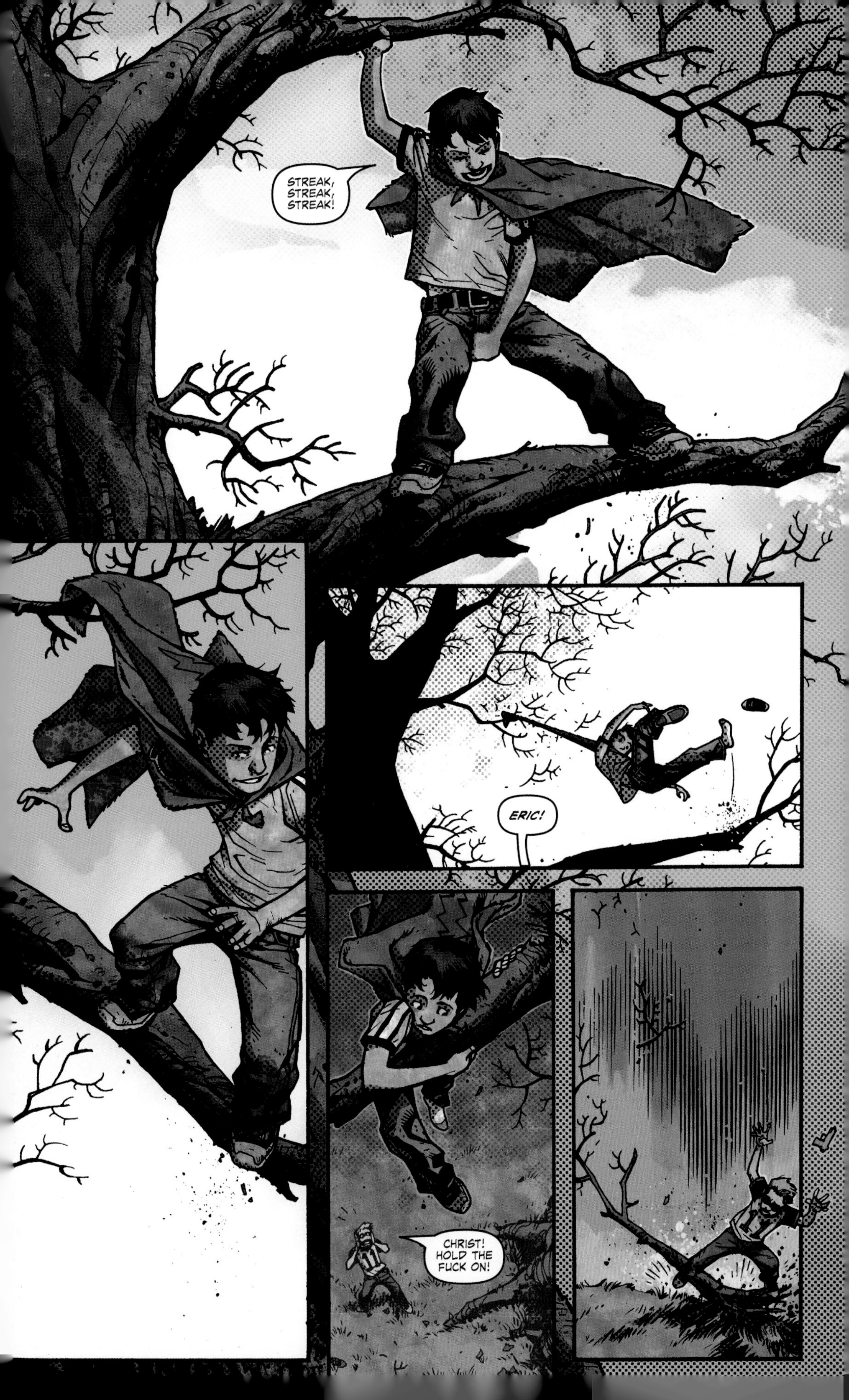
STREAK, STREAK, STREAK!
ERIC!
CHRIST! HOLD THE FUCK ON!

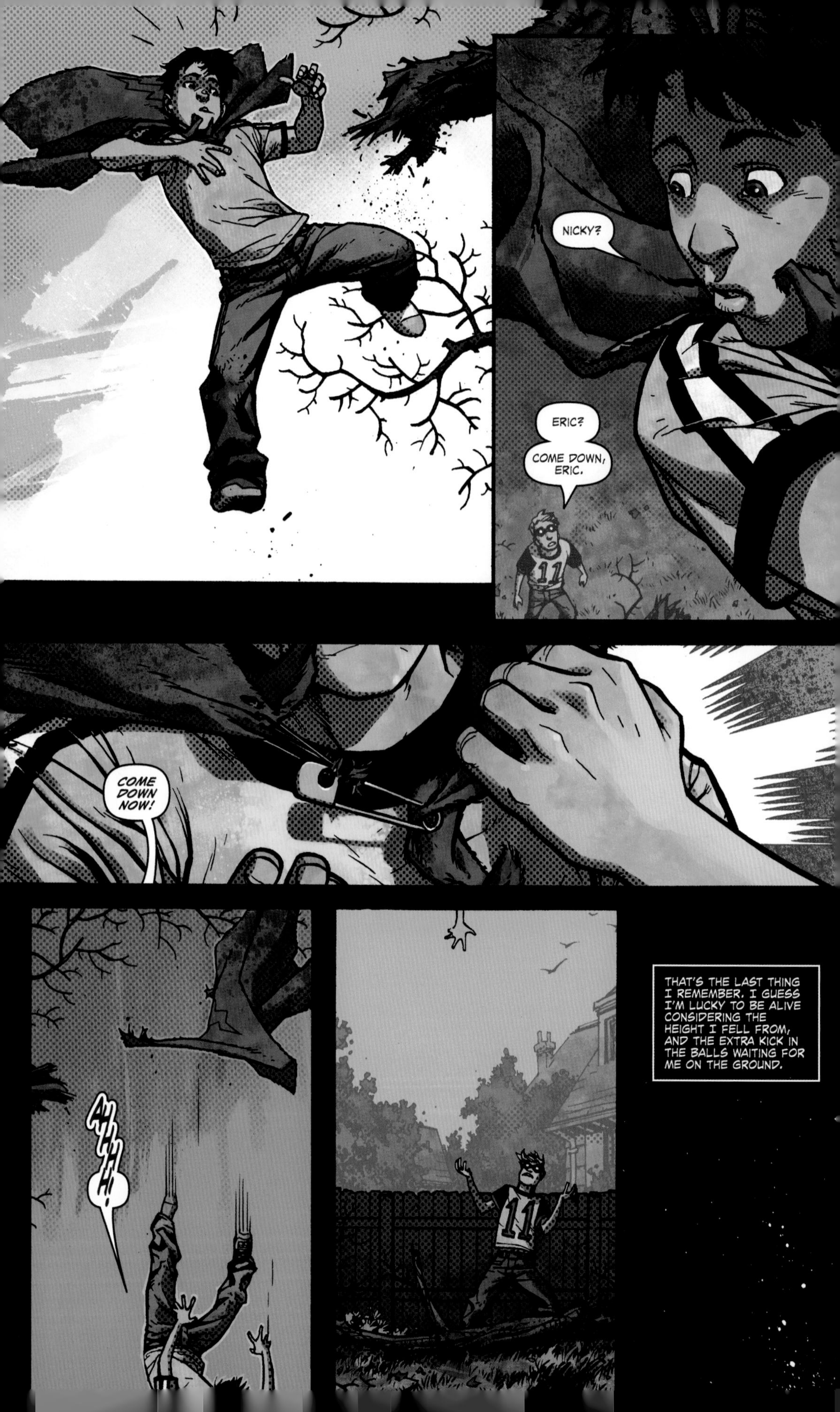
NICKY?
ERIC?
COME DOWN, ERIC.
COME DOWN NOW!
AHHH!
THAT'S THE LAST THING I REMEMBER. I GUESS I'M LUCKY TO BE ALIVE CONSIDERING THE HEIGHT I FELL FROM, AND THE EXTRA KICK IN THE BALLS WAITING FOR ME ON THE GROUND.

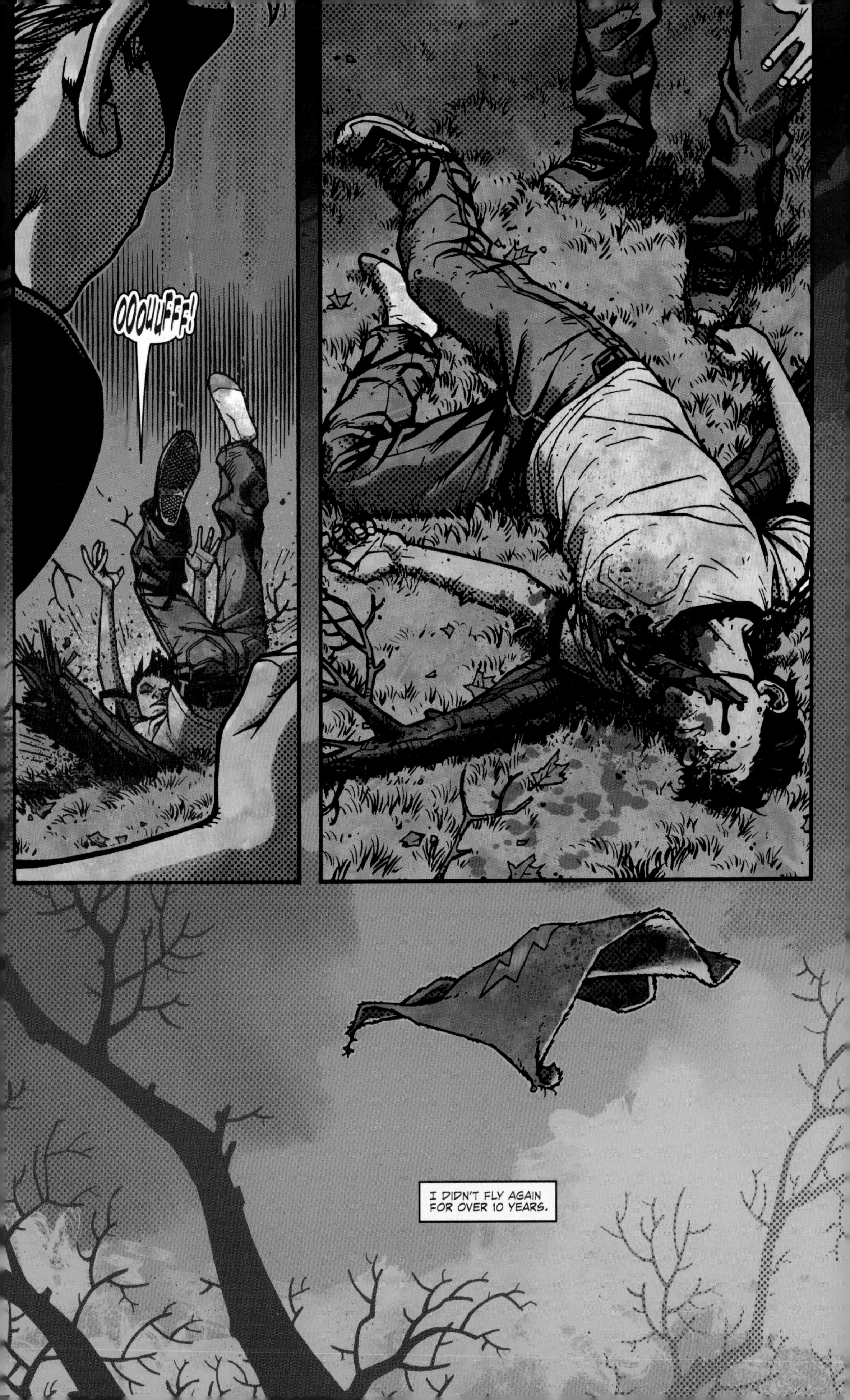
OOOUUFFF!
I DIDN'T FLY AGAIN FOR OVER 10 YEARS.

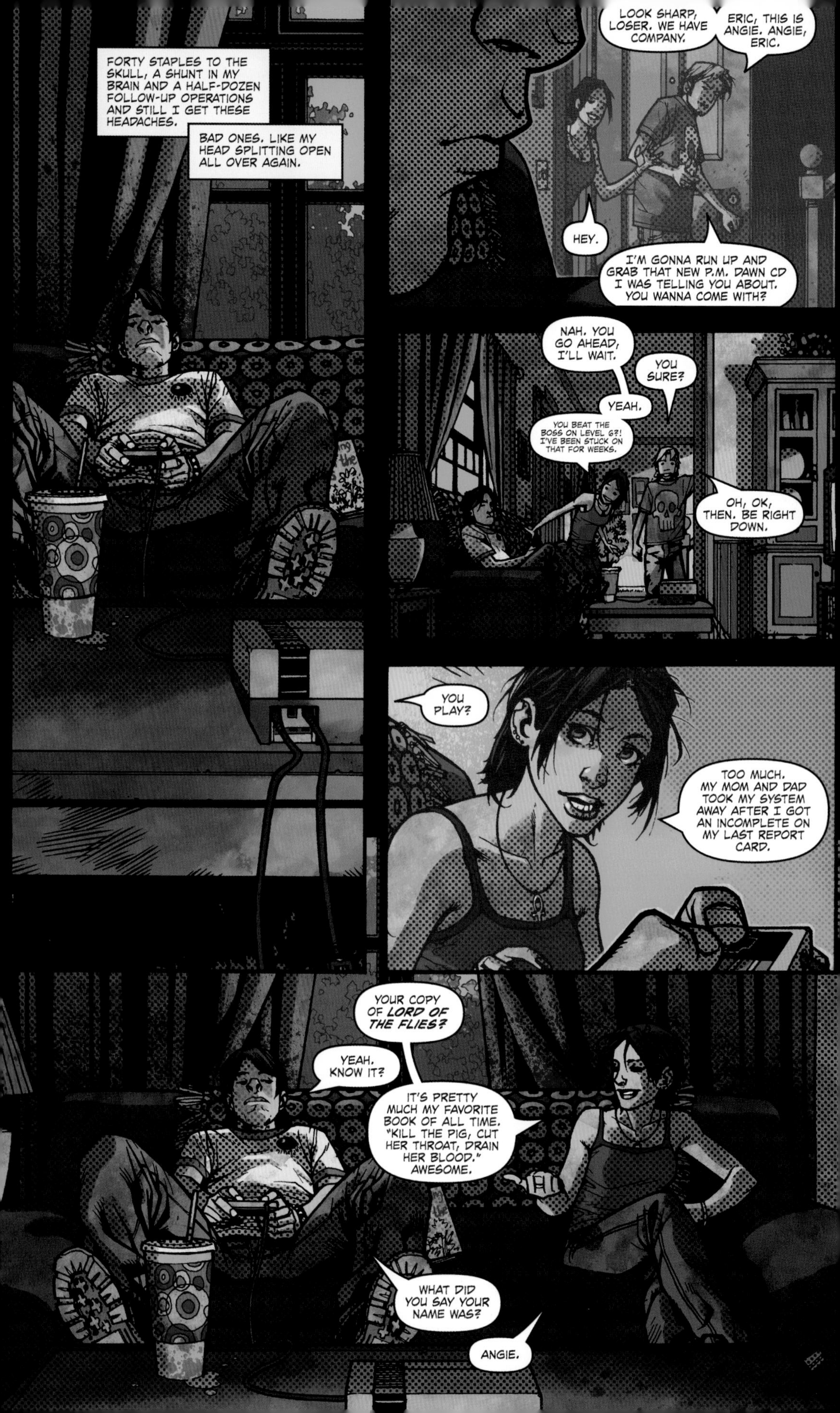
FORTY STAPLES TO THE SKULL, A SHUNT IN MY BRAIN AND A HALF-DOZEN FOLLOW-UP OPERATIONS AND STILL I GET THESE HEADACHES.
BAD ONES. LIKE MY HEAD SPLITTING OPEN ALL OVER AGAIN.
LOOK SHARP, LOSER. WE HAVE COMPANY.
ERIC, THIS IS ANGIE. ANGIE, ERIC.
HEY.
I'M GONNA RUN UP AND GRAB THAT NEW P.M. DAWN CD I WAS TELLING YOU ABOUT. YOU WANNA COME WITH?
NAH. YOU GO AHEAD, I'LL WAIT.
YOU SURE?
YEAH.
YOU BEAT THE BOSS ON LEVEL 6?! I'VE BEEN STUCK ON THAT FOR WEEKS.
OH, OK, THEN. BE RIGHT DOWN.
YOU PLAY?
TOO MUCH. MY MOM AND DAD TOOK MY SYSTEM AWAY AFTER I GOT AN INCOMPLETE ON MY LAST REPORT CARD.
YOUR COPY OF *LORD OF THE FLIES?*
YEAH. KNOW IT?
IT'S PRETTY MUCH MY FAVORITE BOOK OF ALL TIME. "KILL THE PIG, CUT HER THROAT, DRAIN HER BLOOD." AWESOME.
WHAT DID YOU SAY YOUR NAME WAS?
ANGIE.

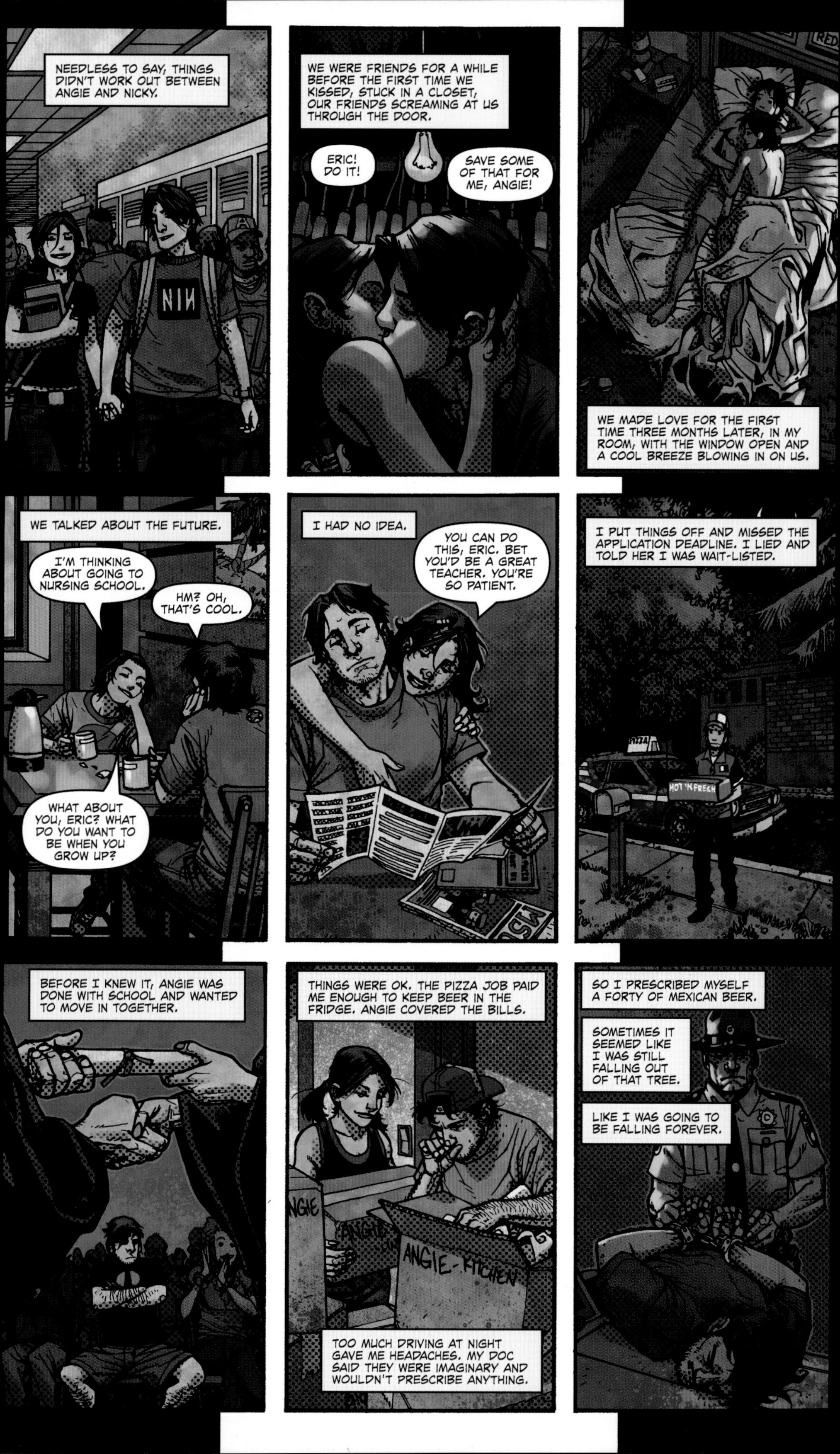
NEEDLESS TO SAY, THINGS DIDN'T WORK OUT BETWEEN ANGIE AND NICKY.
NIN
WE WERE FRIENDS FOR A WHILE BEFORE THE FIRST TIME WE KISSED, STUCK IN A CLOSET, OUR FRIENDS SCREAMING AT US THROUGH THE DOOR.
ERIC! DO IT!
SAVE SOME OF THAT FOR ME, ANGIE!
WE MADE LOVE FOR THE FIRST TIME THREE MONTHS LATER, IN MY ROOM, WITH THE WINDOW OPEN AND A COOL BREEZE BLOWING IN ON US.
WE TALKED ABOUT THE FUTURE.
I'M THINKING ABOUT GOING TO NURSING SCHOOL.
HM? OH, THAT'S COOL.
WHAT ABOUT YOU, ERIC? WHAT DO YOU WANT TO BE WHEN YOU GROW UP?
I HAD NO IDEA.
YOU CAN DO THIS, ERIC. BET YOU'D BE A GREAT TEACHER. YOU'RE SO PATIENT.
I PUT THINGS OFF AND MISSED THE APPLICATION DEADLINE. I LIED AND TOLD HER I WAS WAIT-LISTED.
PIZZA
HOT 'N FRESH
BEFORE I KNEW IT, ANGIE WAS DONE WITH SCHOOL AND WANTED TO MOVE IN TOGETHER.
THINGS WERE OK. THE PIZZA JOB PAID ME ENOUGH TO KEEP BEER IN THE FRIDGE. ANGIE COVERED THE BILLS.
ANGIE
ANGIE-KITCHEN
TOO MUCH DRIVING AT NIGHT GAVE ME HEADACHES. MY DOC SAID THEY WERE IMAGINARY AND WOULDN'T PRESCRIBE ANYTHING.
SO I PRESCRIBED MYSELF A FORTY OF MEXICAN BEER.
SOMETIMES IT SEEMED LIKE I WAS STILL FALLING OUT OF THAT TREE.
LIKE I WAS GOING TO BE FALLING FOREVER.

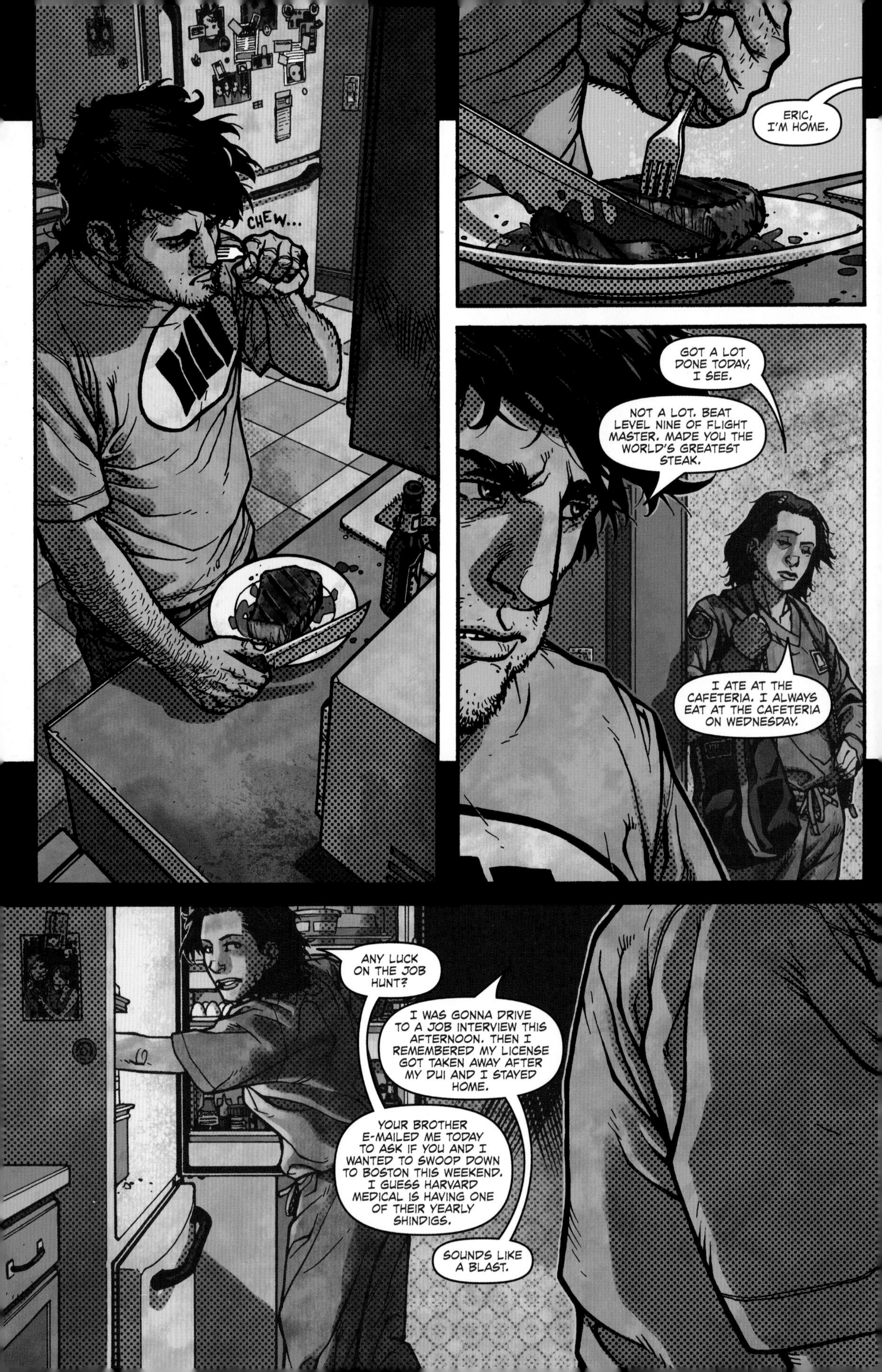
CHEW...
ERIC, I'M HOME.
GOT A LOT DONE TODAY, I SEE.
NOT A LOT. BEAT LEVEL NINE OF FLIGHT MASTER. MADE YOU THE WORLD'S GREATEST STEAK.
I ATE AT THE CAFETERIA. I ALWAYS EAT AT THE CAFETERIA ON WEDNESDAY.
ANY LUCK ON THE JOB HUNT?
I WAS GONNA DRIVE TO A JOB INTERVIEW THIS AFTERNOON. THEN I REMEMBERED MY LICENSE GOT TAKEN AWAY AFTER MY DUI AND I STAYED HOME.
YOUR BROTHER E-MAILED ME TODAY TO ASK IF YOU AND I WANTED TO SWOOP DOWN TO BOSTON THIS WEEKEND. I GUESS HARVARD MEDICAL IS HAVING ONE OF THEIR YEARLY SHINDIGS.
SOUNDS LIKE A BLAST.

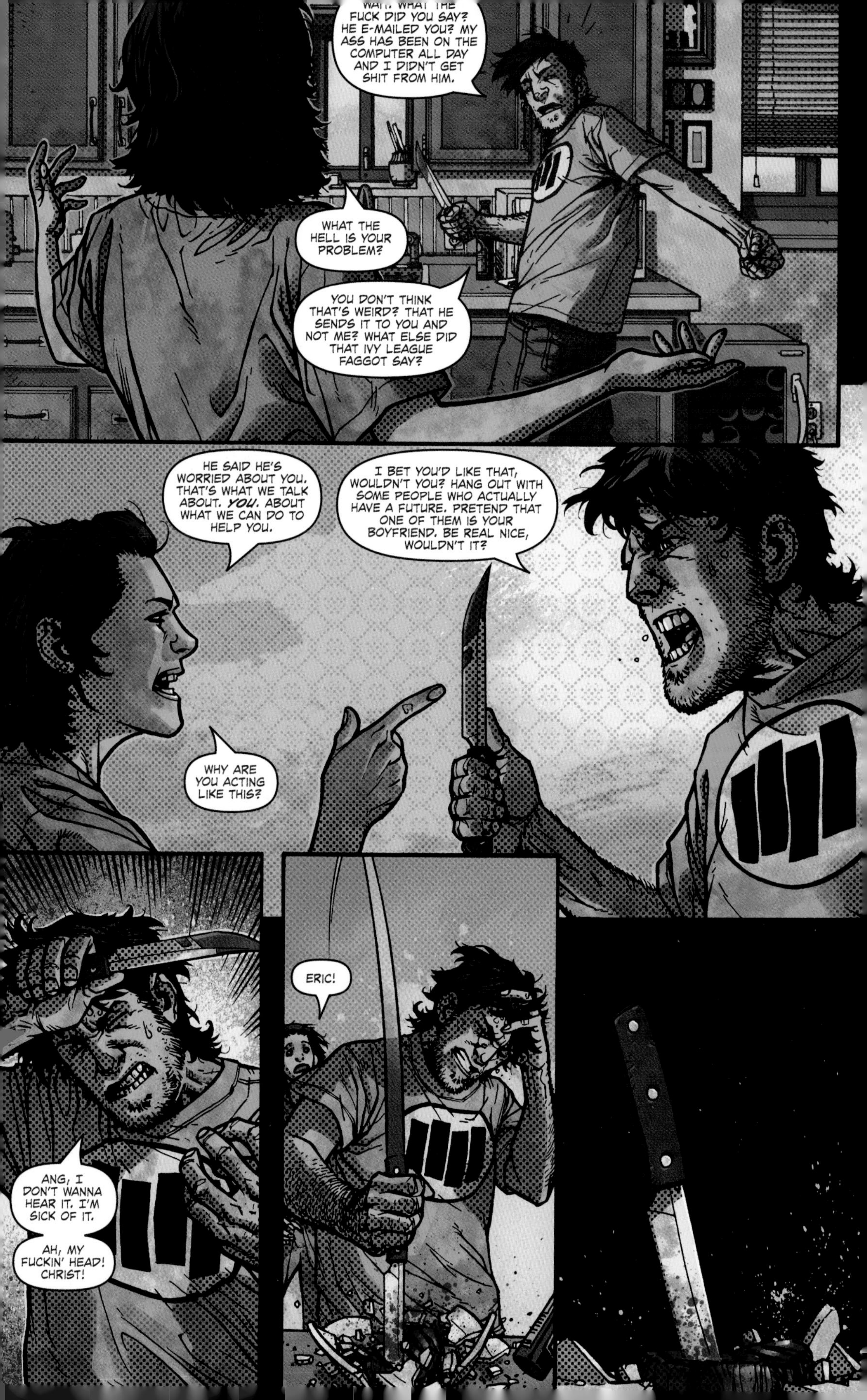
WAIT. WHAT THE FUCK DID YOU SAY? HE E-MAILED YOU? MY ASS HAS BEEN ON THE COMPUTER ALL DAY AND I DIDN'T GET SHIT FROM HIM.
WHAT THE HELL IS YOUR PROBLEM?
YOU DON'T THINK THAT'S WEIRD? THAT HE SENDS IT TO YOU AND NOT ME? WHAT ELSE DID THAT IVY LEAGUE FAGGOT SAY?
HE SAID HE'S WORRIED ABOUT YOU. THAT'S WHAT WE TALK ABOUT. *YOU*. ABOUT WHAT WE CAN DO TO HELP YOU.
I BET YOU'D LIKE THAT, WOULDN'T YOU? HANG OUT WITH SOME PEOPLE WHO ACTUALLY HAVE A FUTURE. PRETEND THAT ONE OF THEM IS YOUR BOYFRIEND. BE REAL NICE, WOULDN'T IT?
WHY ARE YOU ACTING LIKE THIS?
ANG, I DON'T WANNA HEAR IT. I'M SICK OF IT.
AH, MY FUCKIN' HEAD! CHRIST!
ERIC!

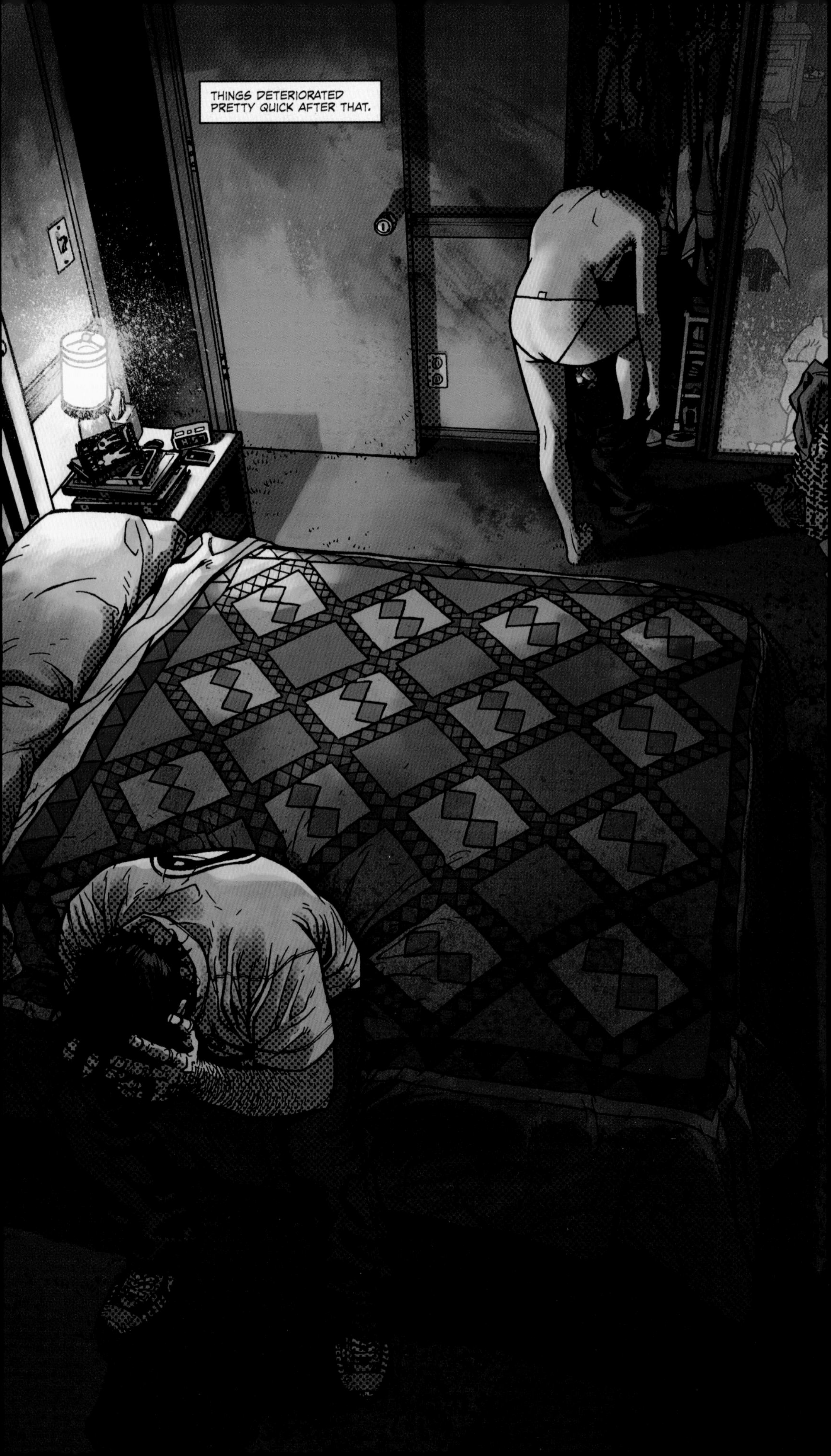
THINGS DETERIORATED PRETTY QUICK AFTER THAT.

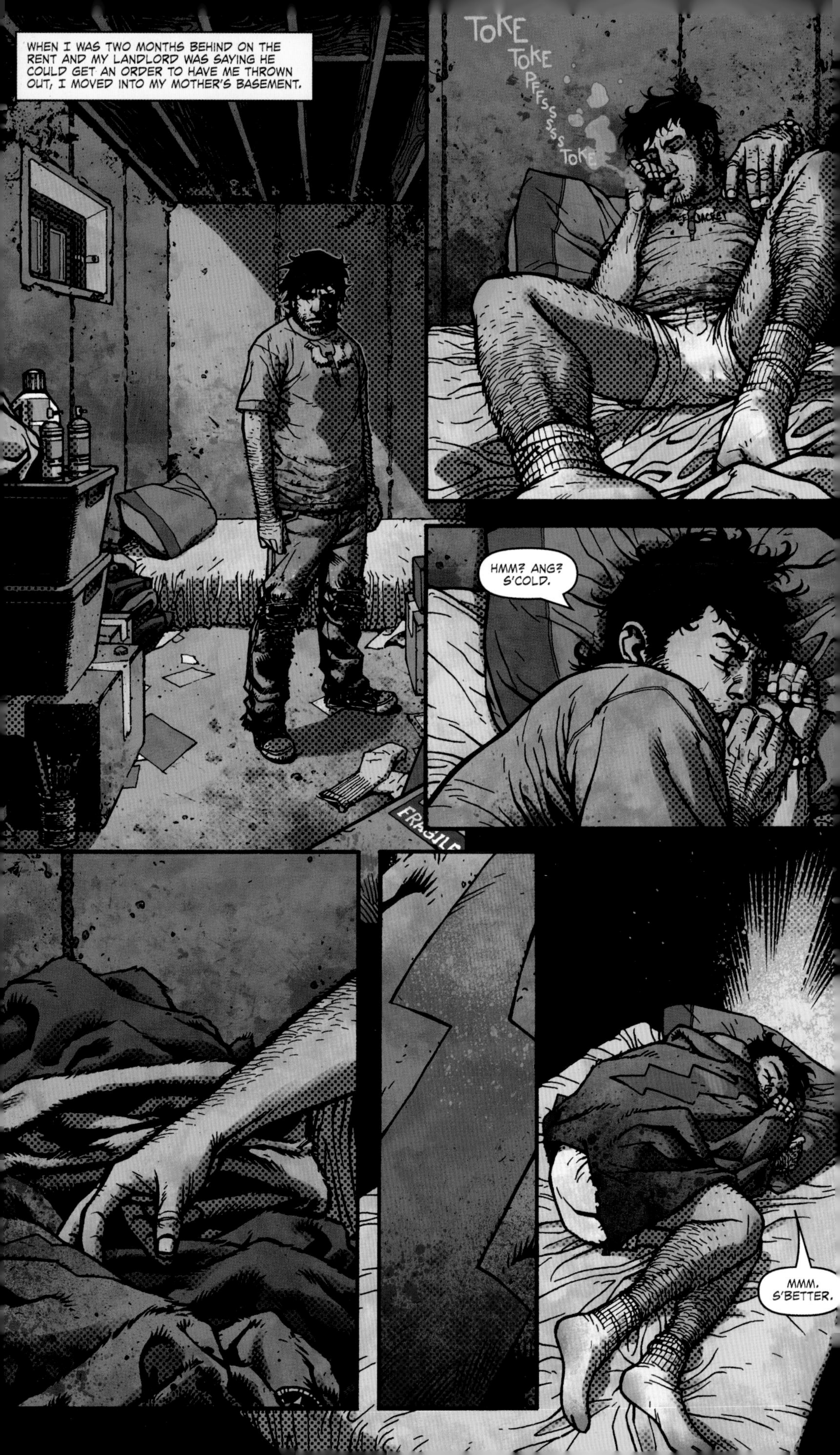
WHEN I WAS TWO MONTHS BEHIND ON THE RENT AND MY LANDLORD WAS SAYING HE COULD GET AN ORDER TO HAVE ME THROWN OUT, I MOVED INTO MY MOTHER'S BASEMENT.
FRAGILE
TOKE
TOKE
PFFSSSSS
TOKE
HMM? ANG? S'COLD.
MMM. S'BETTER.

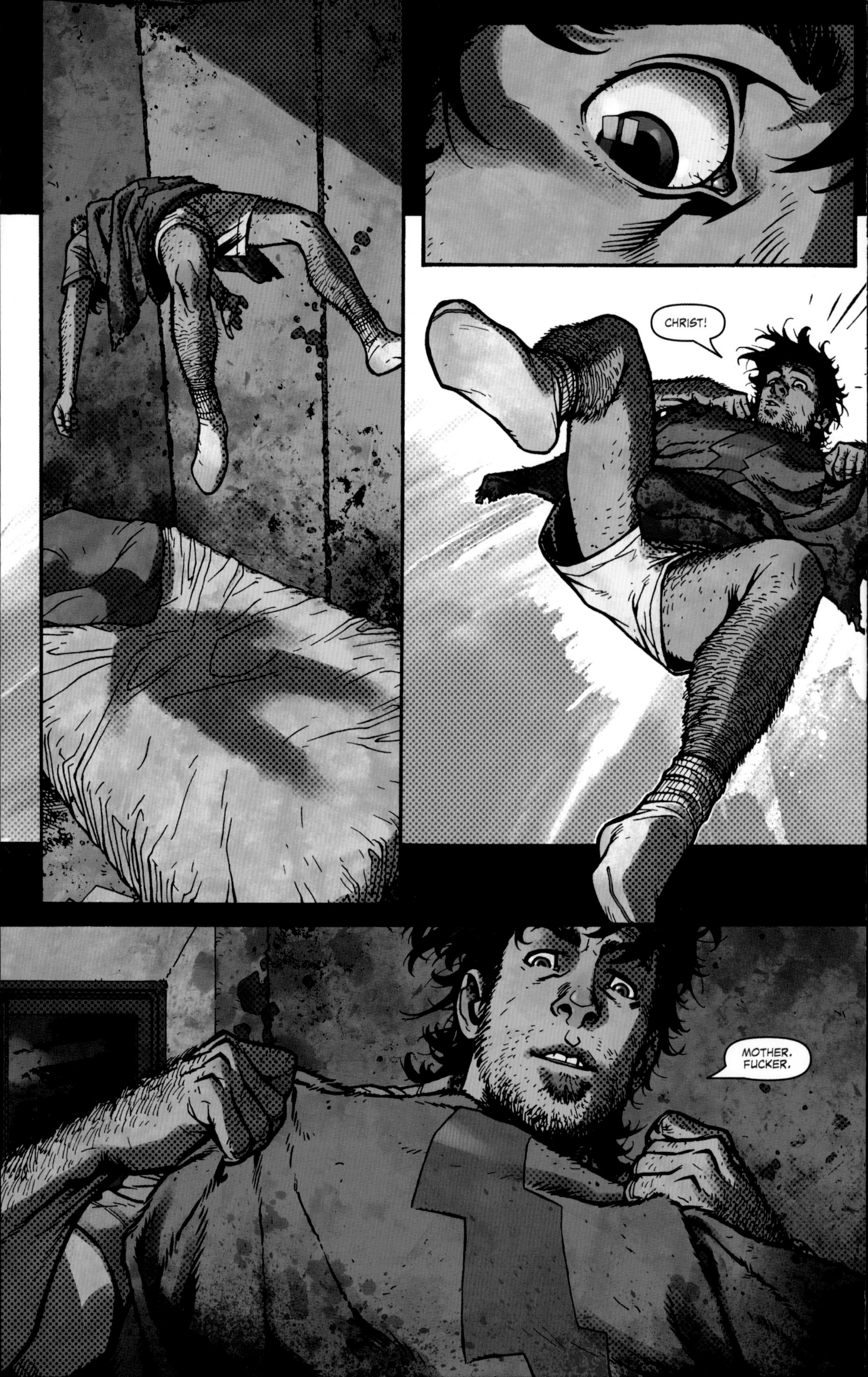
CHRIST!
MOTHER. FUCKER.

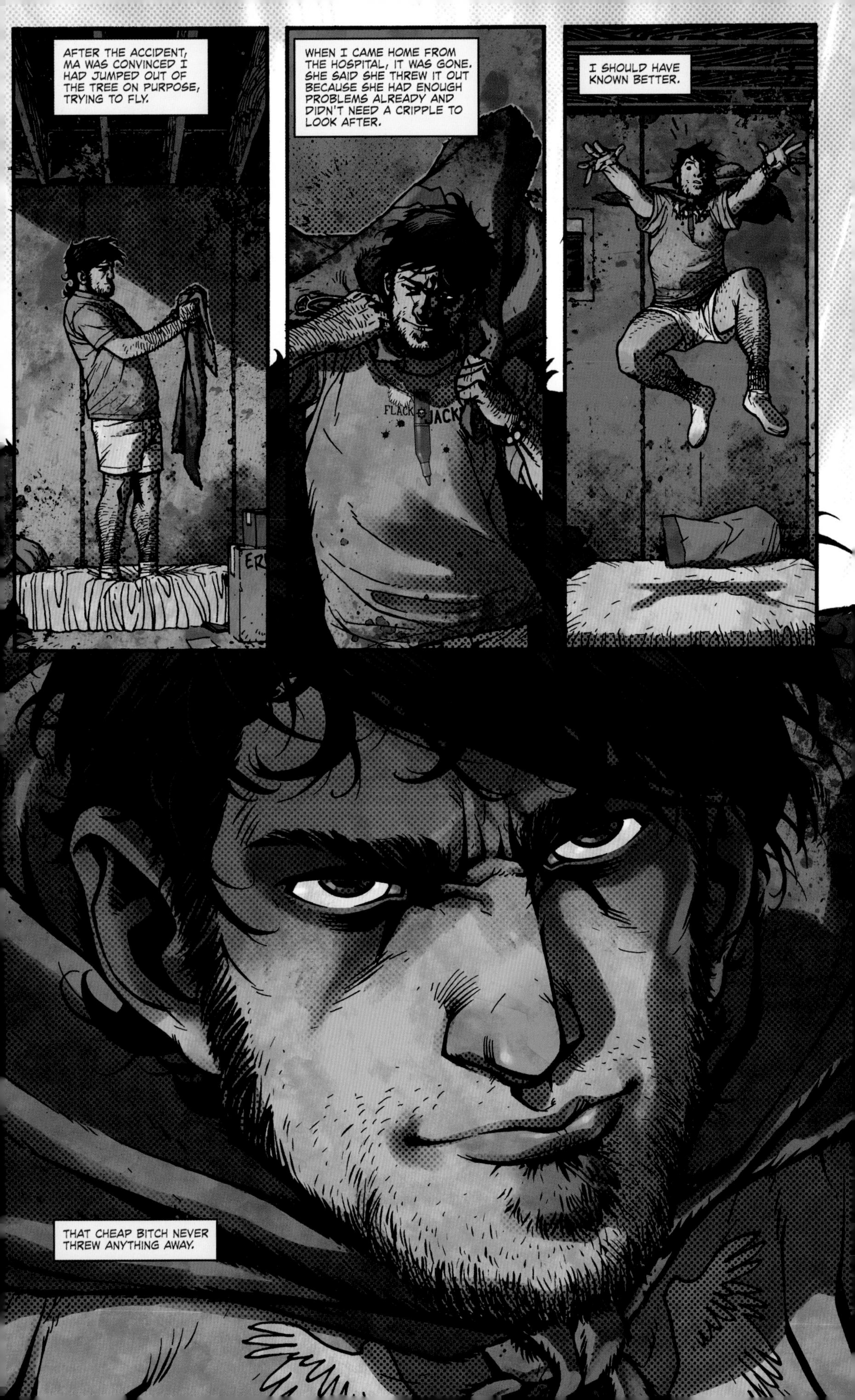
AFTER THE ACCIDENT, MA WAS CONVINCED I HAD JUMPED OUT OF THE TREE ON PURPOSE, TRYING TO FLY.
WHEN I CAME HOME FROM THE HOSPITAL, IT WAS GONE. SHE SAID SHE THREW IT OUT BECAUSE SHE HAD ENOUGH PROBLEMS ALREADY AND DIDN'T NEED A CRIPPLE TO LOOK AFTER.
FLACK JACK
I SHOULD HAVE KNOWN BETTER.
THAT CHEAP BITCH NEVER THREW ANYTHING AWAY.

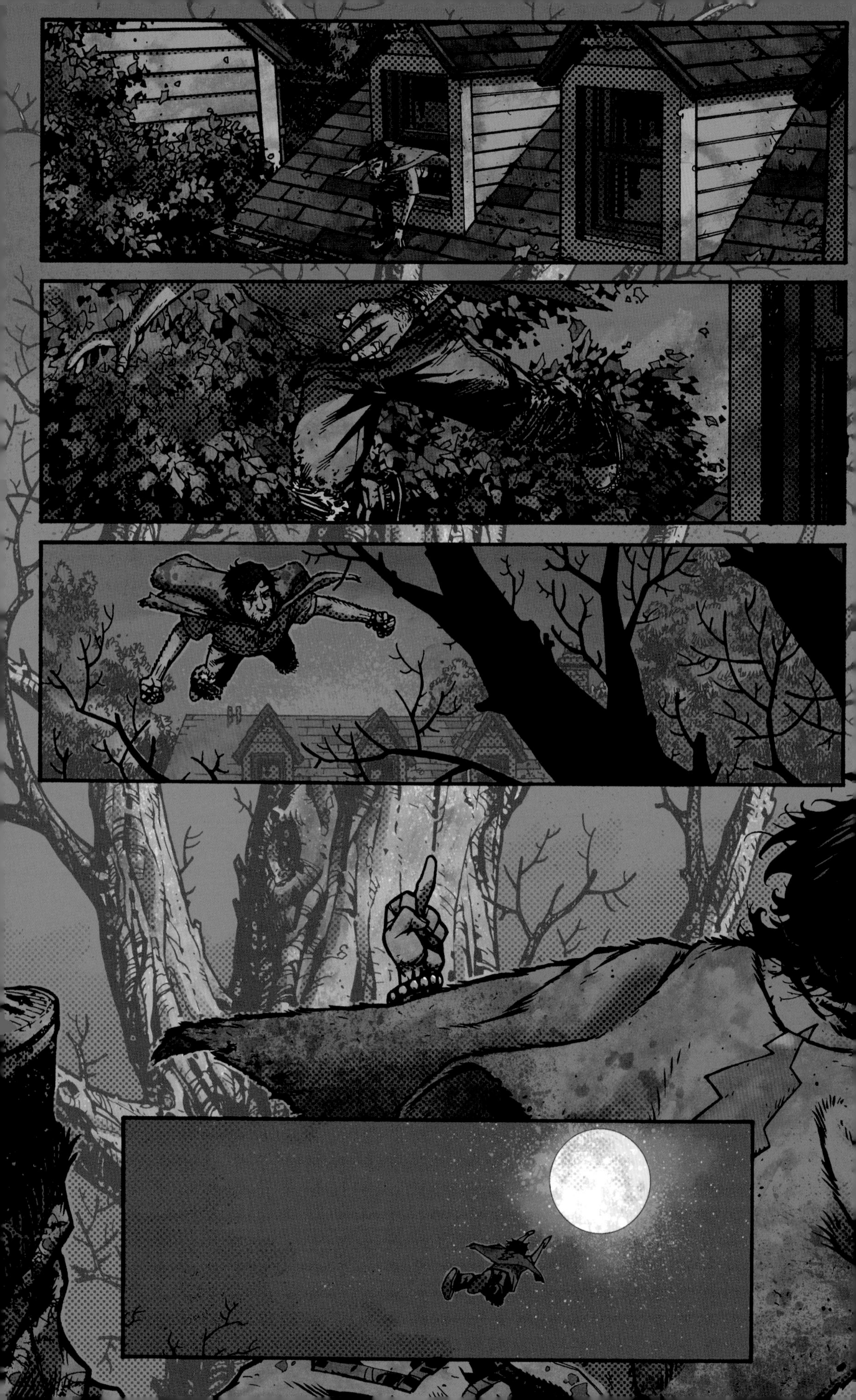

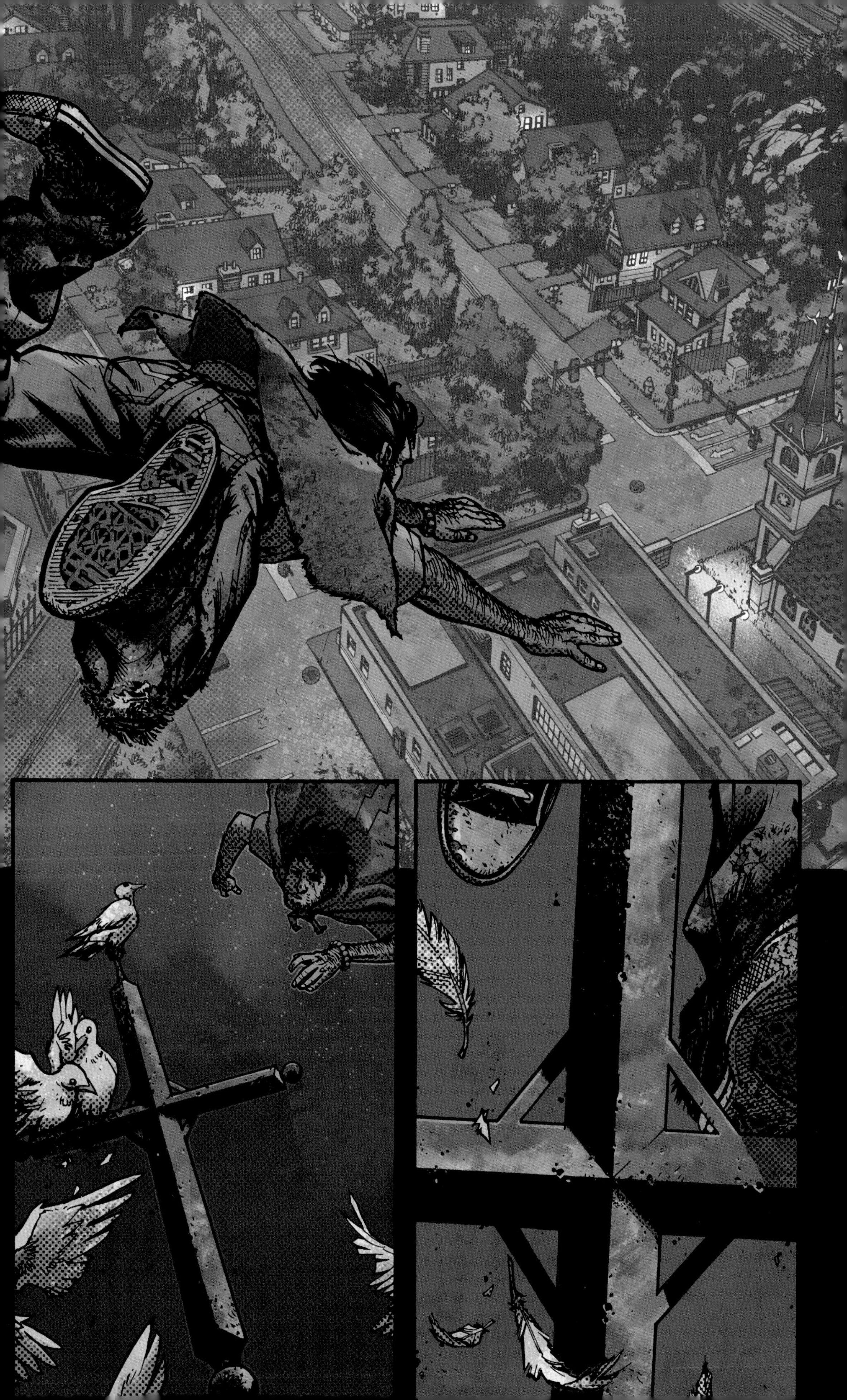

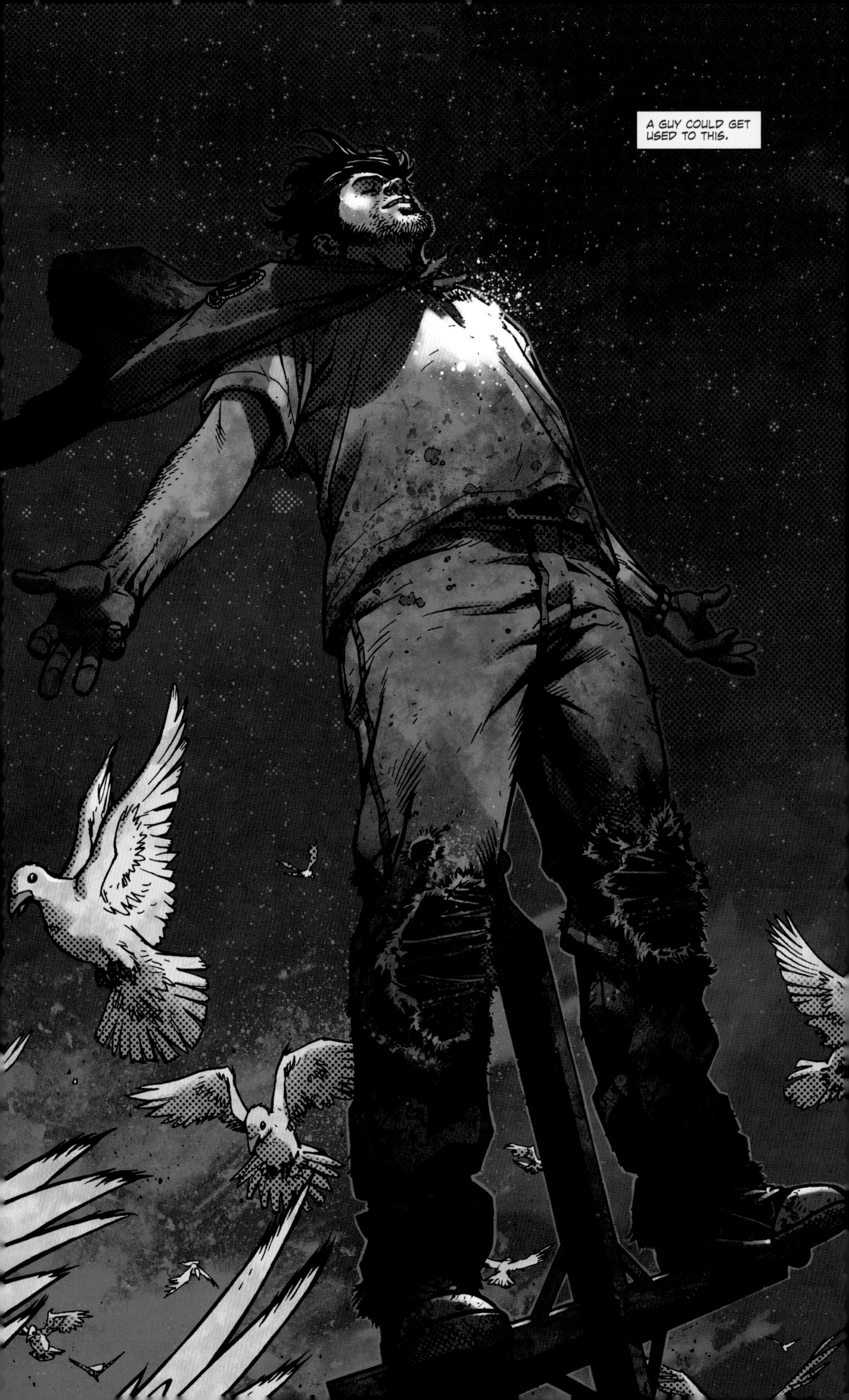
A GUY COULD GET USED TO THIS.

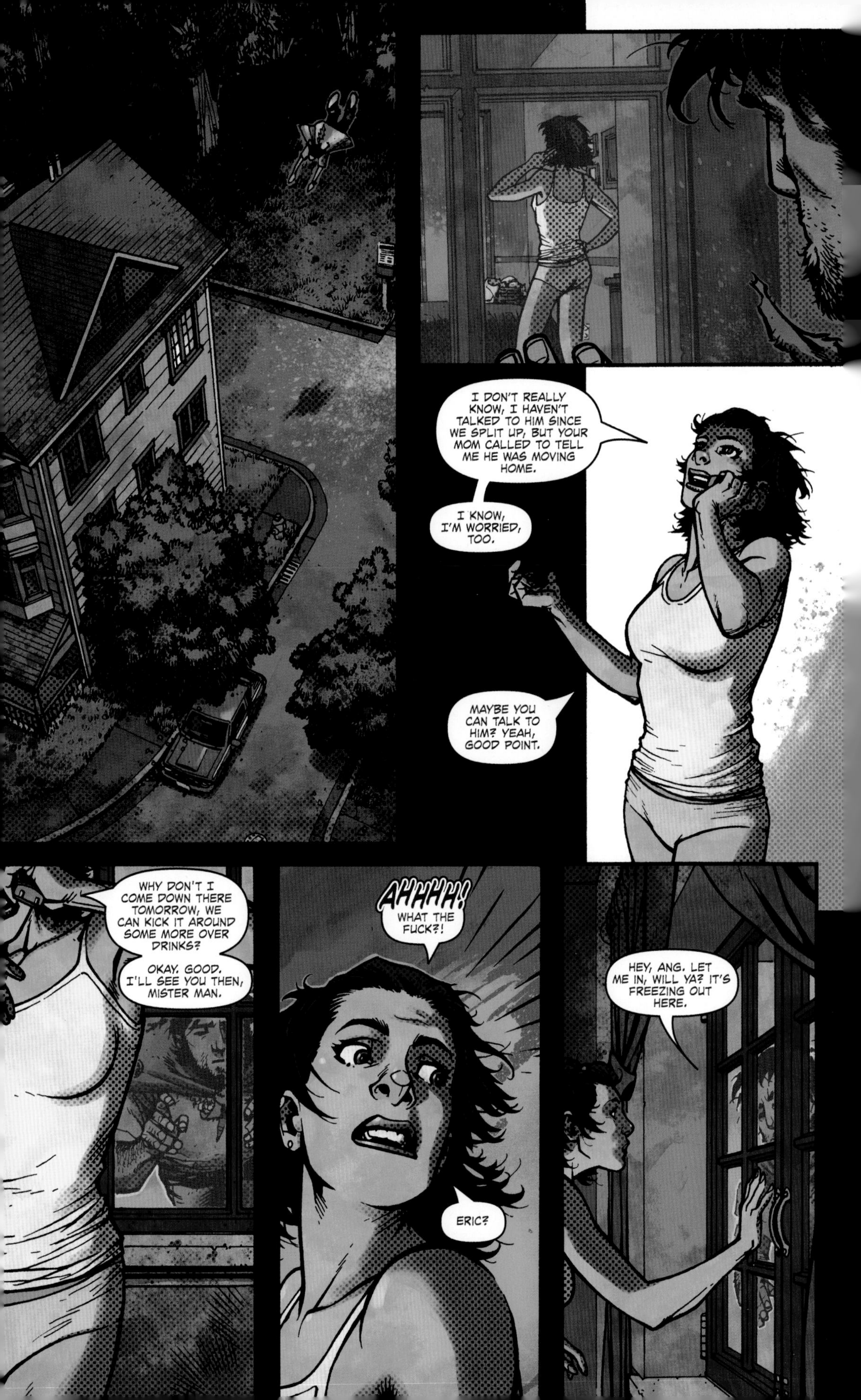

I DON'T REALLY KNOW, I HAVEN'T TALKED TO HIM SINCE WE SPLIT UP, BUT YOUR MOM CALLED TO TELL ME HE WAS MOVING HOME.
I KNOW, I'M WORRIED, TOO.
MAYBE YOU CAN TALK TO HIM? YEAH, GOOD POINT.
WHY DON'T I COME DOWN THERE TOMORROW, WE CAN KICK IT AROUND SOME MORE OVER DRINKS?
OKAY. GOOD. I'LL SEE YOU THEN, MISTER MAN.
AHHHH!
WHAT THE FUCK?!
ERIC?
HEY, ANG. LET ME IN, WILL YA? IT'S FREEZING OUT HERE.

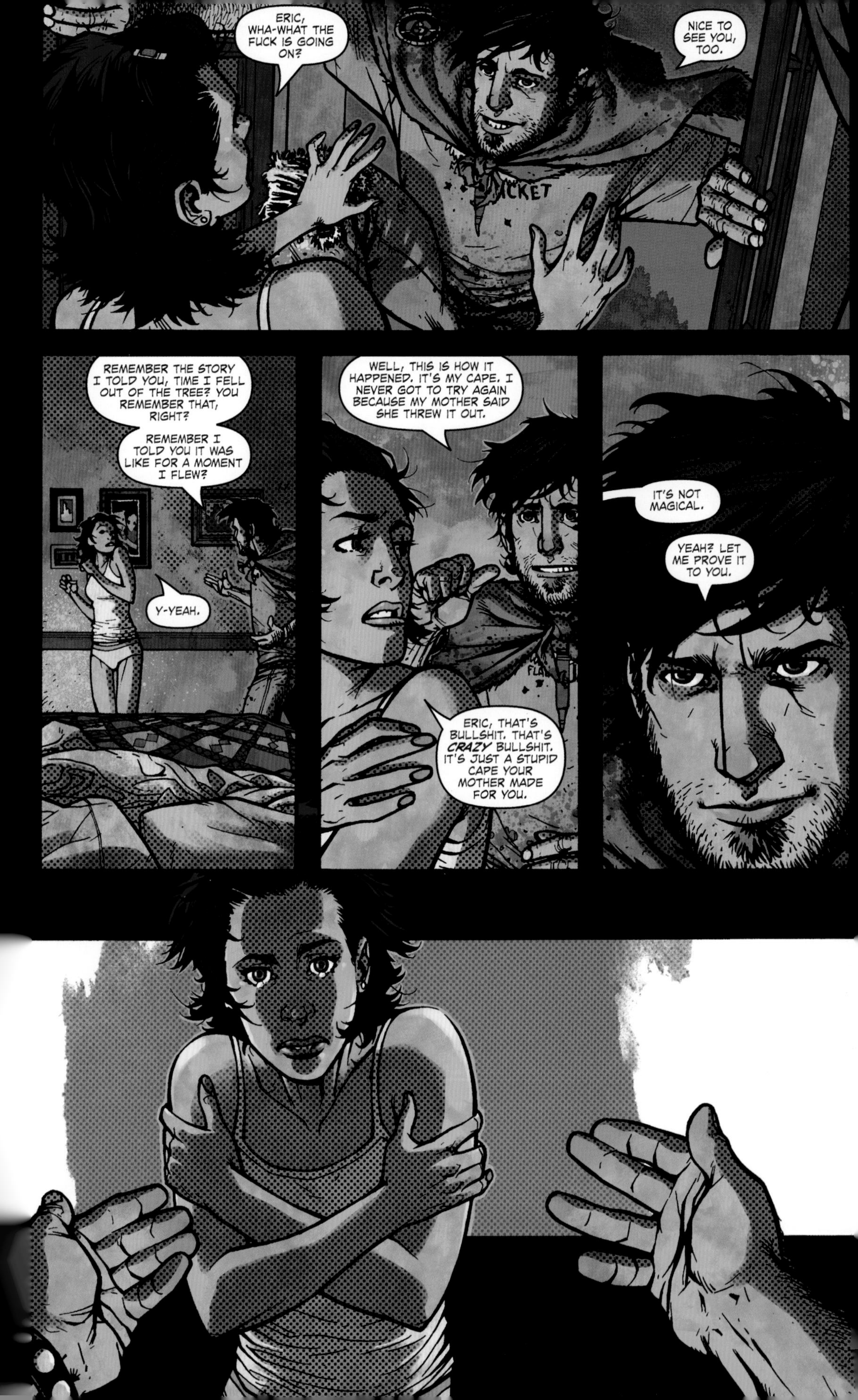
ERIC, WHA-WHAT THE FUCK IS GOING ON?
NICE TO SEE YOU, TOO.
REMEMBER THE STORY I TOLD YOU, TIME I FELL OUT OF THE TREE? YOU REMEMBER THAT, RIGHT?
REMEMBER I TOLD YOU IT WAS LIKE FOR A MOMENT I FLEW?
Y-YEAH.
WELL, THIS IS HOW IT HAPPENED. IT'S MY CAPE. I NEVER GOT TO TRY AGAIN BECAUSE MY MOTHER SAID SHE THREW IT OUT.
ERIC, THAT'S BULLSHIT. THAT'S *CRAZY* BULLSHIT. IT'S JUST A STUPID CAPE YOUR MOTHER MADE FOR YOU.
IT'S NOT MAGICAL.
YEAH? LET ME PROVE IT TO YOU.

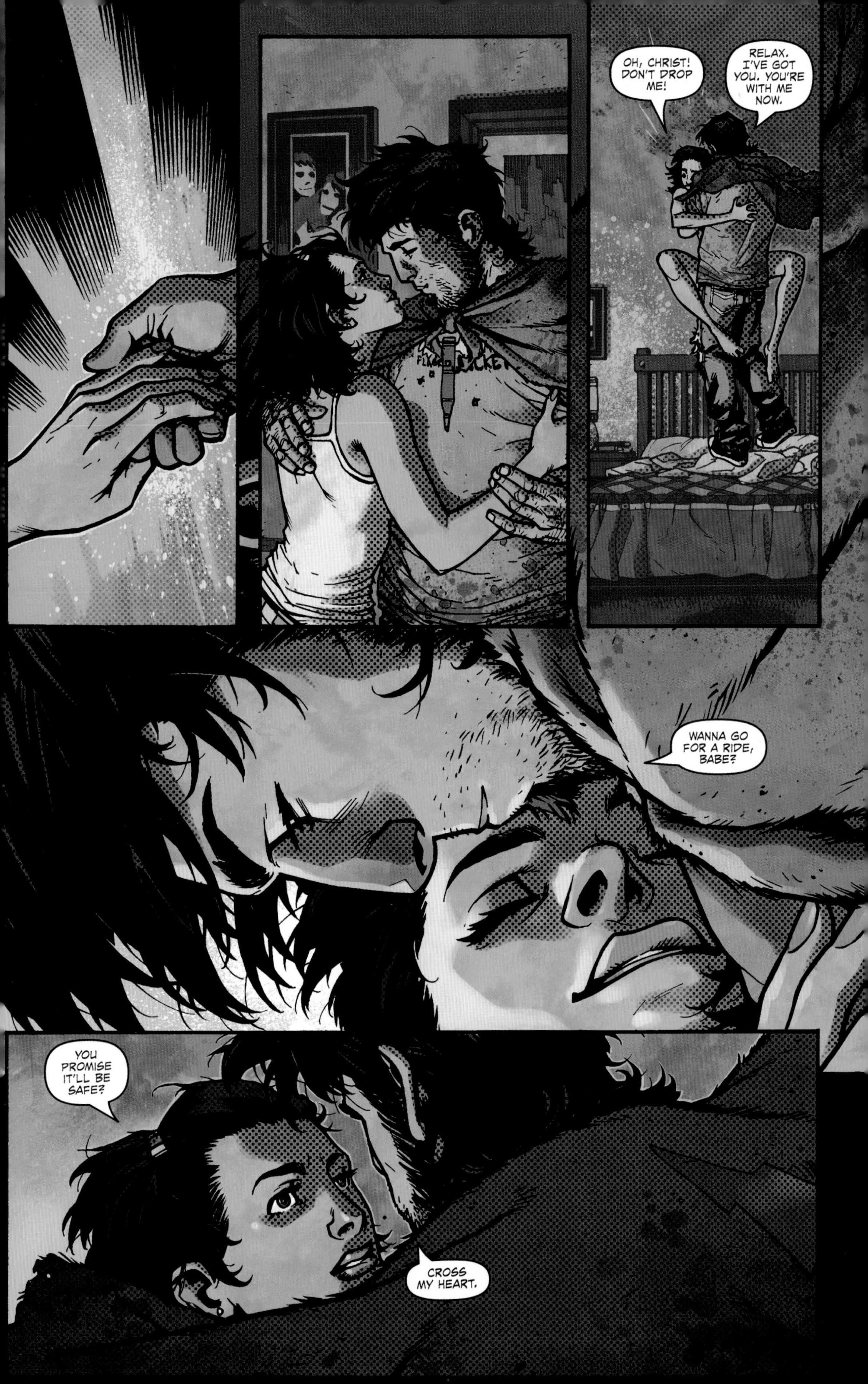
OH, CHRIST! DON'T DROP ME!
RELAX. I'VE GOT YOU. YOU'RE WITH ME NOW.
WANNA GO FOR A RIDE, BABE?
YOU PROMISE IT'LL BE SAFE?
CROSS MY HEART.

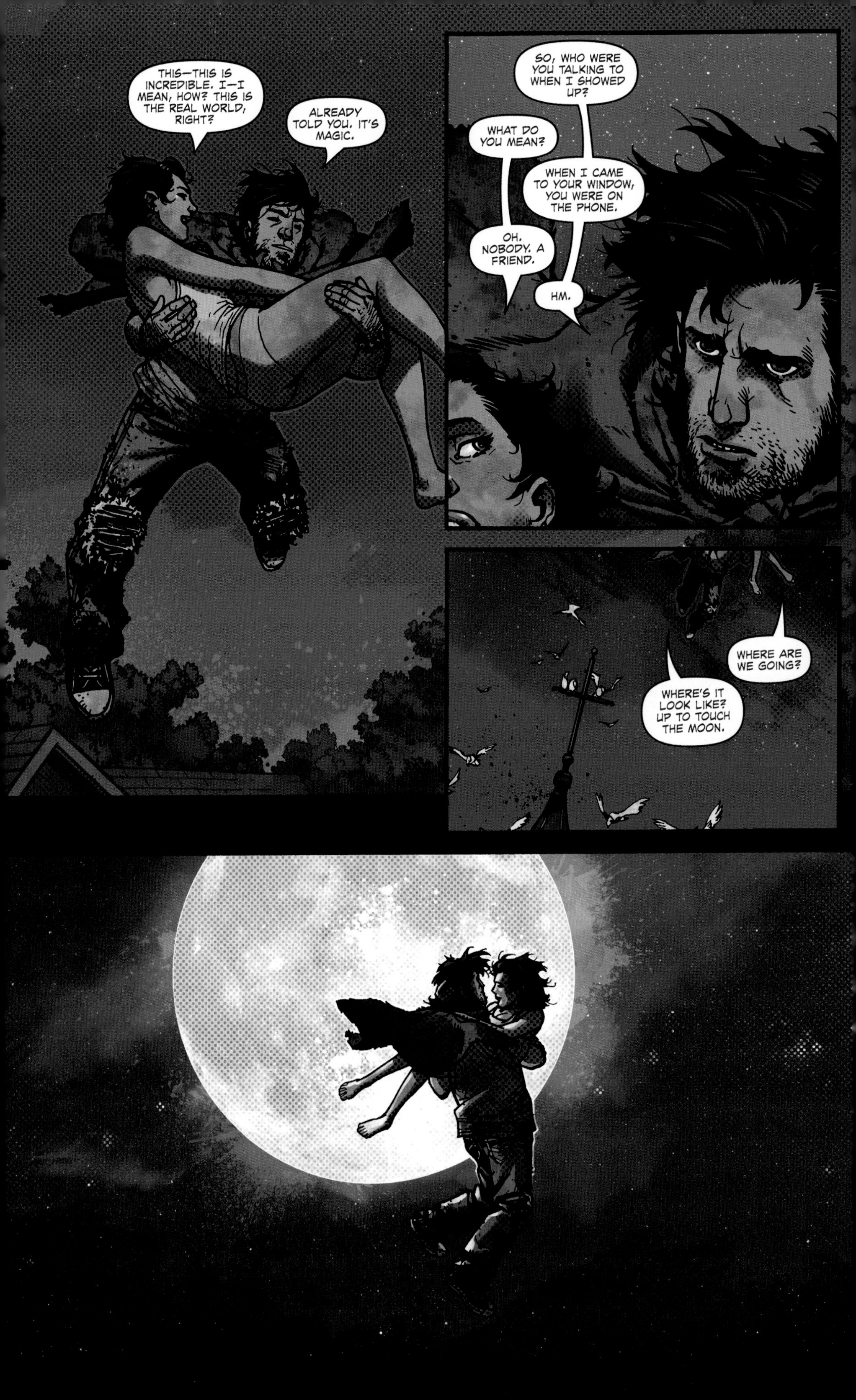
THIS—THIS IS INCREDIBLE. I—I MEAN, HOW? THIS IS THE REAL WORLD, RIGHT?
ALREADY TOLD YOU. IT'S MAGIC.
SO, WHO WERE YOU TALKING TO WHEN I SHOWED UP?
WHAT DO YOU MEAN?
WHEN I CAME TO YOUR WINDOW, YOU WERE ON THE PHONE.
OH. NOBODY. A FRIEND.
HM.
WHERE ARE WE GOING?
WHERE'S IT LOOK LIKE? UP TO TOUCH THE MOON.

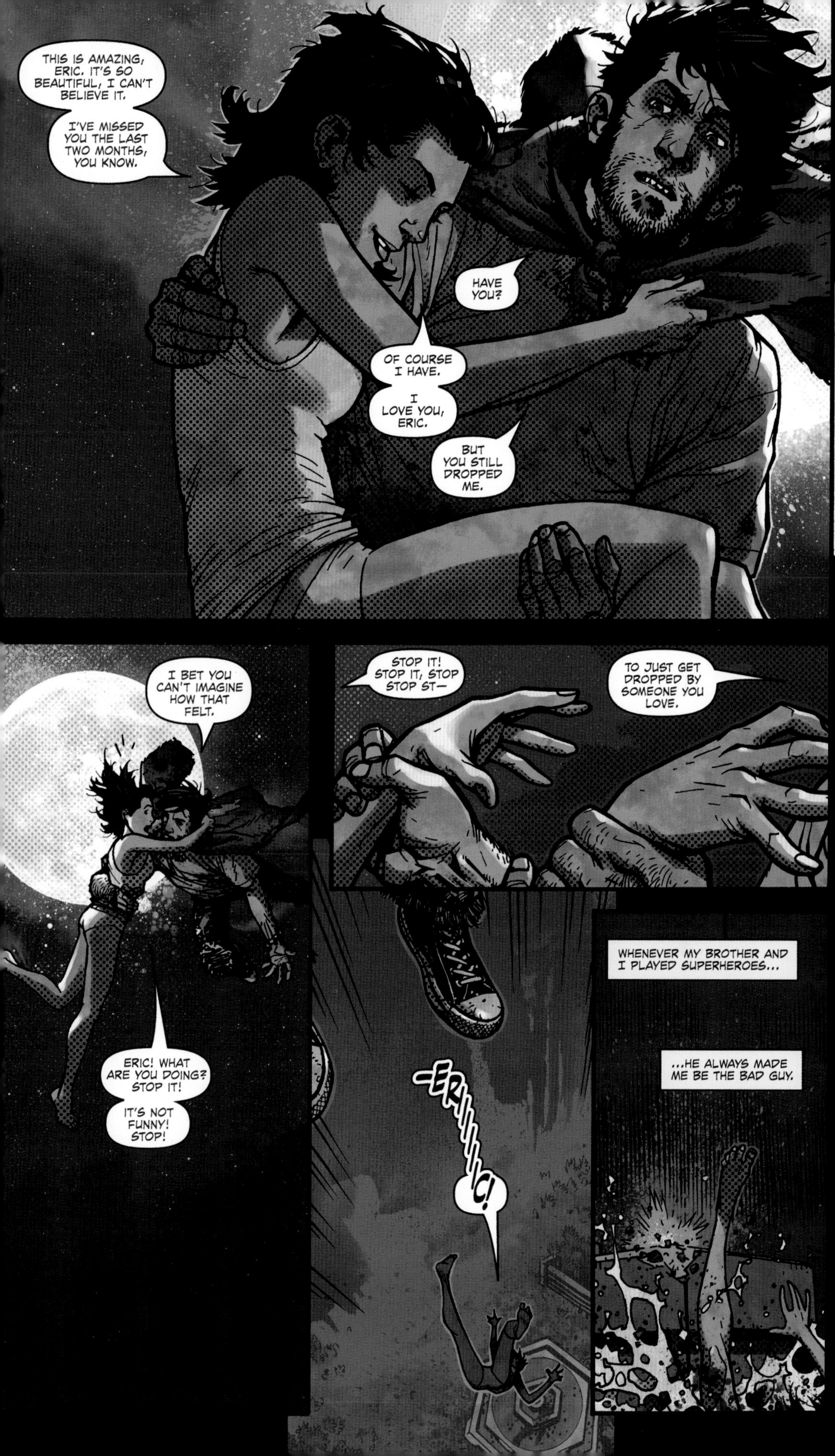
THIS IS AMAZING, ERIC. IT'S SO BEAUTIFUL, I CAN'T BELIEVE IT.
I'VE MISSED YOU THE LAST TWO MONTHS, YOU KNOW.
HAVE YOU?
OF COURSE I HAVE.
I LOVE YOU, ERIC.
BUT YOU STILL DROPPED ME.
I BET YOU CAN'T IMAGINE HOW THAT FELT.
ERIC! WHAT ARE YOU DOING? STOP IT!
IT'S NOT FUNNY! STOP!
STOP IT! STOP IT, STOP STOP ST—
TO JUST GET DROPPED BY SOMEONE YOU LOVE.
-ERIIIIIIC!
WHENEVER MY BROTHER AND I PLAYED SUPERHEROES...
...HE ALWAYS MADE ME BE THE BAD GUY.

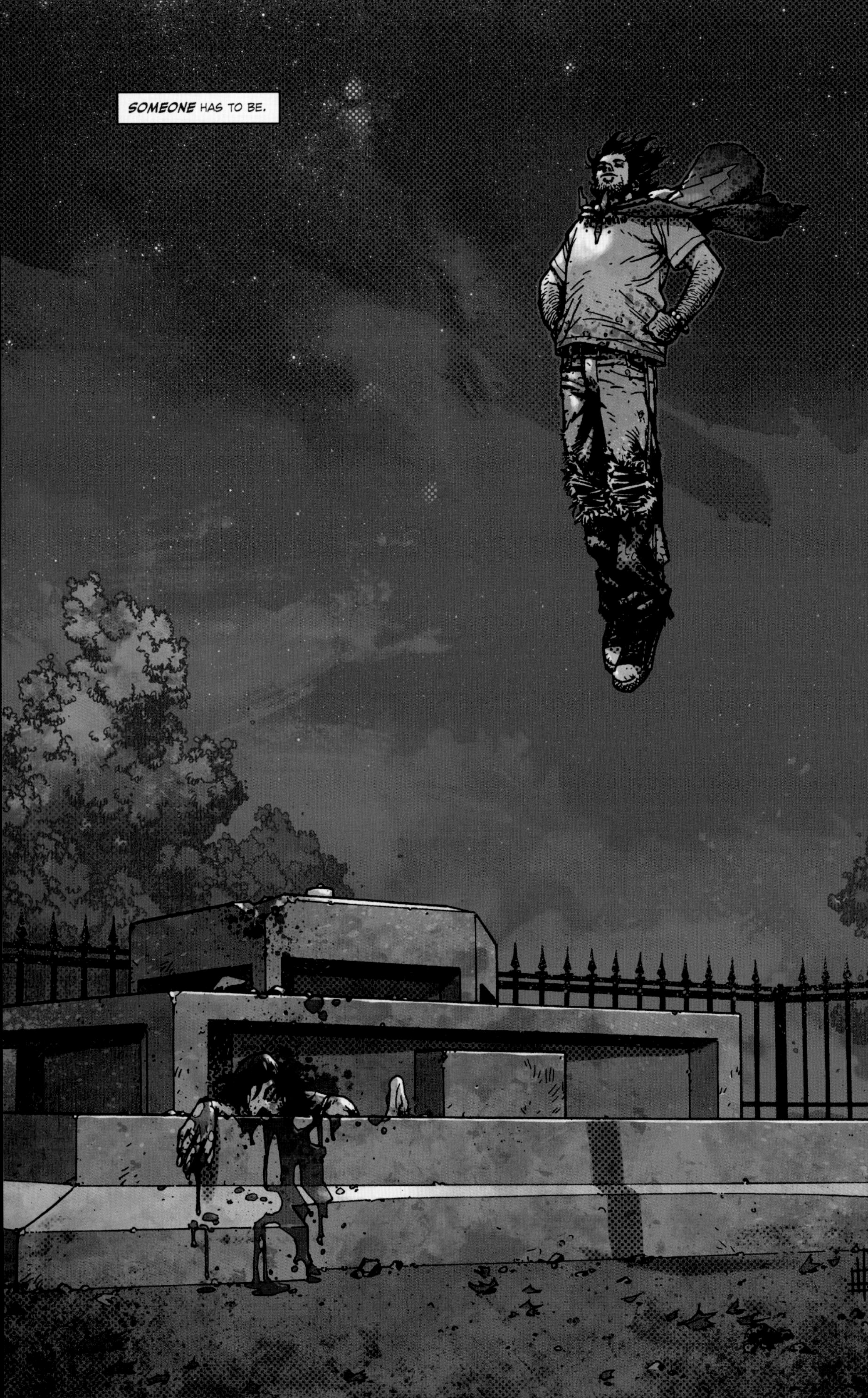
SOMEONE HAS TO BE.

"Evil is unspectacular and always human and shares our bed and eats at our own table."

—W.H. Auden

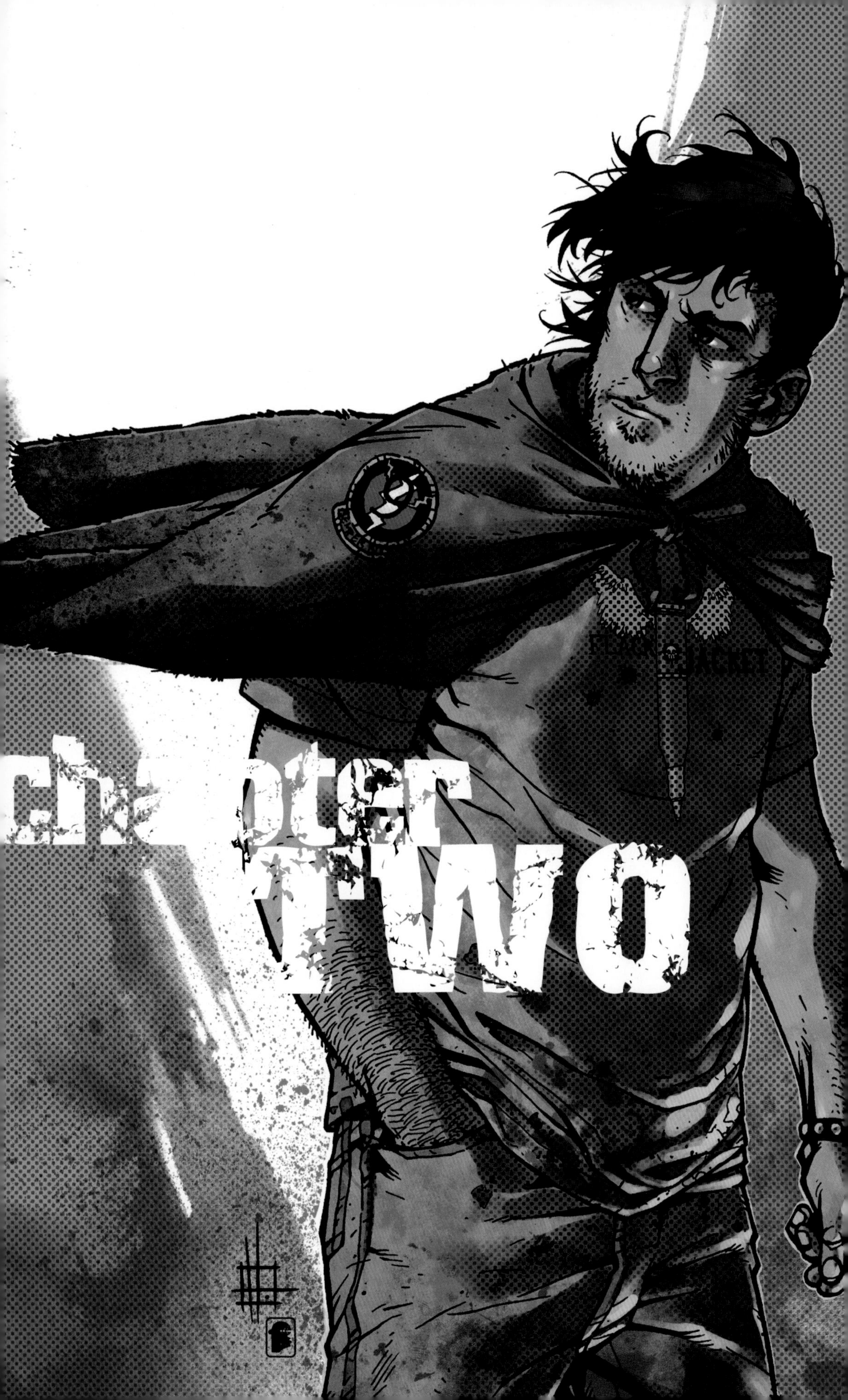
chapter
TWO

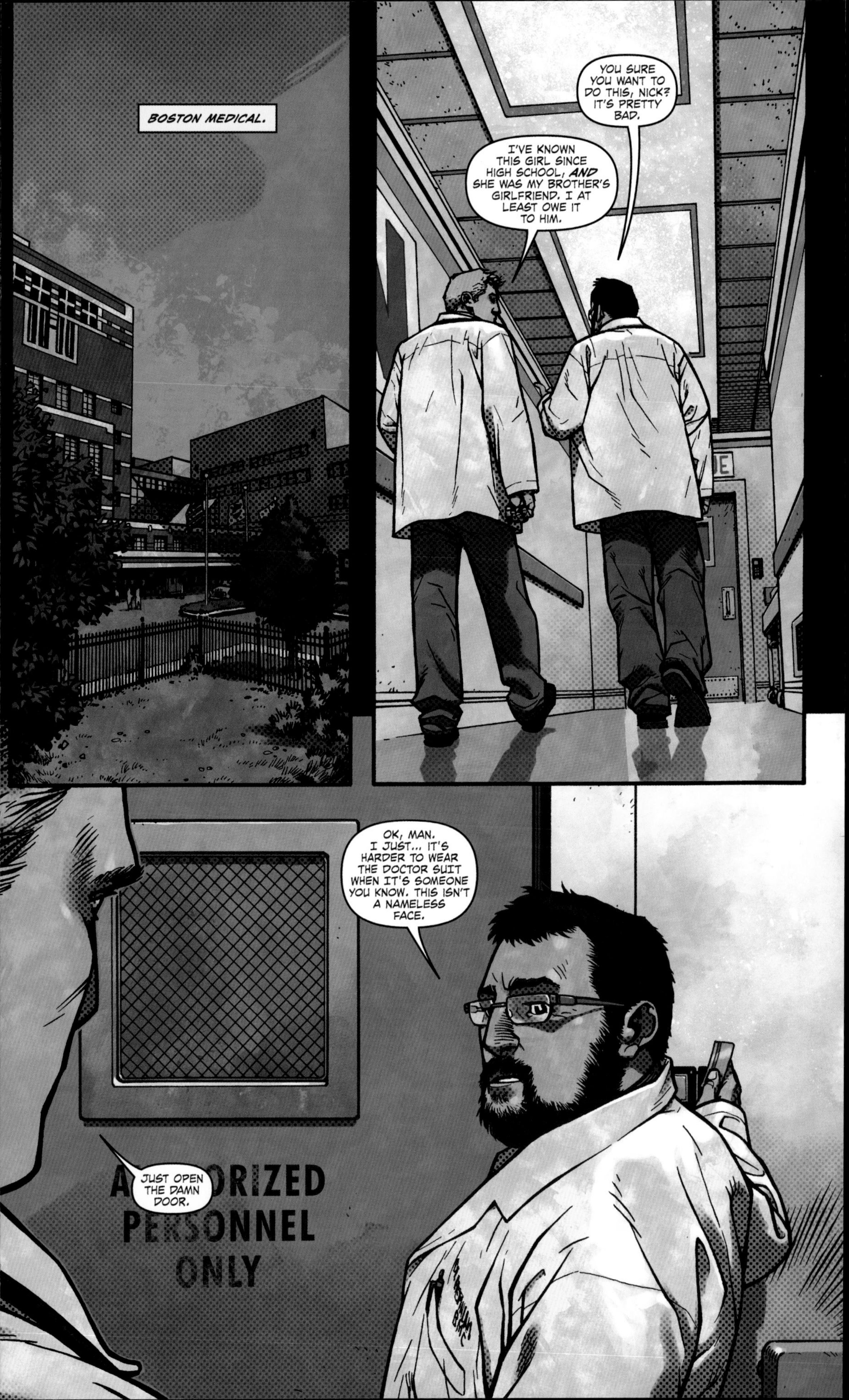
BOSTON MEDICAL.
YOU SURE YOU WANT TO DO THIS, NICK? IT'S PRETTY BAD.
I'VE KNOWN THIS GIRL SINCE HIGH SCHOOL, AND SHE WAS MY BROTHER'S GIRLFRIEND. I AT LEAST OWE IT TO HIM.
OK, MAN. I JUST... IT'S HARDER TO WEAR THE DOCTOR SUIT WHEN IT'S SOMEONE YOU KNOW. THIS ISN'T A NAMELESS FACE.
JUST OPEN THE DAMN DOOR.
PERSONNEL
ONLY

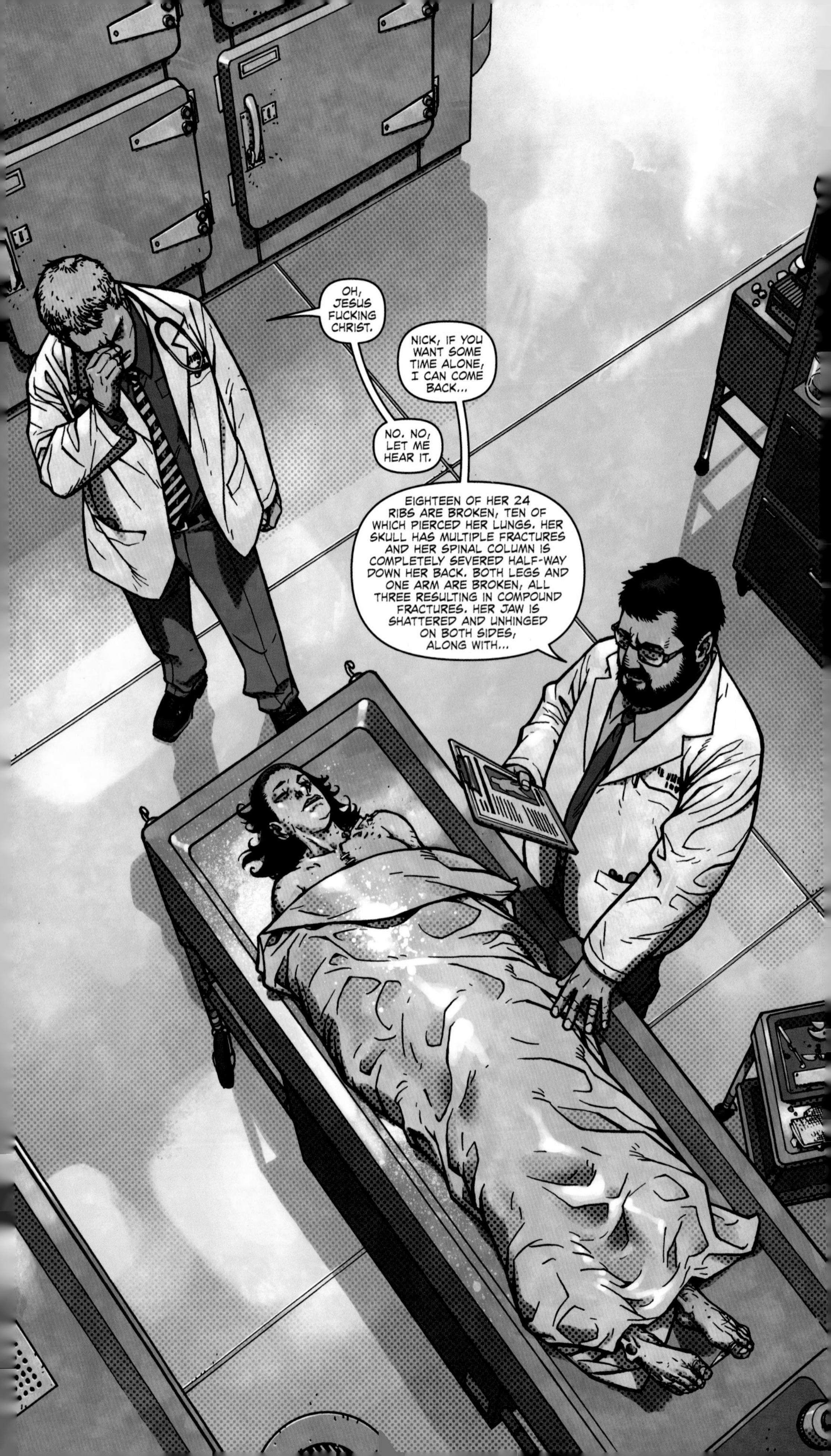
OH, JESUS FUCKING CHRIST.
NICK, IF YOU WANT SOME TIME ALONE, I CAN COME BACK...
NO. NO, LET ME HEAR IT.
EIGHTEEN OF HER 24 RIBS ARE BROKEN, TEN OF WHICH PIERCED HER LUNGS. HER SKULL HAS MULTIPLE FRACTURES AND HER SPINAL COLUMN IS COMPLETELY SEVERED HALF-WAY DOWN HER BACK. BOTH LEGS AND ONE ARM ARE BROKEN, ALL THREE RESULTING IN COMPOUND FRACTURES. HER JAW IS SHATTERED AND UNHINGED ON BOTH SIDES, ALONG WITH...

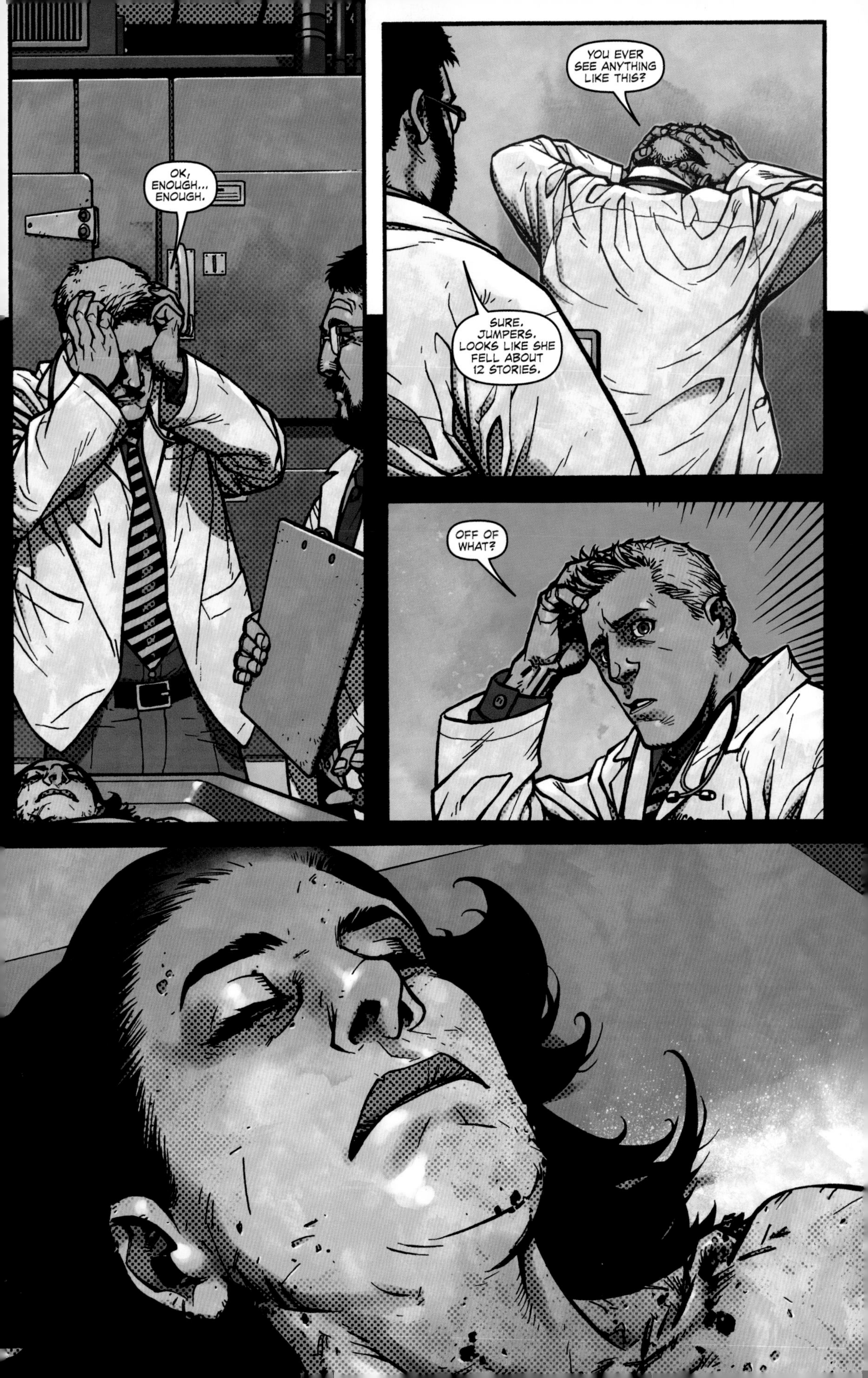
OK, ENOUGH... ENOUGH.
YOU EVER SEE ANYTHING LIKE THIS?
SURE. JUMPERS. LOOKS LIKE SHE FELL ABOUT 12 STORIES.
OFF OF WHAT?

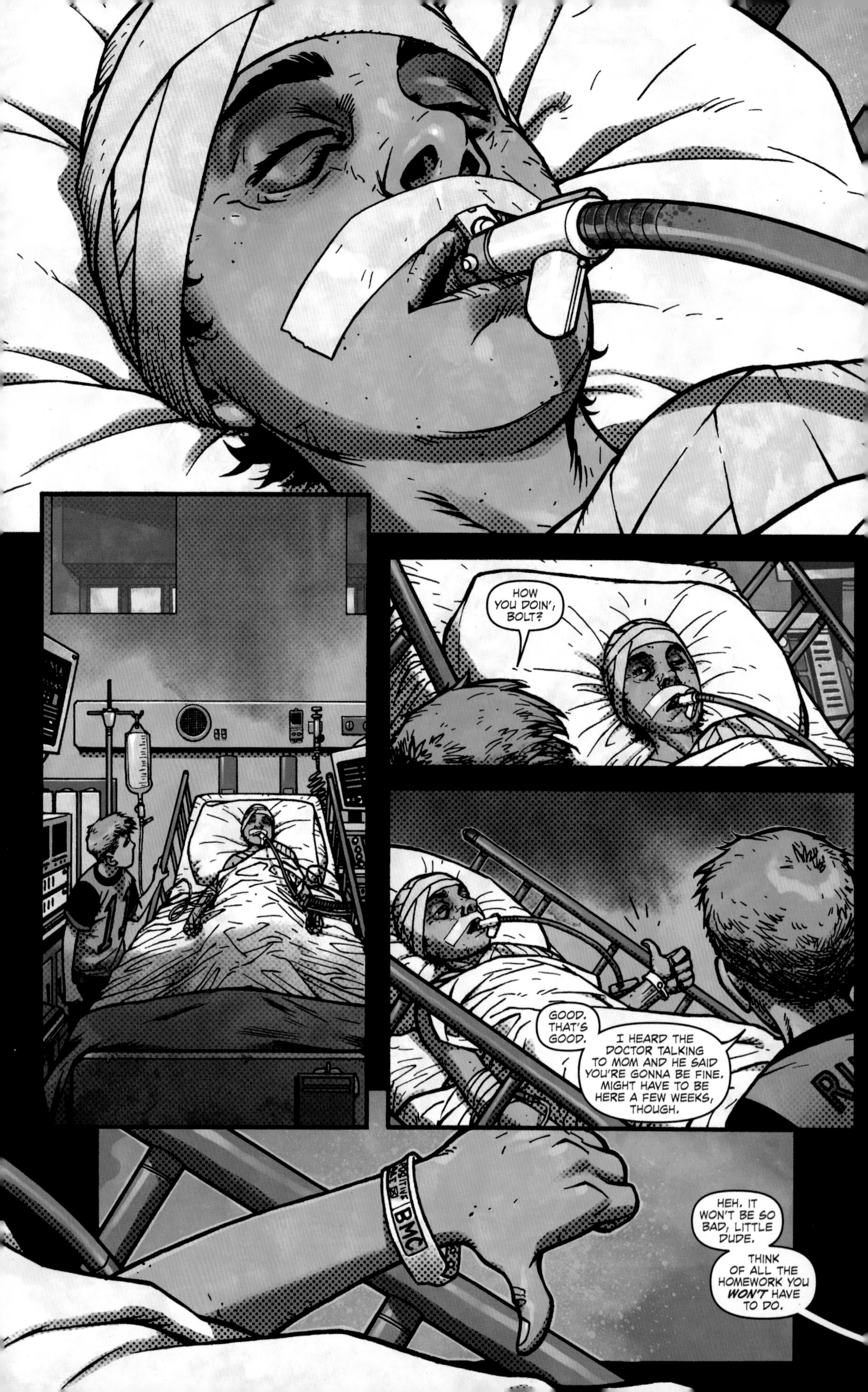
HOW YOU DOIN', BOLT?
GOOD. THAT'S GOOD.
I HEARD THE DOCTOR TALKING TO MOM AND HE SAID YOU'RE GONNA BE FINE. MIGHT HAVE TO BE HERE A FEW WEEKS, THOUGH.
BMC
HEH. IT WON'T BE SO BAD, LITTLE DUDE.
THINK OF ALL THE HOMEWORK YOU *WON'T* HAVE TO DO.

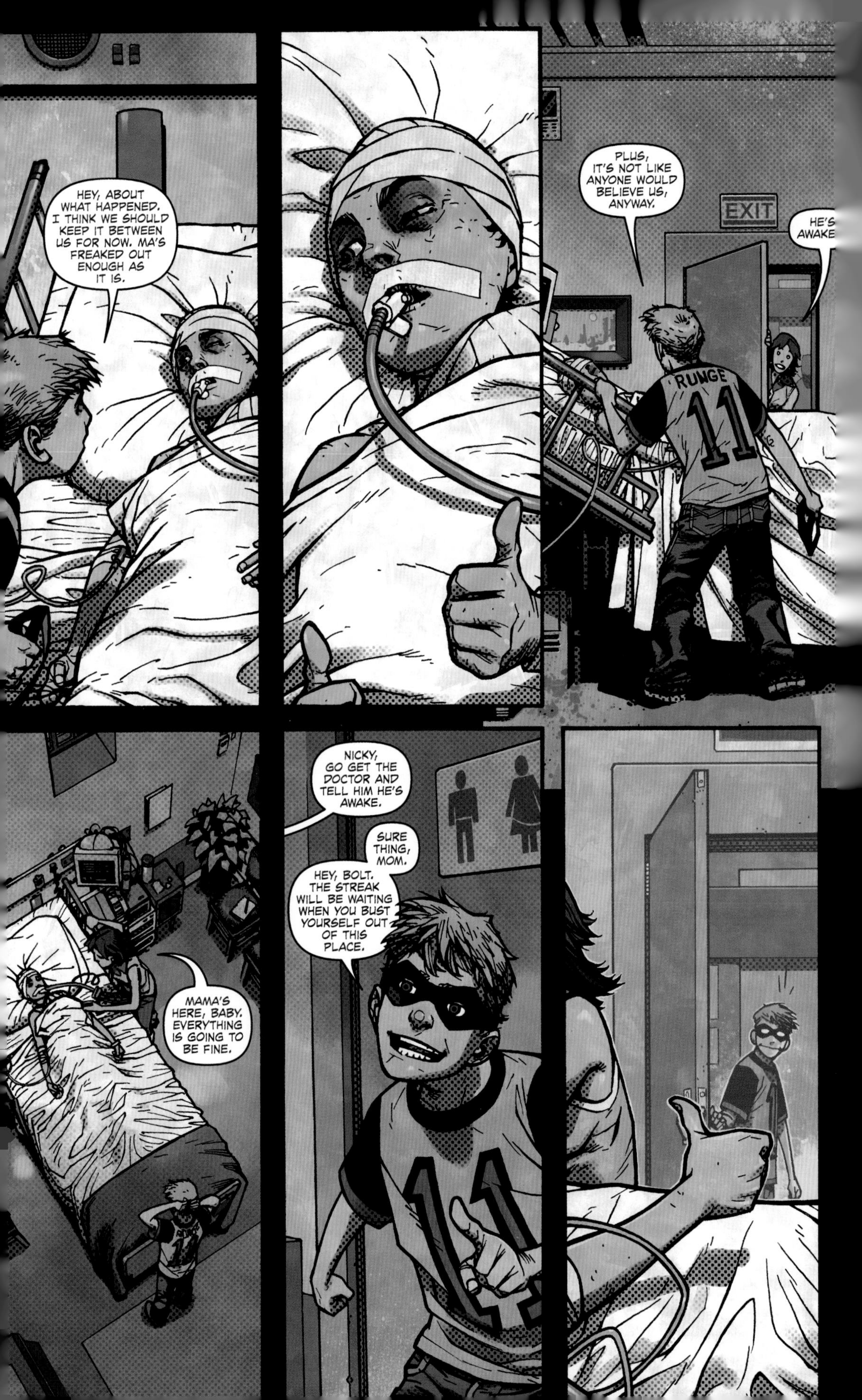
HEY, ABOUT WHAT HAPPENED. I THINK WE SHOULD KEEP IT BETWEEN US FOR NOW. MA'S FREAKED OUT ENOUGH AS IT IS.
PLUS, IT'S NOT LIKE ANYONE WOULD BELIEVE US, ANYWAY.
EXIT
HE'S AWAKE
RUNGE 11
MAMA'S HERE, BABY. EVERYTHING IS GOING TO BE FINE.
NICKY, GO GET THE DOCTOR AND TELL HIM HE'S AWAKE.
SURE THING, MOM.
HEY, BOLT. THE STREAK WILL BE WAITING WHEN YOU BUST YOURSELF OUT OF THIS PLACE.

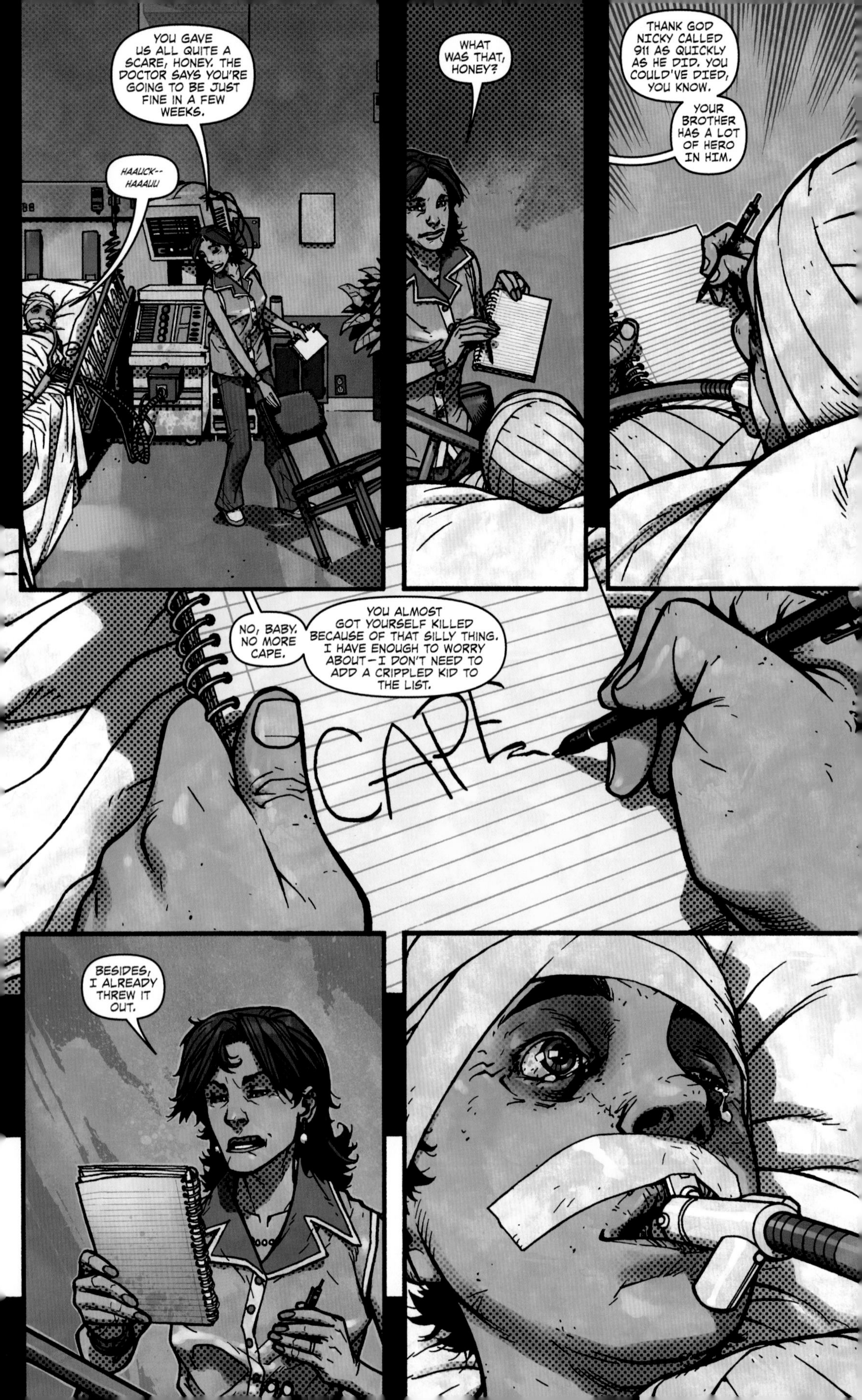
YOU GAVE US ALL QUITE A SCARE, HONEY. THE DOCTOR SAYS YOU'RE GOING TO BE JUST FINE IN A FEW WEEKS.
HAAUCK-- HAAAUU
WHAT WAS THAT, HONEY?
THANK GOD NICKY CALLED 911 AS QUICKLY AS HE DID. YOU COULD'VE DIED, YOU KNOW.
YOUR BROTHER HAS A LOT OF HERO IN HIM.
CAPE
NO, BABY. NO MORE CAPE.
YOU ALMOST GOT YOURSELF KILLED BECAUSE OF THAT SILLY THING. I HAVE ENOUGH TO WORRY ABOUT—I DON'T NEED TO ADD A CRIPPLED KID TO THE LIST.
BESIDES, I ALREADY THREW IT OUT.

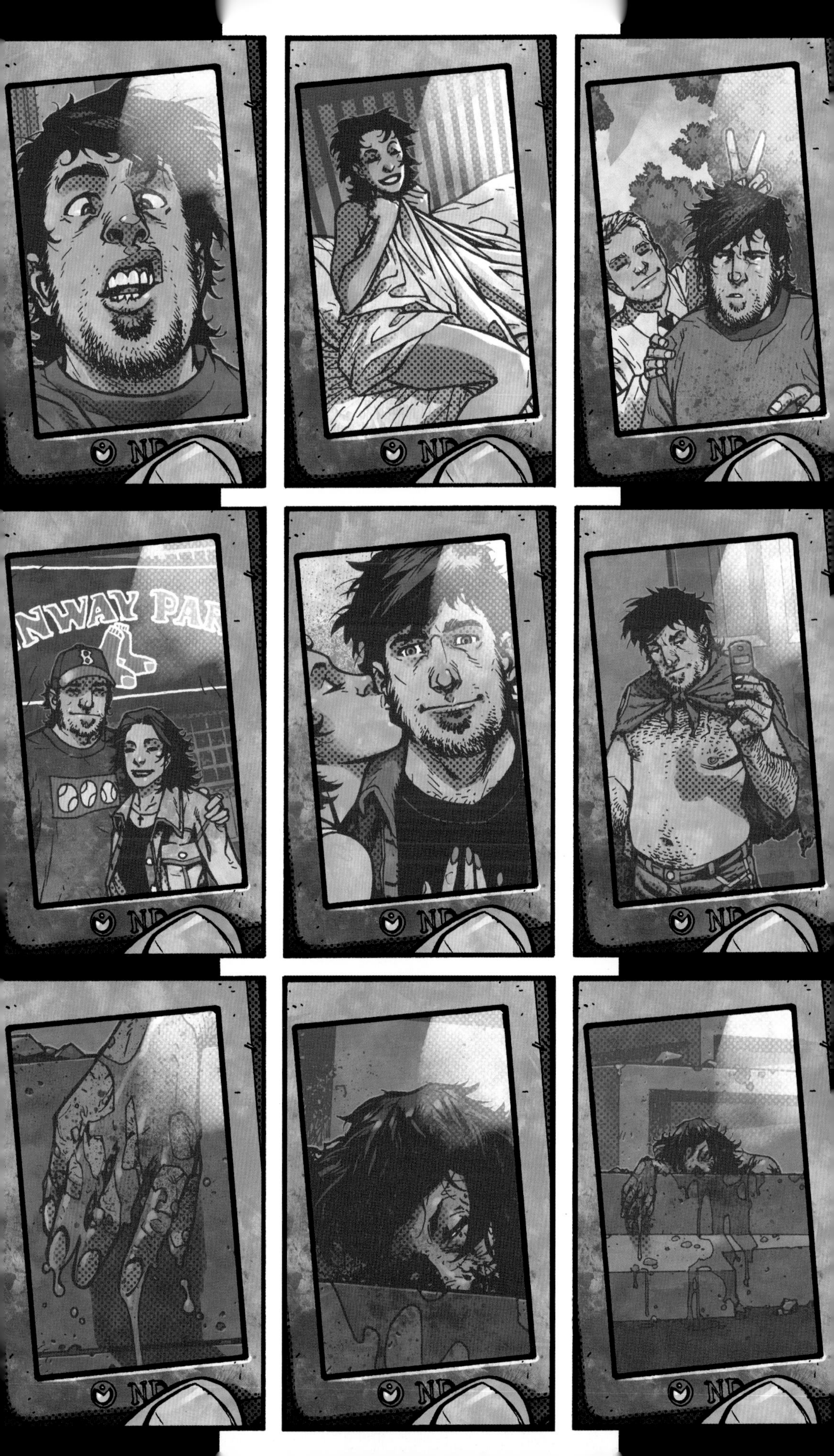
NWAY PAR

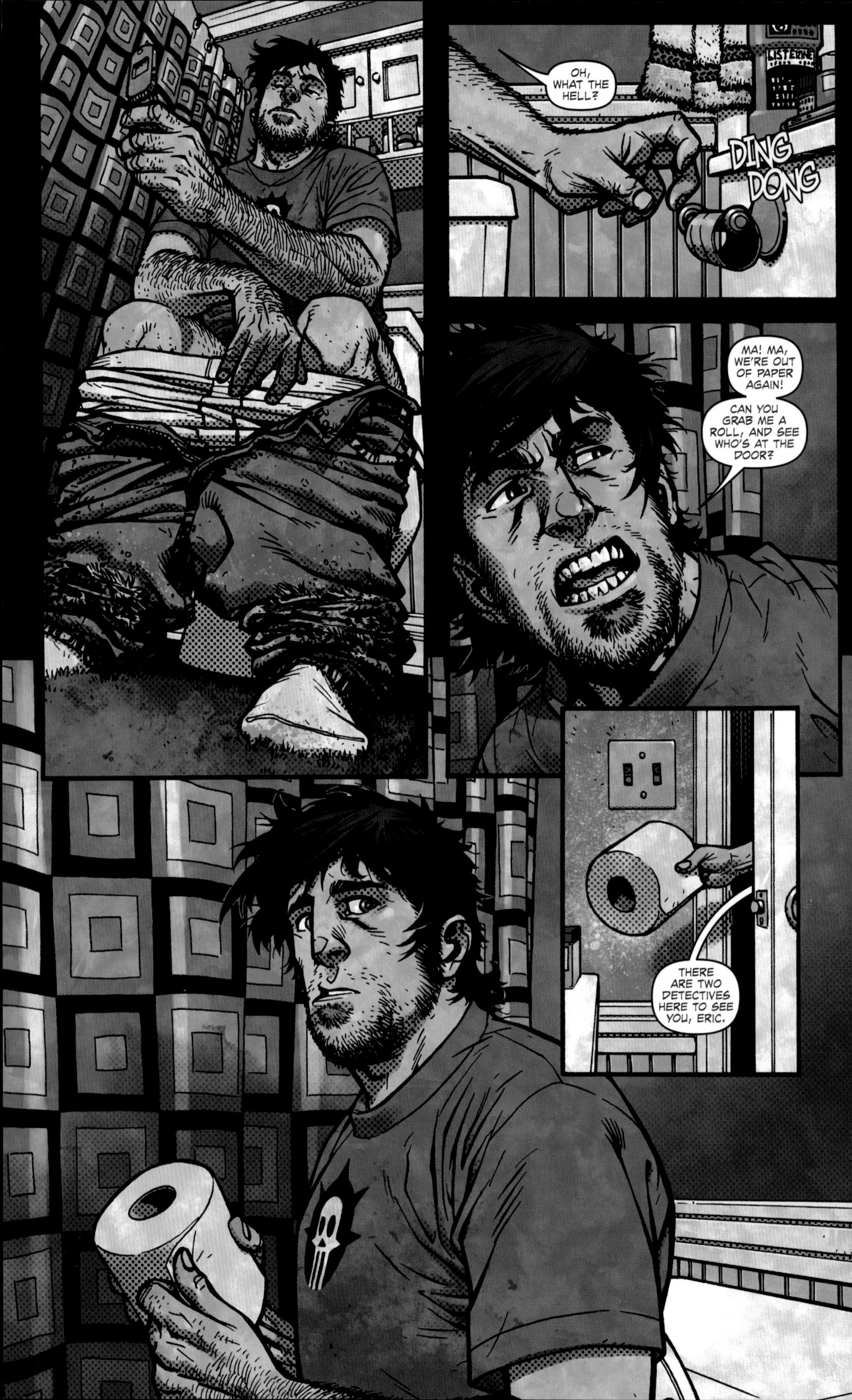
OH, WHAT THE HELL?
DING DONG
MA! MA, WE'RE OUT OF PAPER AGAIN!
CAN YOU GRAB ME A ROLL, AND SEE WHO'S AT THE DOOR?
THERE ARE TWO DETECTIVES HERE TO SEE YOU, ERIC.

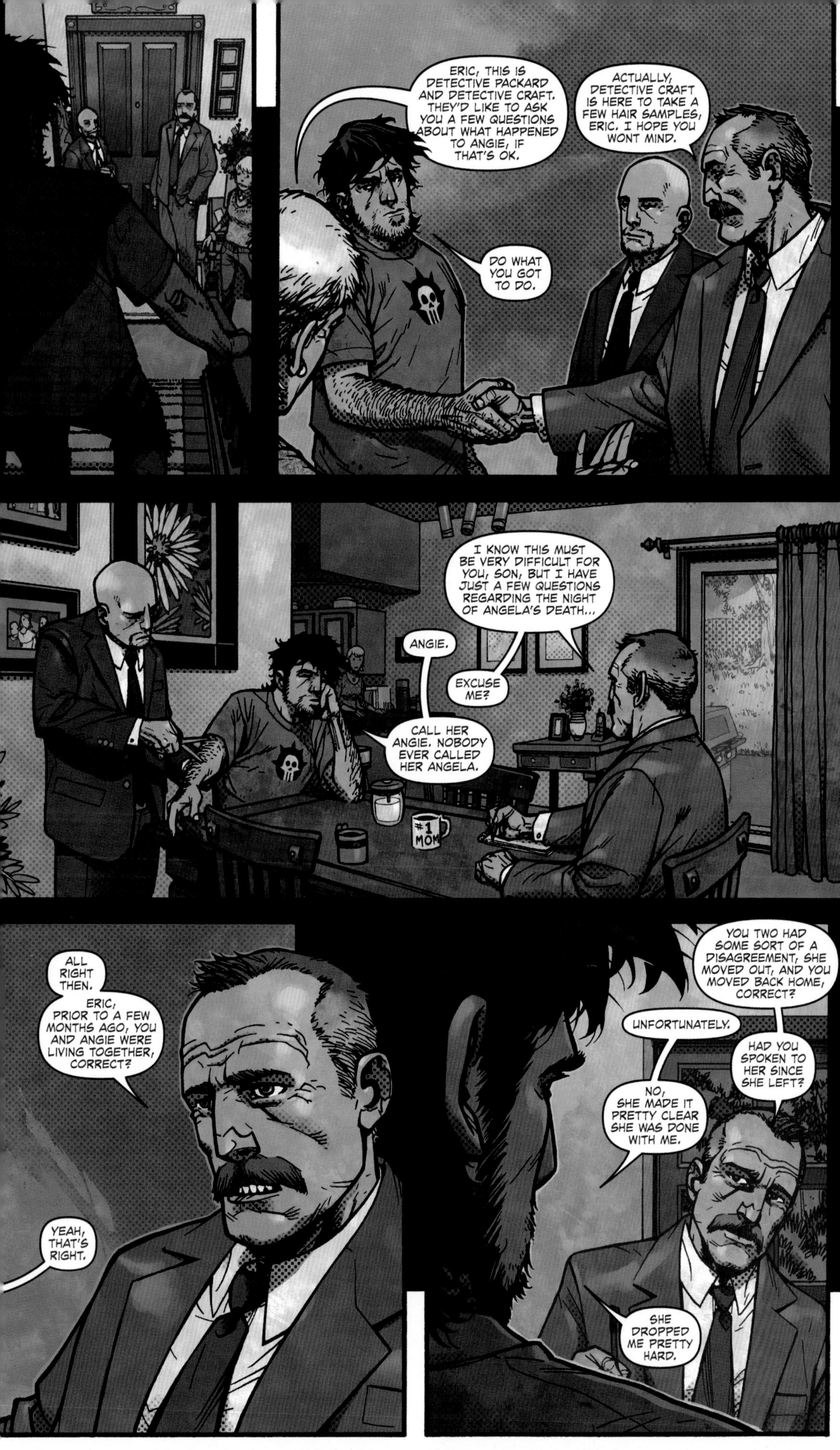
ERIC, THIS IS DETECTIVE PACKARD AND DETECTIVE CRAFT. THEY'D LIKE TO ASK YOU A FEW QUESTIONS ABOUT WHAT HAPPENED TO ANGIE, IF THAT'S OK.
ACTUALLY, DETECTIVE CRAFT IS HERE TO TAKE A FEW HAIR SAMPLES, ERIC. I HOPE YOU WONT MIND.
DO WHAT YOU GOT TO DO.
I KNOW THIS MUST BE VERY DIFFICULT FOR YOU, SON, BUT I HAVE JUST A FEW QUESTIONS REGARDING THE NIGHT OF ANGELA'S DEATH...
ANGIE.
EXCUSE ME?
CALL HER ANGIE. NOBODY EVER CALLED HER ANGELA.
#1 MOM
ALL RIGHT THEN.
ERIC, PRIOR TO A FEW MONTHS AGO, YOU AND ANGIE WERE LIVING TOGETHER, CORRECT?
YEAH, THAT'S RIGHT.
YOU TWO HAD SOME SORT OF A DISAGREEMENT, SHE MOVED OUT, AND YOU MOVED BACK HOME, CORRECT?
UNFORTUNATELY.
HAD YOU SPOKEN TO HER SINCE SHE LEFT?
NO, SHE MADE IT PRETTY CLEAR SHE WAS DONE WITH ME.
SHE DROPPED ME PRETTY HARD.

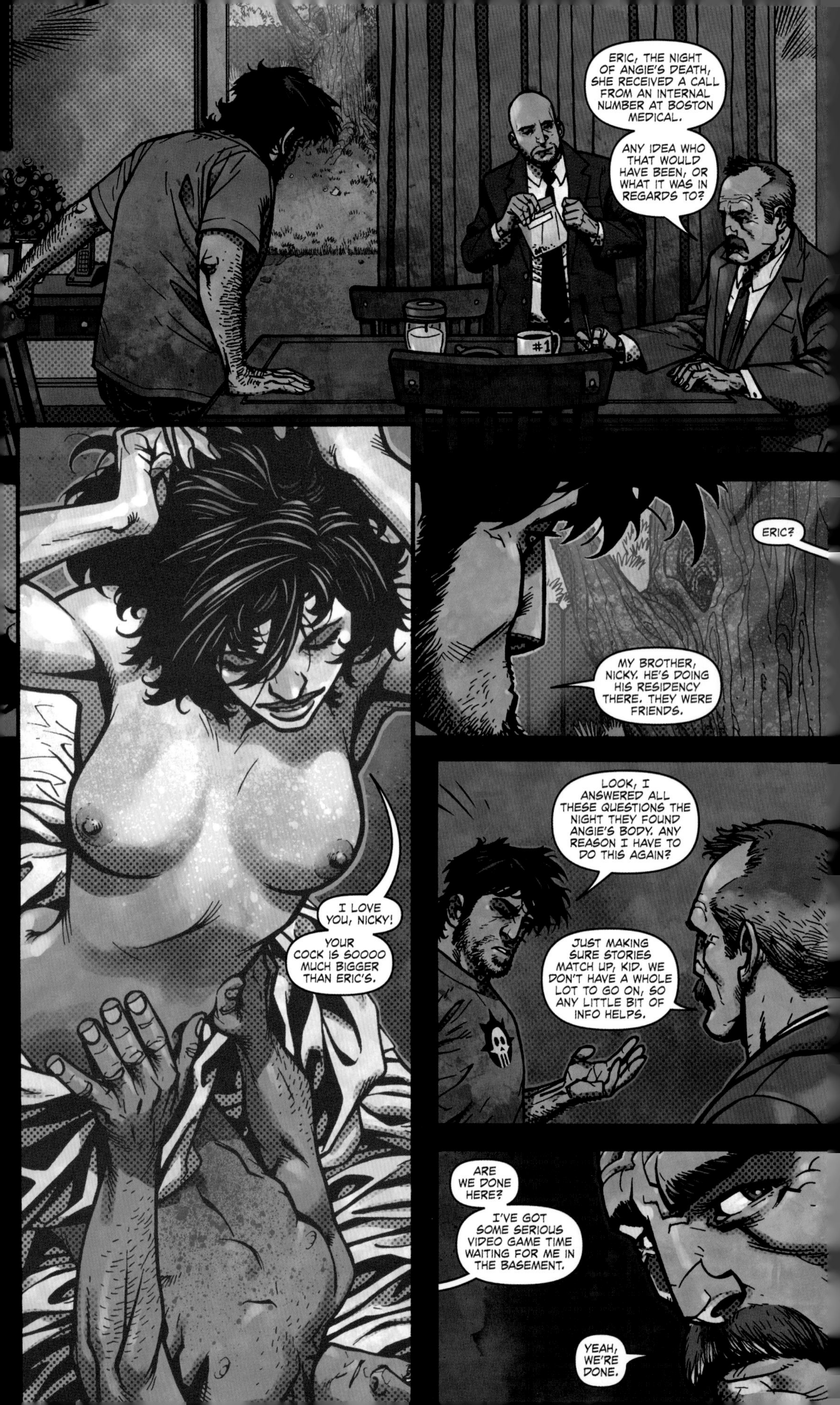
ERIC, THE NIGHT OF ANGIE'S DEATH, SHE RECEIVED A CALL FROM AN INTERNAL NUMBER AT BOSTON MEDICAL.
ANY IDEA WHO THAT WOULD HAVE BEEN, OR WHAT IT WAS IN REGARDS TO?
I LOVE YOU, NICKY!
YOUR COCK IS SOOOO MUCH BIGGER THAN ERIC'S.
ERIC?
MY BROTHER, NICKY. HE'S DOING HIS RESIDENCY THERE. THEY WERE FRIENDS.
LOOK, I ANSWERED ALL THESE QUESTIONS THE NIGHT THEY FOUND ANGIE'S BODY. ANY REASON I HAVE TO DO THIS AGAIN?
JUST MAKING SURE STORIES MATCH UP, KID. WE DON'T HAVE A WHOLE LOT TO GO ON, SO ANY LITTLE BIT OF INFO HELPS.
ARE WE DONE HERE?
I'VE GOT SOME SERIOUS VIDEO GAME TIME WAITING FOR ME IN THE BASEMENT.
YEAH, WE'RE DONE.

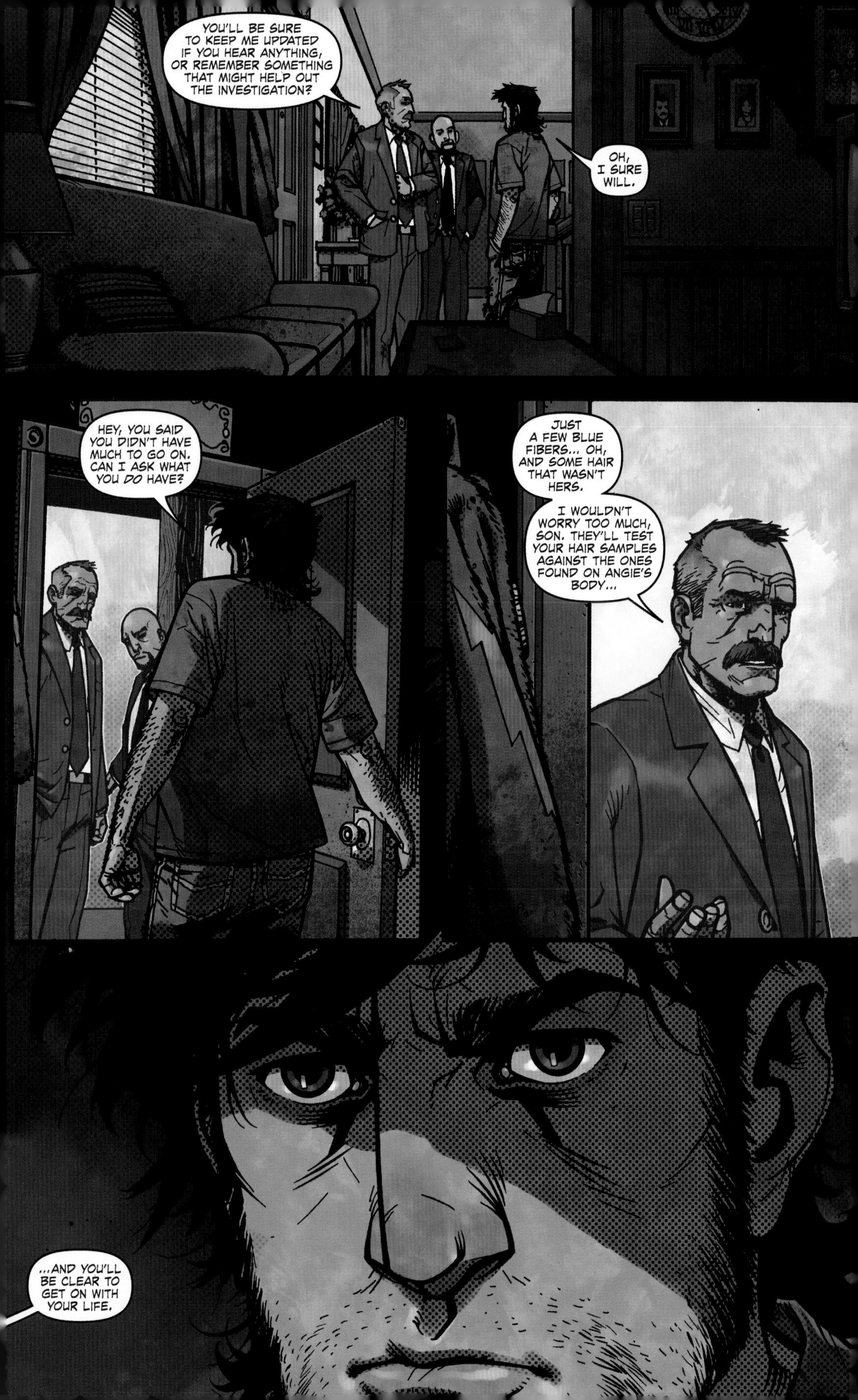
YOU'LL BE SURE TO KEEP ME UPDATED IF YOU HEAR ANYTHING, OR REMEMBER SOMETHING THAT MIGHT HELP OUT THE INVESTIGATION?
OH, I SURE WILL.
HEY, YOU SAID YOU DIDN'T HAVE MUCH TO GO ON. CAN I ASK WHAT YOU *DO* HAVE?
JUST A FEW BLUE FIBERS... OH, AND SOME HAIR THAT WASN'T HERS.
I WOULDN'T WORRY TOO MUCH, SON. THEY'LL TEST YOUR HAIR SAMPLES AGAINST THE ONES FOUND ON ANGIE'S BODY...
...AND YOU'LL BE CLEAR TO GET ON WITH YOUR LIFE.

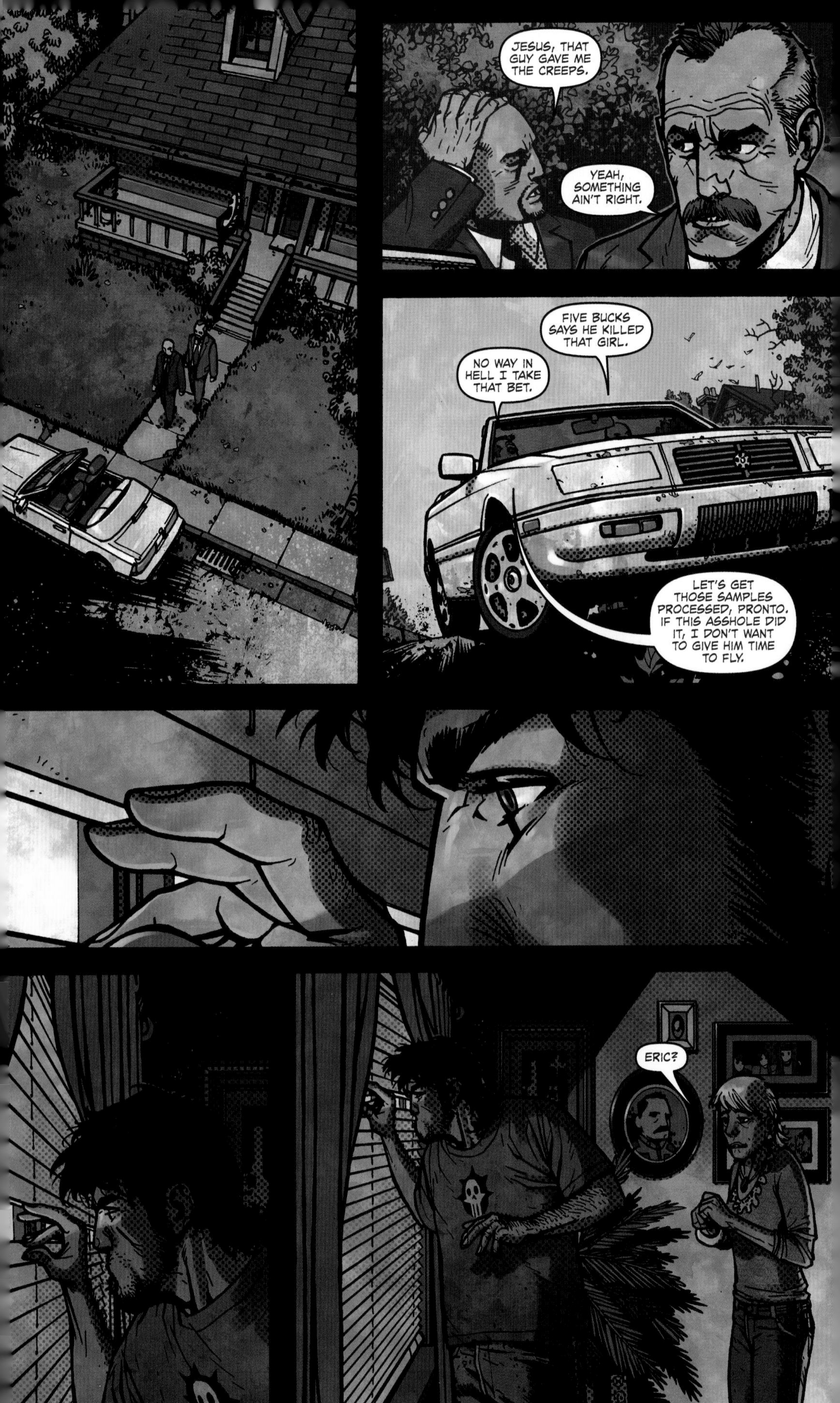
JESUS, THAT GUY GAVE ME THE CREEPS.
YEAH, SOMETHING AIN'T RIGHT.
FIVE BUCKS SAYS HE KILLED THAT GIRL.
NO WAY IN HELL I TAKE THAT BET.
LET'S GET THOSE SAMPLES PROCESSED, PRONTO. IF THIS ASSHOLE DID IT, I DON'T WANT TO GIVE HIM TIME TO FLY.
ERIC?

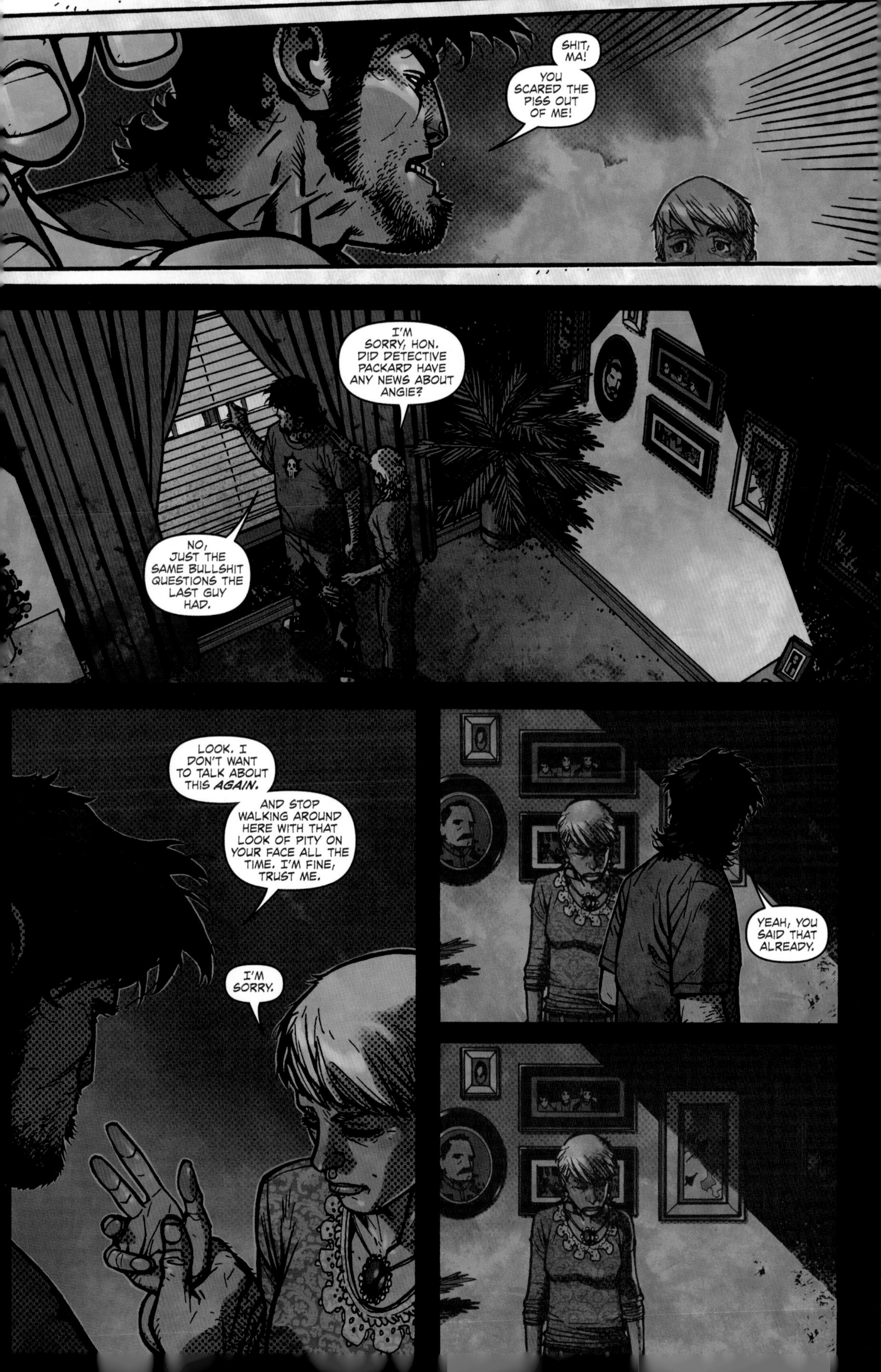
SHIT, MA!
YOU SCARED THE PISS OUT OF ME!
I'M SORRY, HON. DID DETECTIVE PACKARD HAVE ANY NEWS ABOUT ANGIE?
NO, JUST THE SAME BULLSHIT QUESTIONS THE LAST GUY HAD.
LOOK. I DON'T WANT TO TALK ABOUT THIS AGAIN.
AND STOP WALKING AROUND HERE WITH THAT LOOK OF PITY ON YOUR FACE ALL THE TIME. I'M FINE, TRUST ME.
I'M SORRY.
YEAH, YOU SAID THAT ALREADY.

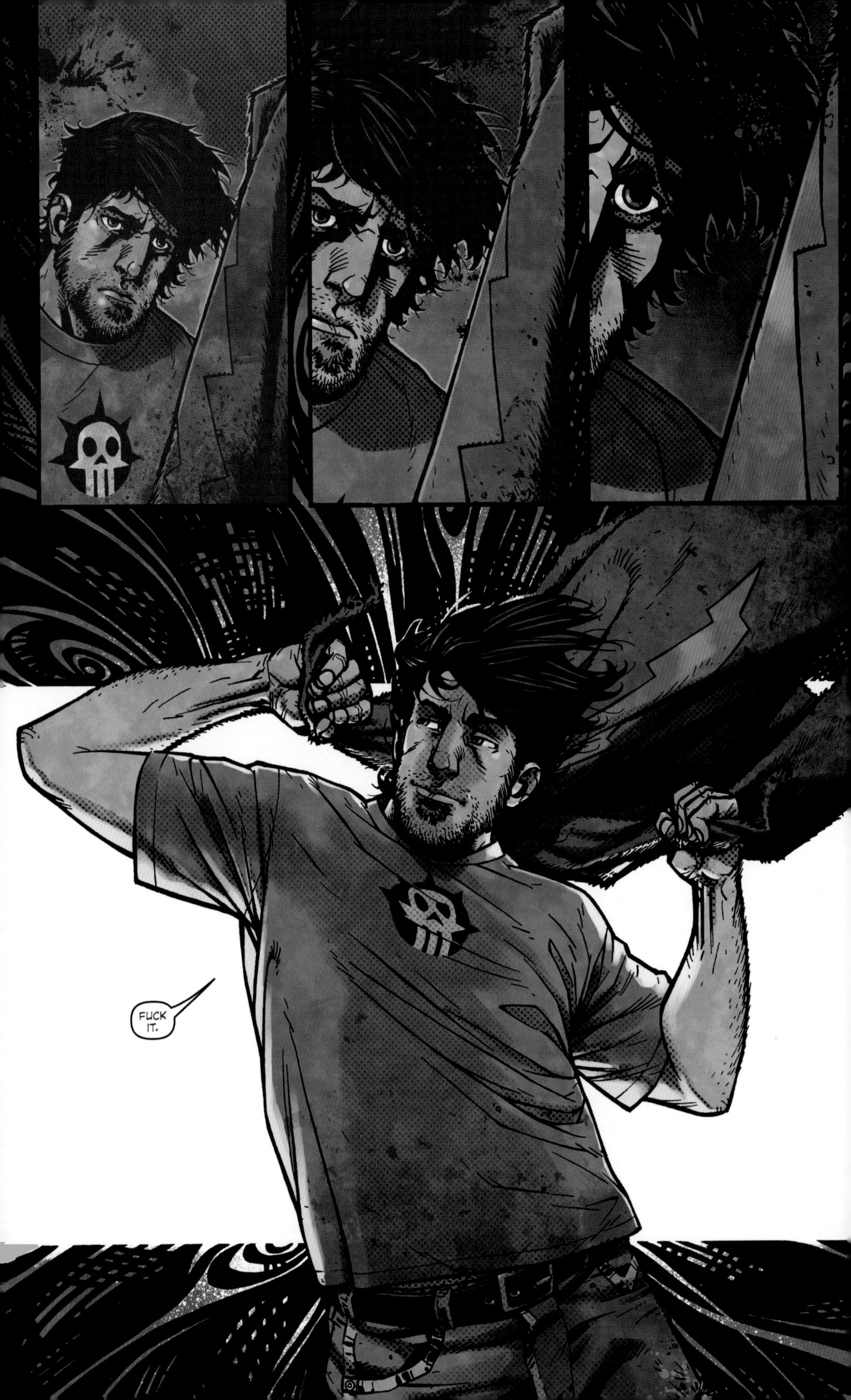
FUCK IT.

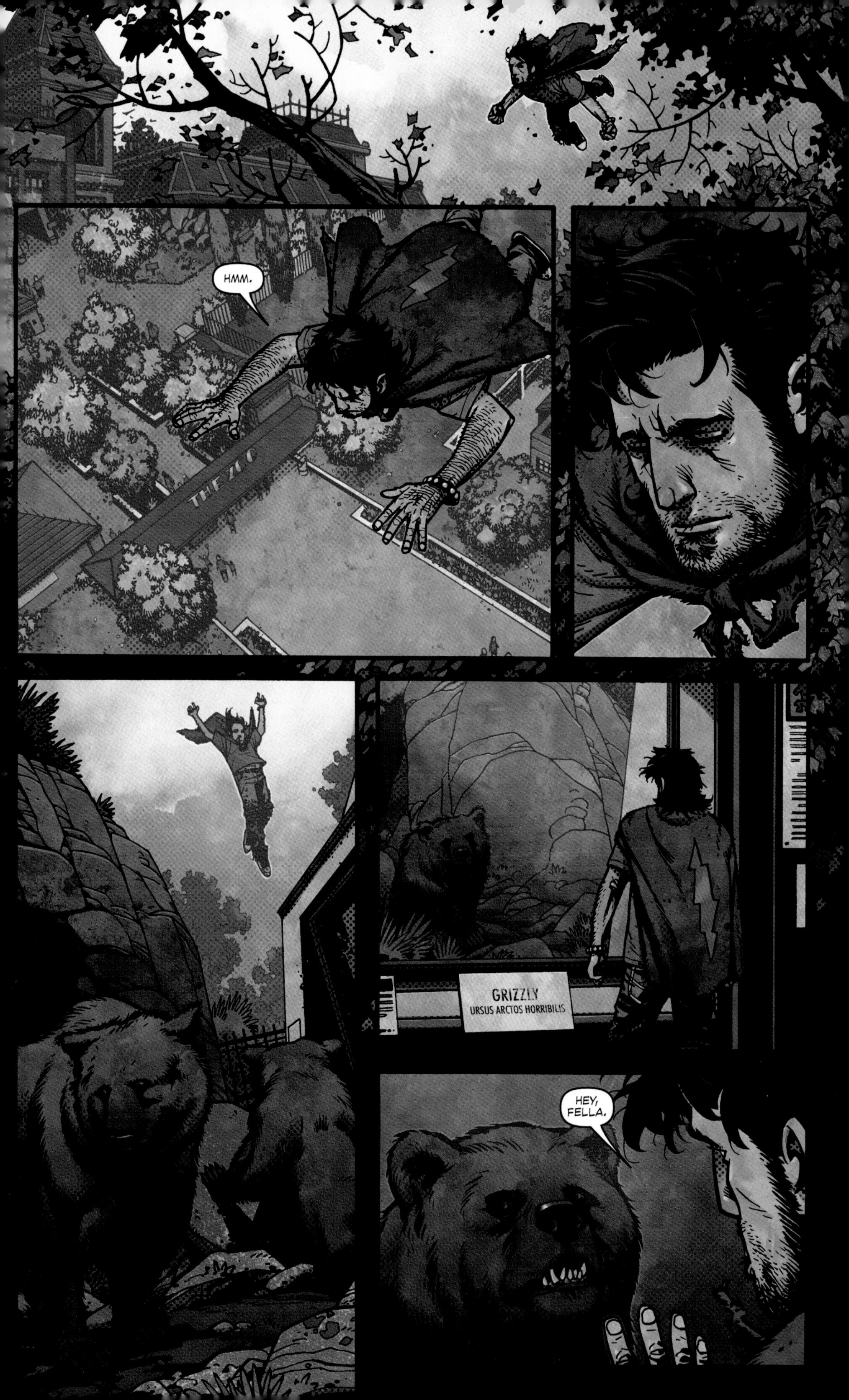
HMM.
THE ZOO
GRIZZLY
URSUS ARCTOS HORRIBILIS
HEY, FELLA.

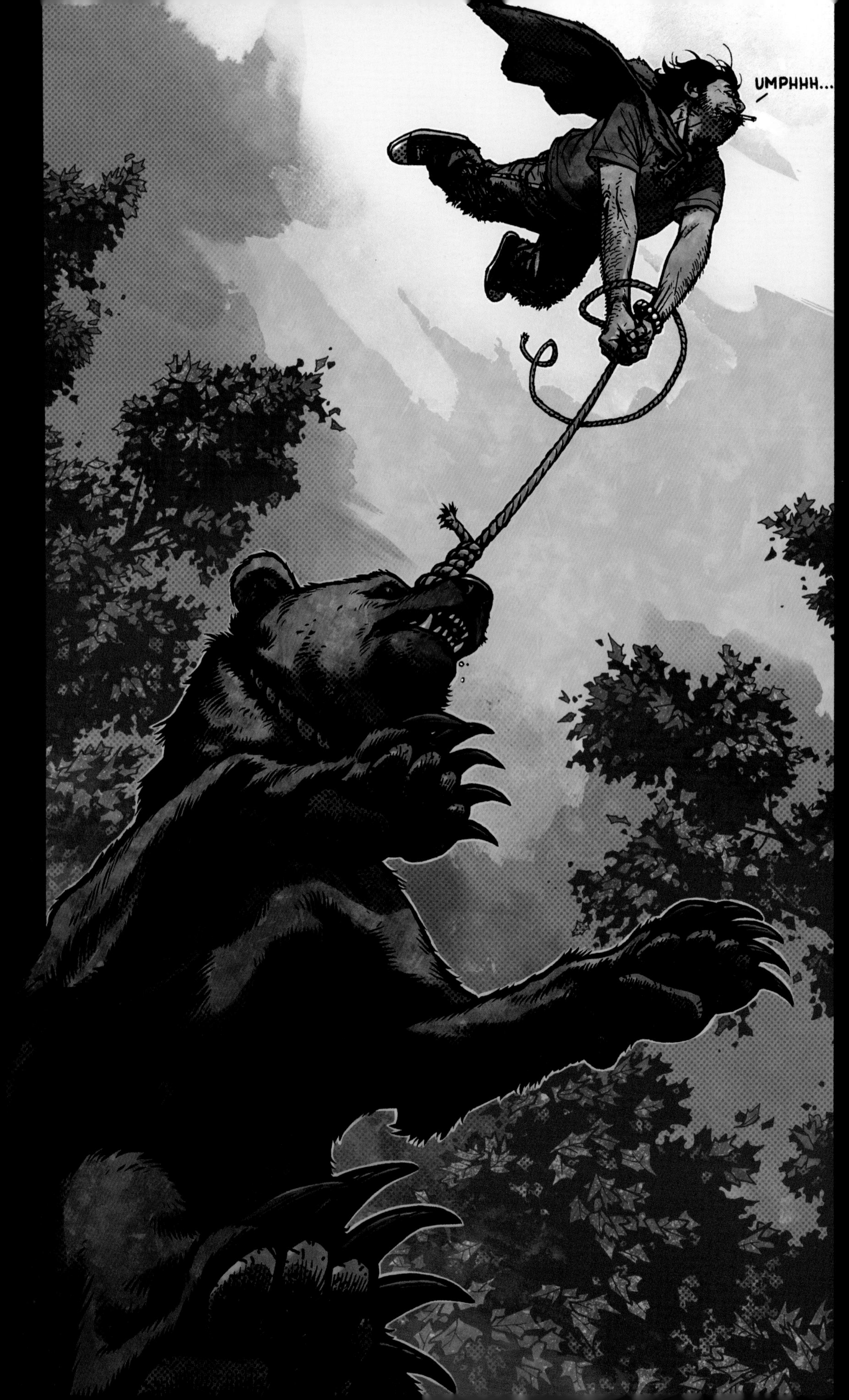
UMPHHH...

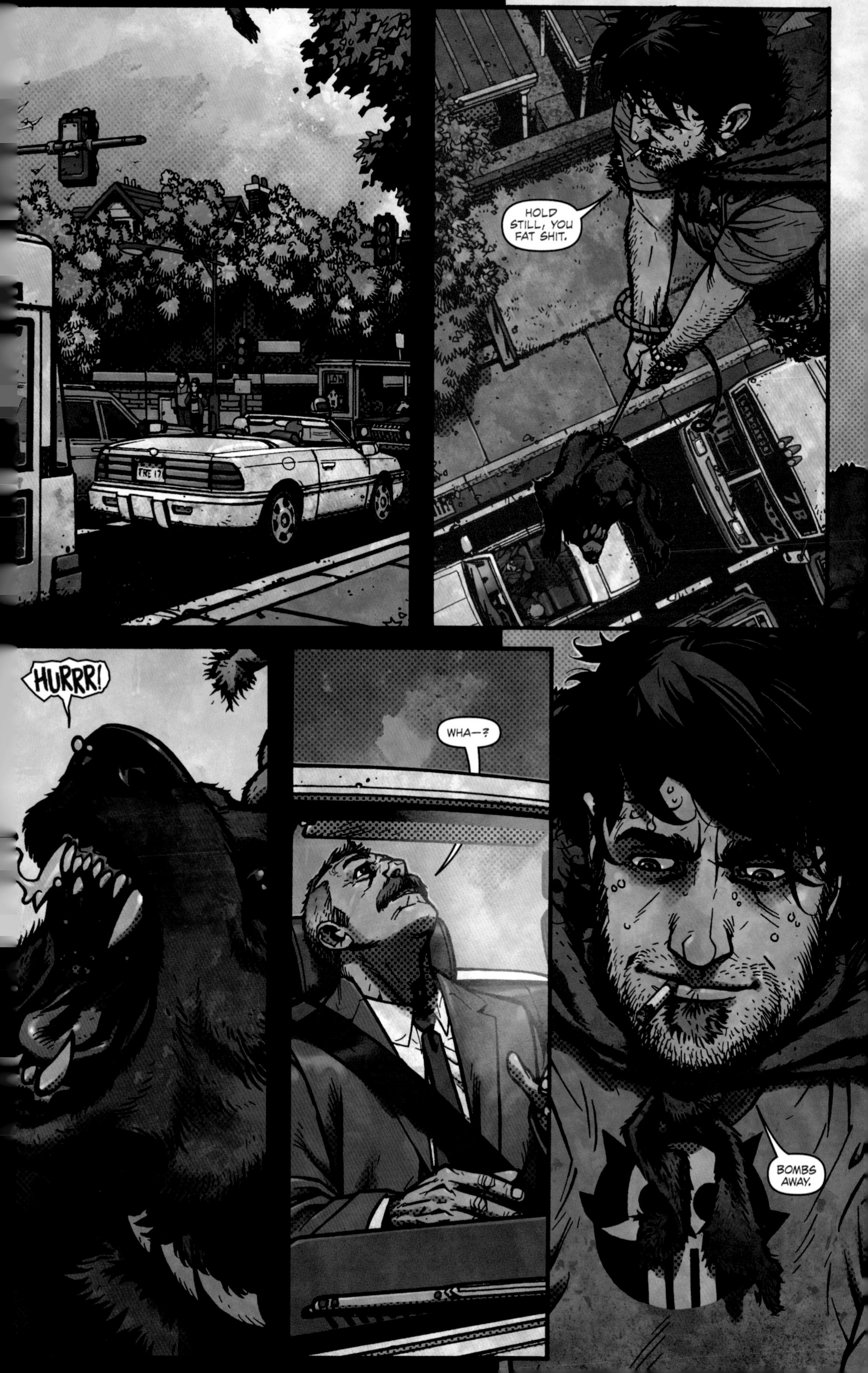
HOLD STILL, YOU FAT SHIT.
HURRR!
WHA—?
BOMBS AWAY.

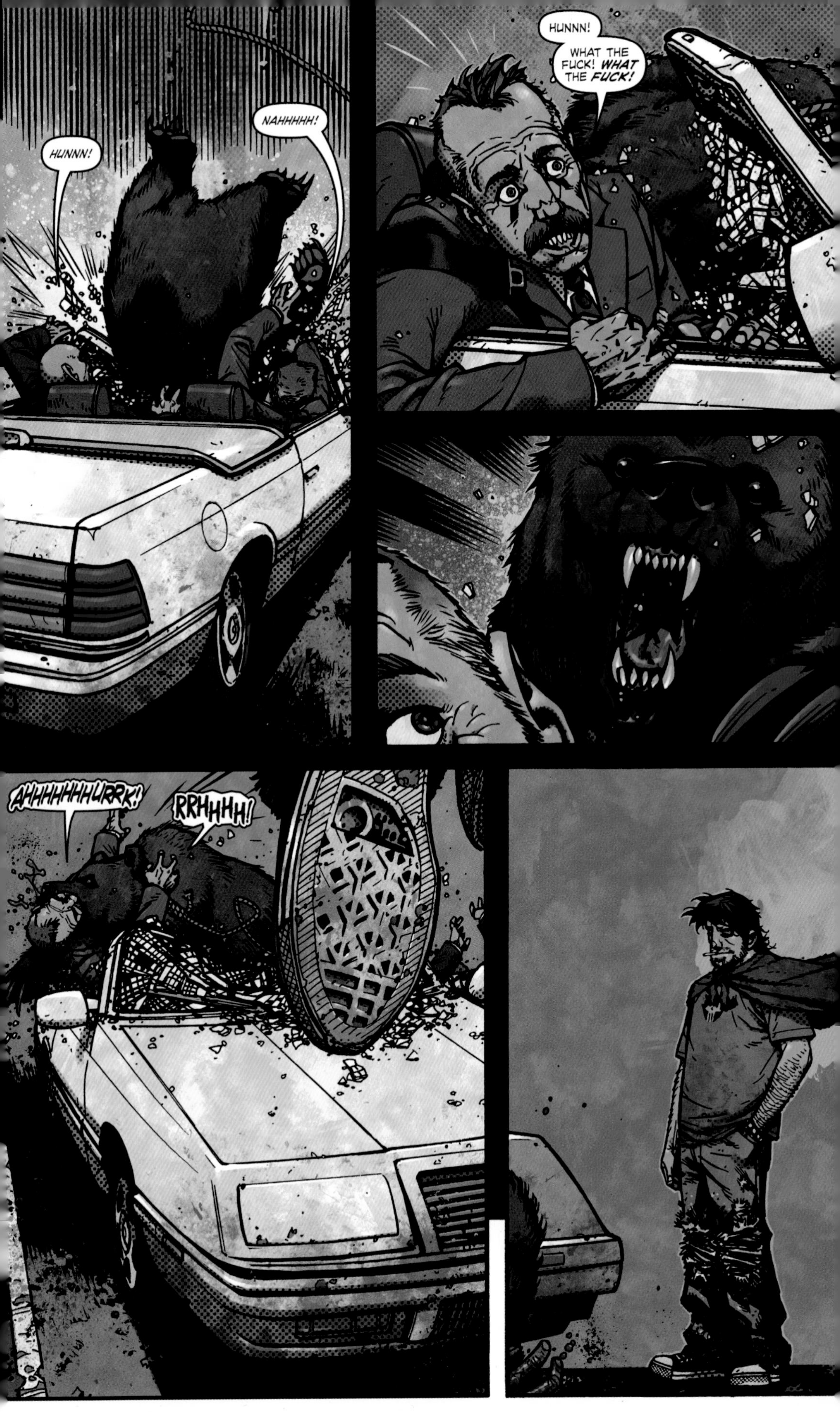
HUNNN!
NAHHHHHH!
HUNNN!
WHAT THE FUCK! WHAT THE FUCK!
AHHHHHHHHURRK!
RRHHHH!

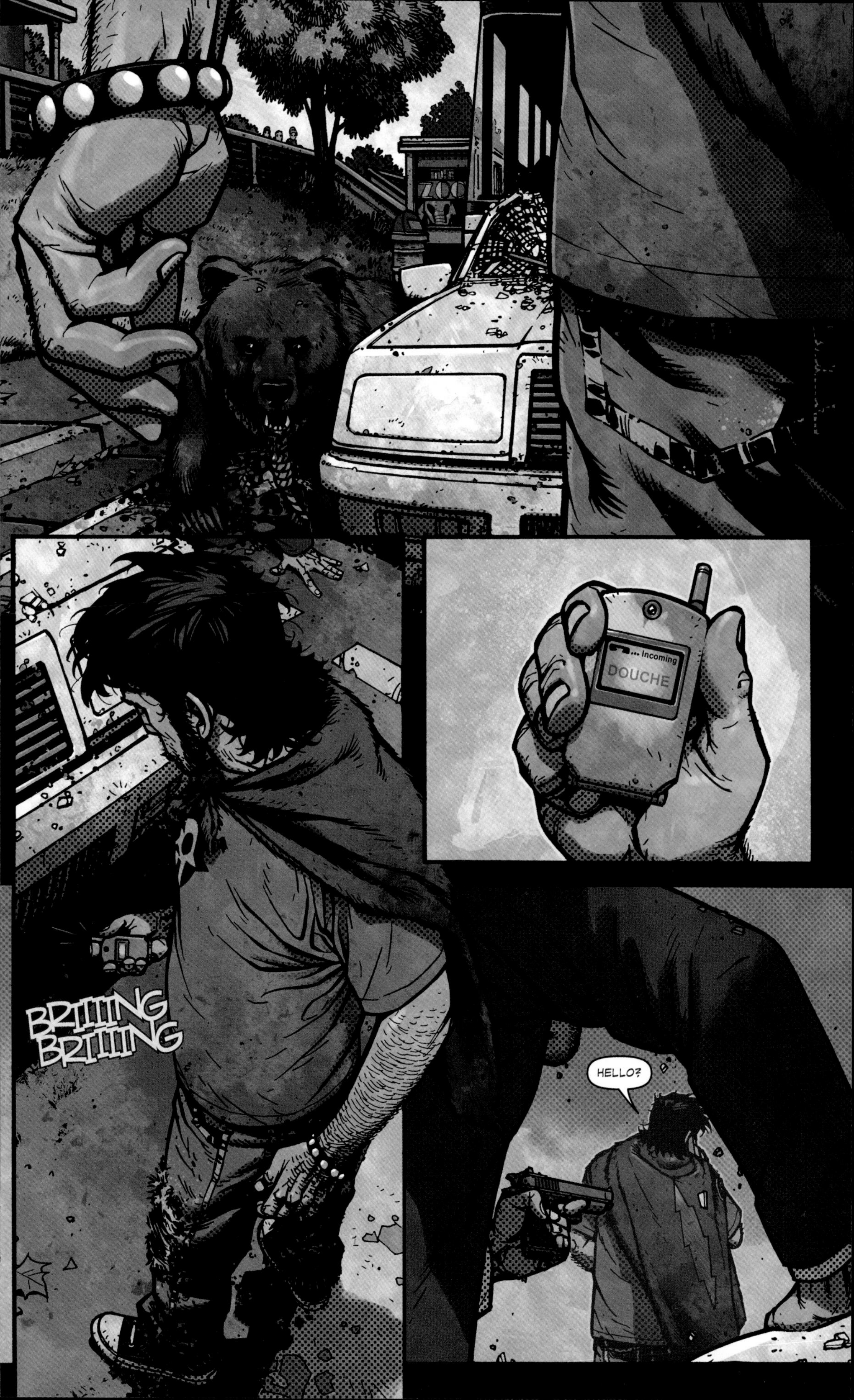
Incoming
DOUCHE
BRIIIING
BRIIIING
HELLO?

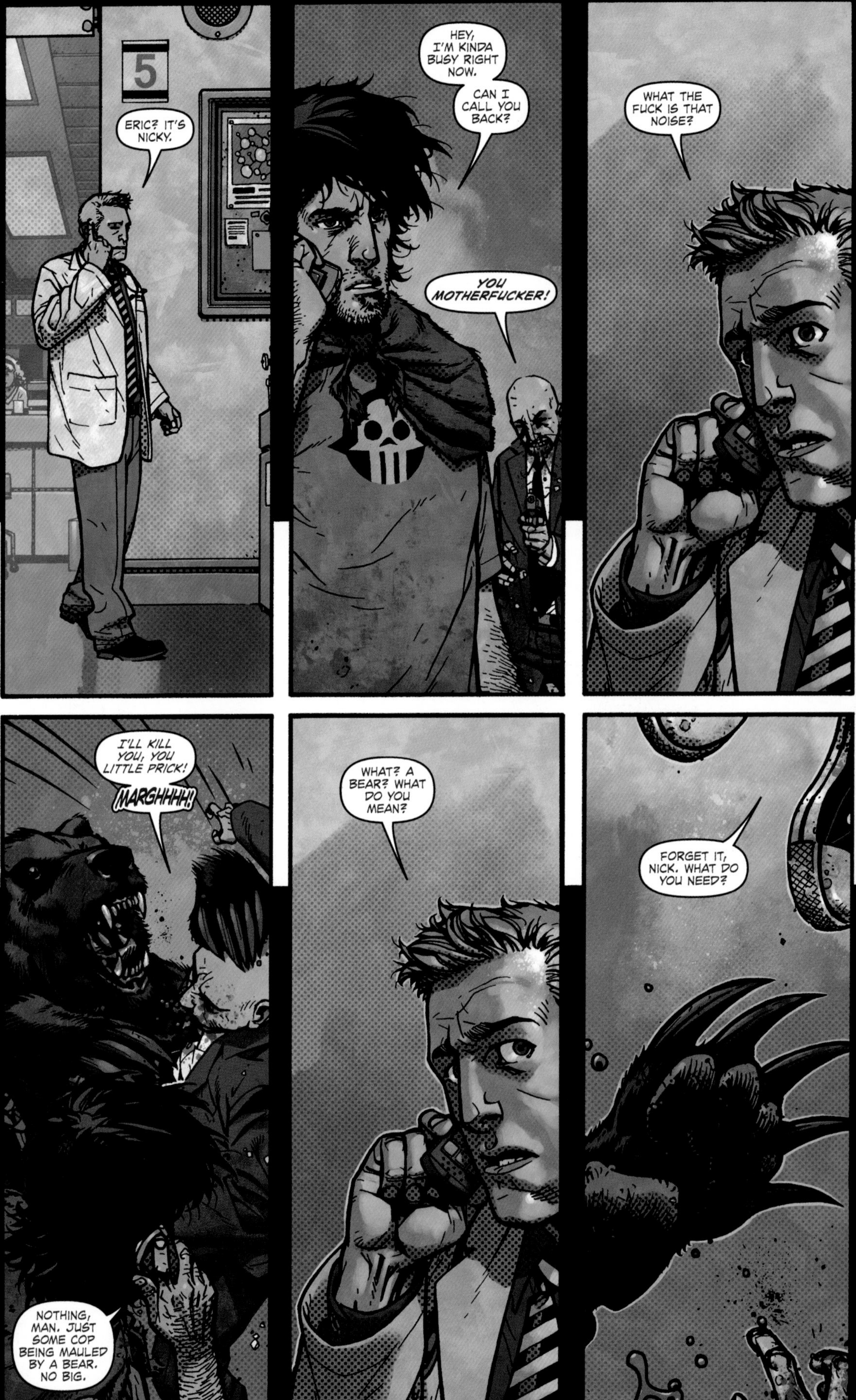
ERIC? IT'S NICKY.
HEY, I'M KINDA BUSY RIGHT NOW.
CAN I CALL YOU BACK?
YOU MOTHERFUCKER!
WHAT THE FUCK IS THAT NOISE?
I'LL KILL YOU, YOU LITTLE PRICK!
MARGHHHH!
NOTHING, MAN. JUST SOME COP BEING MAULED BY A BEAR. NO BIG.
WHAT? A BEAR? WHAT DO YOU MEAN?
FORGET IT, NICK. WHAT DO YOU NEED?

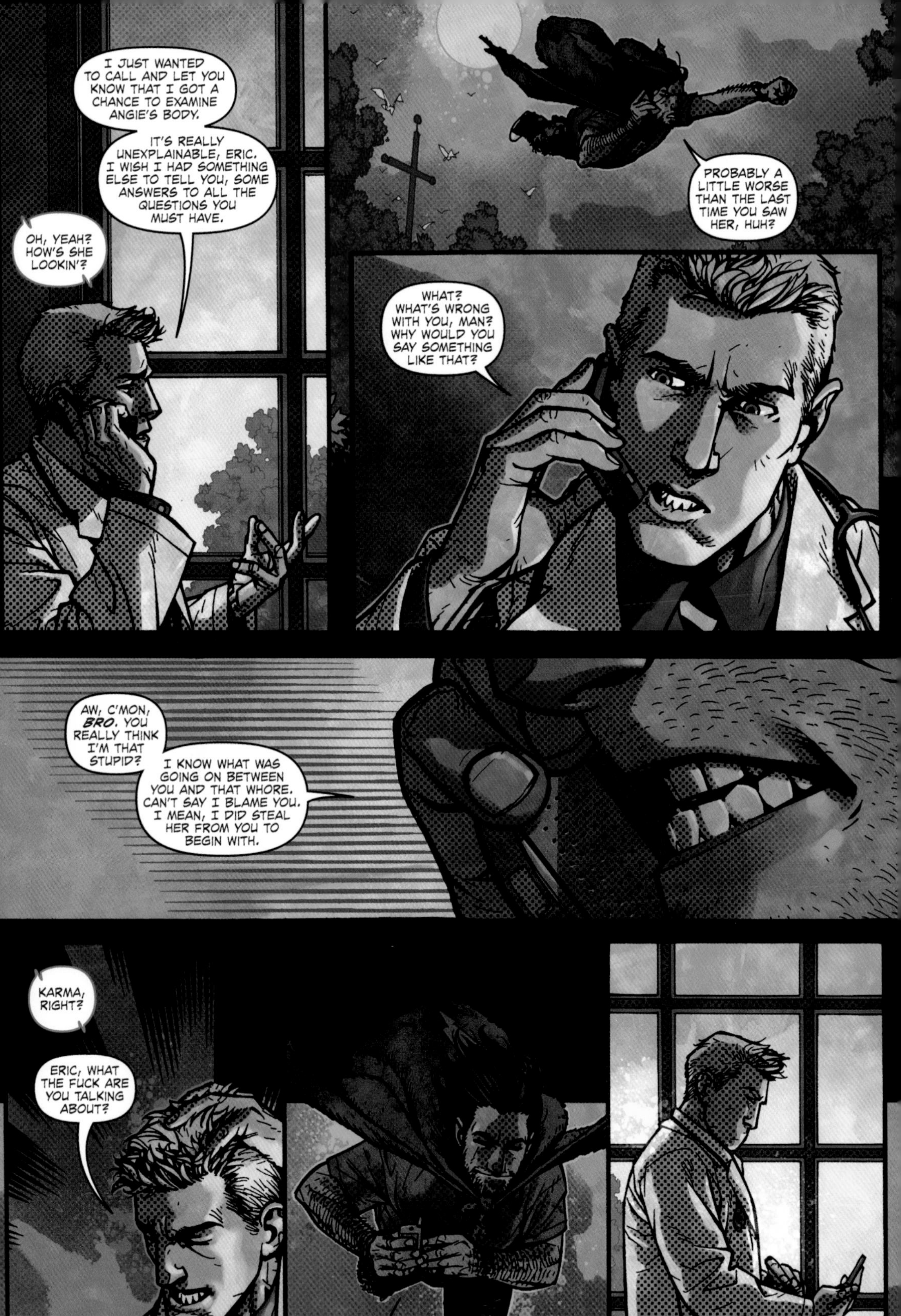

I JUST WANTED TO CALL AND LET YOU KNOW THAT I GOT A CHANCE TO EXAMINE ANGIE'S BODY.
IT'S REALLY UNEXPLAINABLE, ERIC. I WISH I HAD SOMETHING ELSE TO TELL YOU, SOME ANSWERS TO ALL THE QUESTIONS YOU MUST HAVE.
OH, YEAH? HOW'S SHE LOOKIN'?
PROBABLY A LITTLE WORSE THAN THE LAST TIME YOU SAW HER, HUH?
WHAT? WHAT'S WRONG WITH YOU, MAN? WHY WOULD YOU SAY SOMETHING LIKE THAT?
AW, C'MON, BRO. YOU REALLY THINK I'M THAT STUPID?
I KNOW WHAT WAS GOING ON BETWEEN YOU AND THAT WHORE. CAN'T SAY I BLAME YOU. I MEAN, I DID STEAL HER FROM YOU TO BEGIN WITH.
KARMA, RIGHT?
ERIC, WHAT THE FUCK ARE YOU TALKING ABOUT?
CLICK.

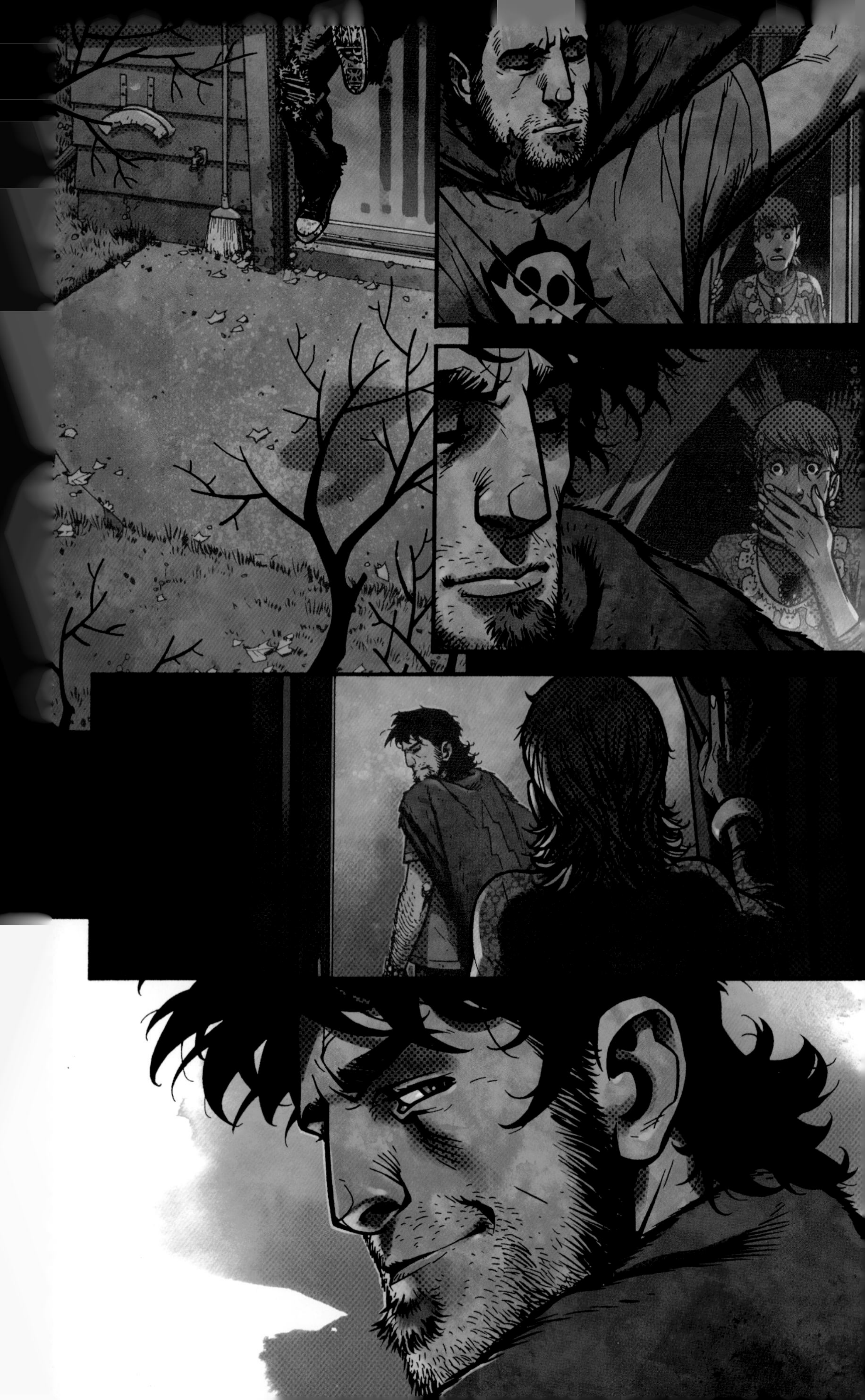

"A man must dream a long time in order to act
with grandeur, and dreaming is nursed in darkness."
—Jean Genet

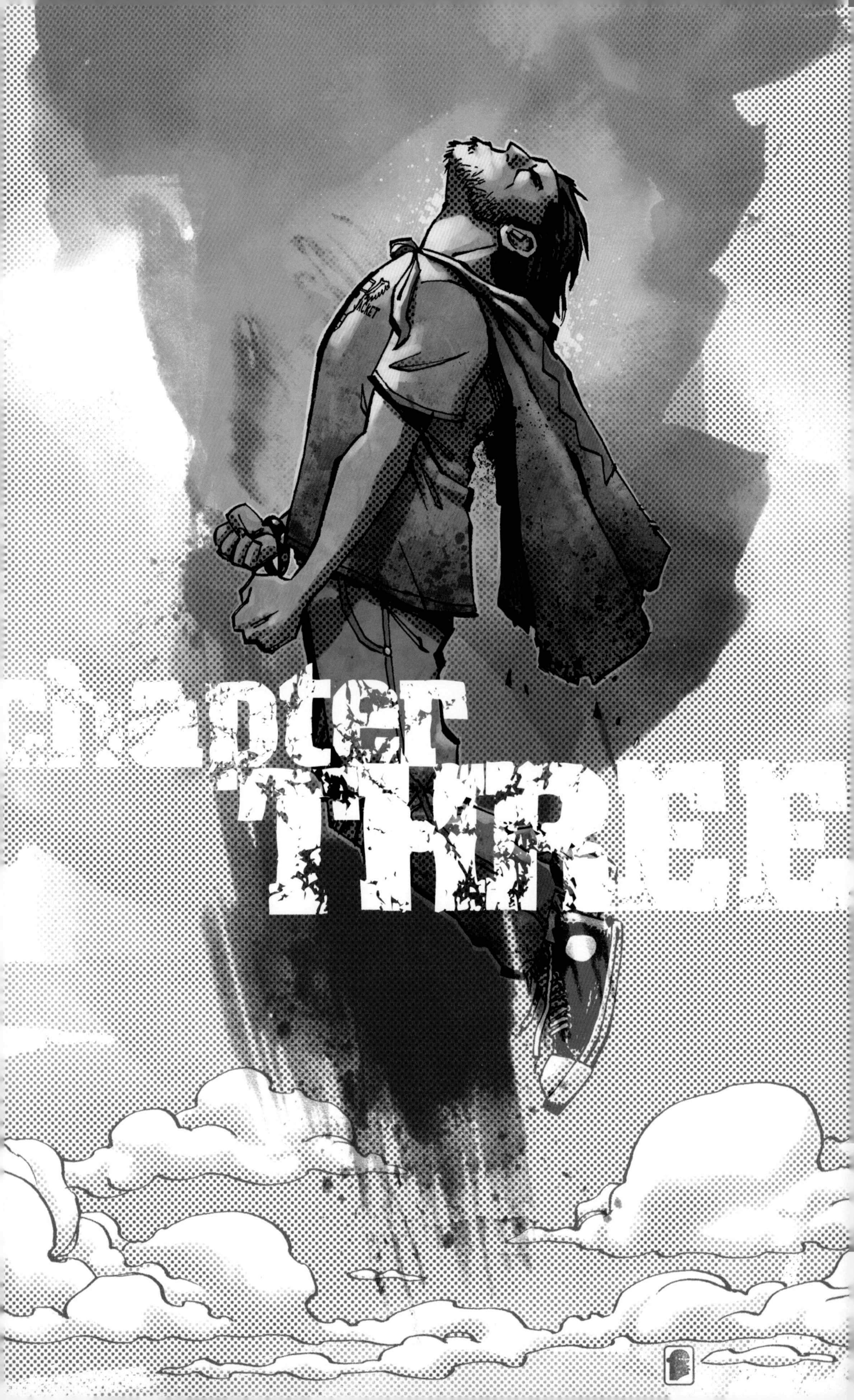
chapter
THREE

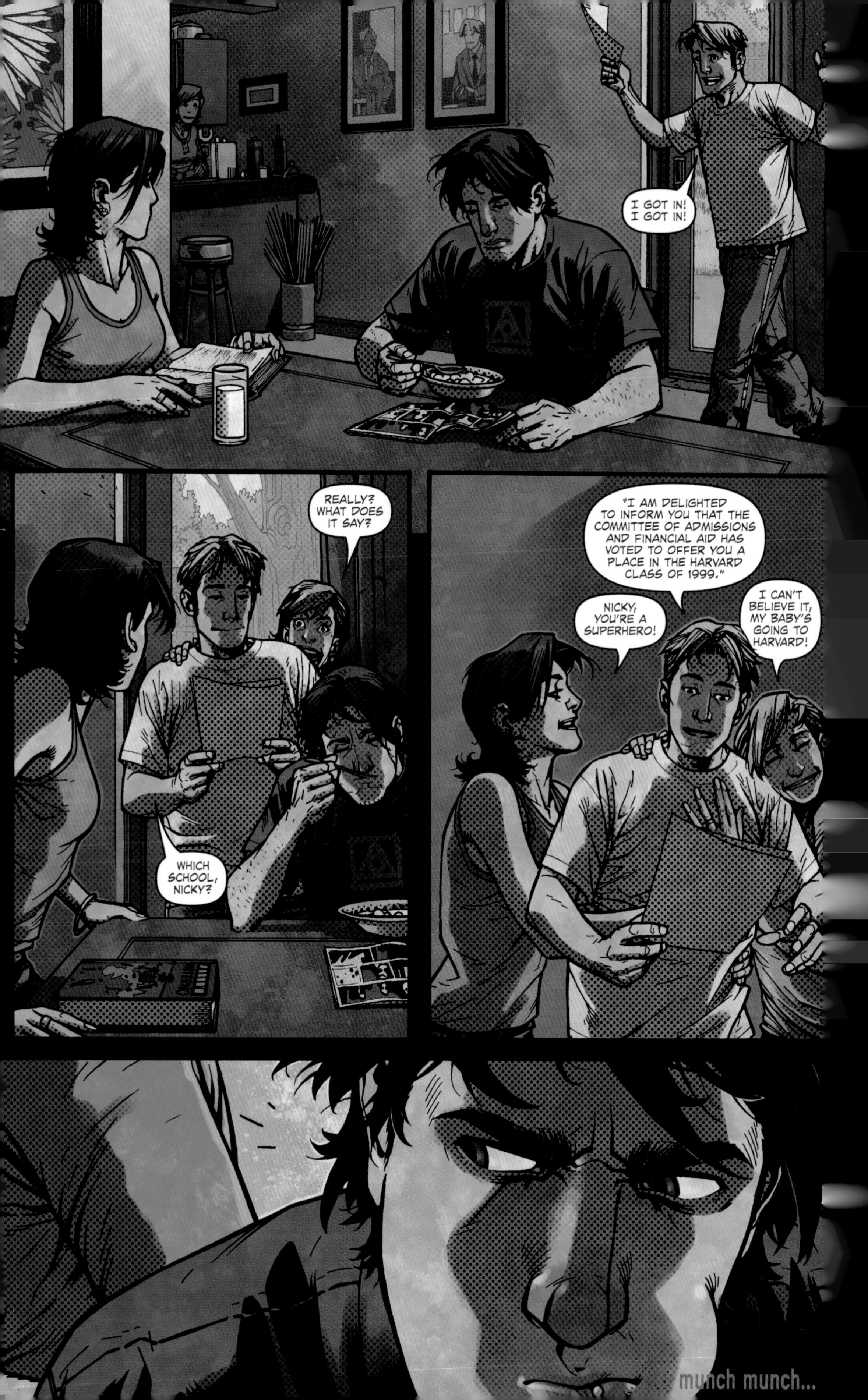
I GOT IN! I GOT IN!
REALLY? WHAT DOES IT SAY?
WHICH SCHOOL, NICKY?
"I AM DELIGHTED TO INFORM YOU THAT THE COMMITTEE OF ADMISSIONS AND FINANCIAL AID HAS VOTED TO OFFER YOU A PLACE IN THE HARVARD CLASS OF 1999."
NICKY, YOU'RE A SUPERHERO!
I CAN'T BELIEVE IT, MY BABY'S GOING TO HARVARD!
munch munch...

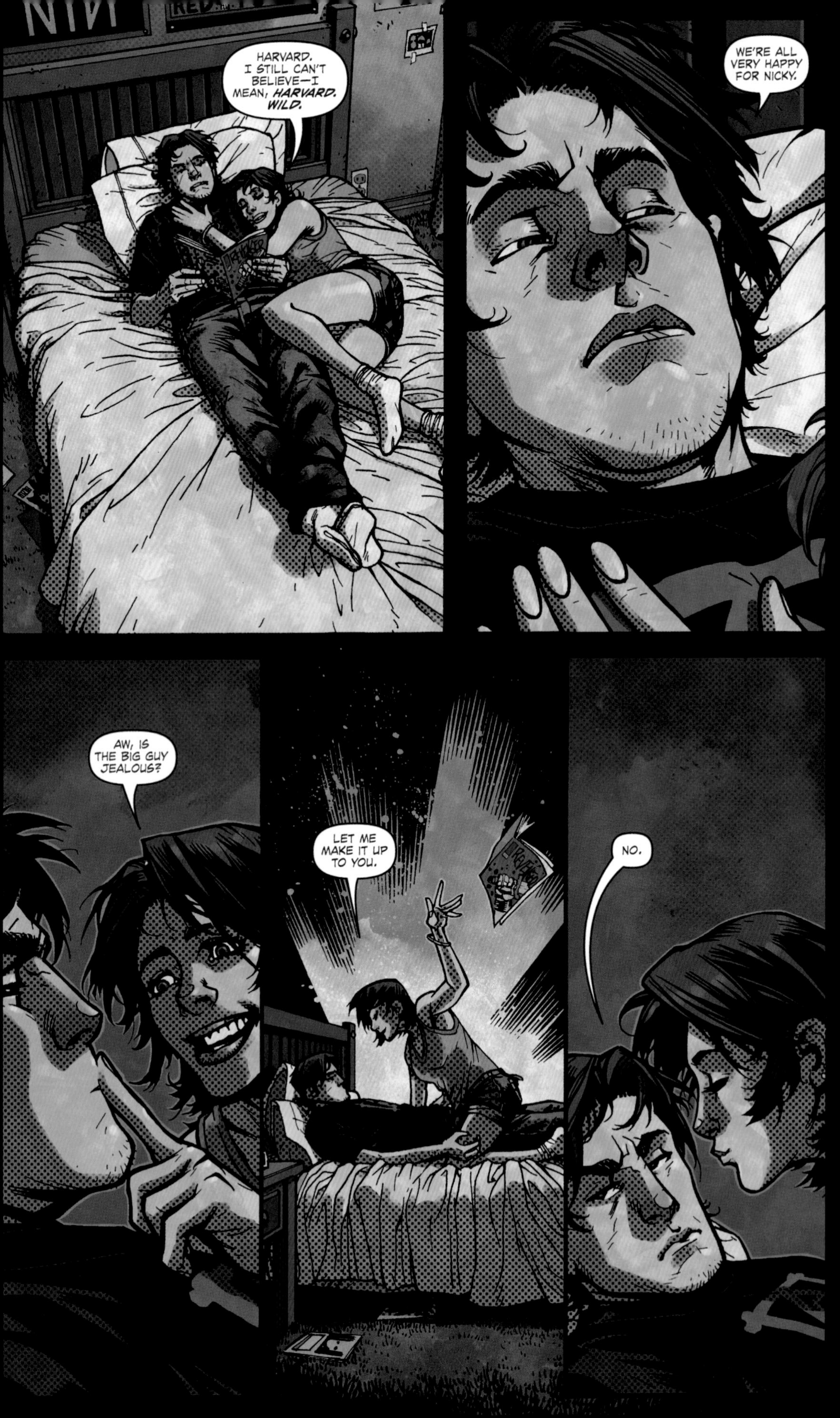
HARVARD. I STILL CAN'T BELIEVE—I MEAN, HARVARD. WILD.
WE'RE ALL VERY HAPPY FOR NICKY.
AW, IS THE BIG GUY JEALOUS?
LET ME MAKE IT UP TO YOU.
NO.

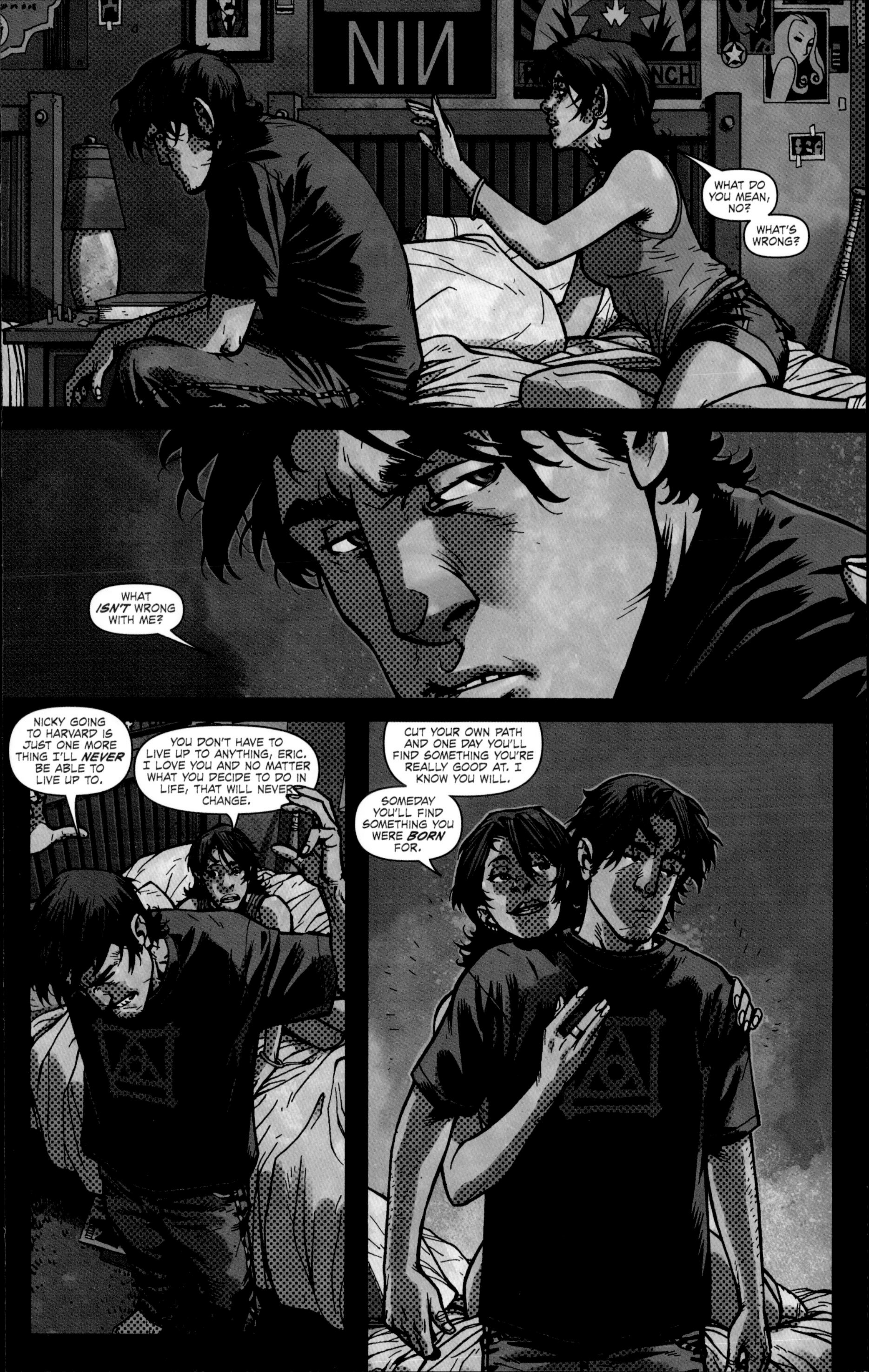
NIN
WHAT DO YOU MEAN, NO?
WHAT'S WRONG?
WHAT *ISN'T* WRONG WITH ME?
NICKY GOING TO HARVARD IS JUST ONE MORE THING I'LL ***NEVER*** BE ABLE TO LIVE UP TO.
YOU DON'T HAVE TO LIVE UP TO ANYTHING, ERIC. I LOVE YOU AND NO MATTER WHAT YOU DECIDE TO DO IN LIFE, THAT WILL NEVER CHANGE.
CUT YOUR OWN PATH AND ONE DAY YOU'LL FIND SOMETHING YOU'RE REALLY GOOD AT. I KNOW YOU WILL.
SOMEDAY YOU'LL FIND SOMETHING YOU WERE ***BORN*** FOR.

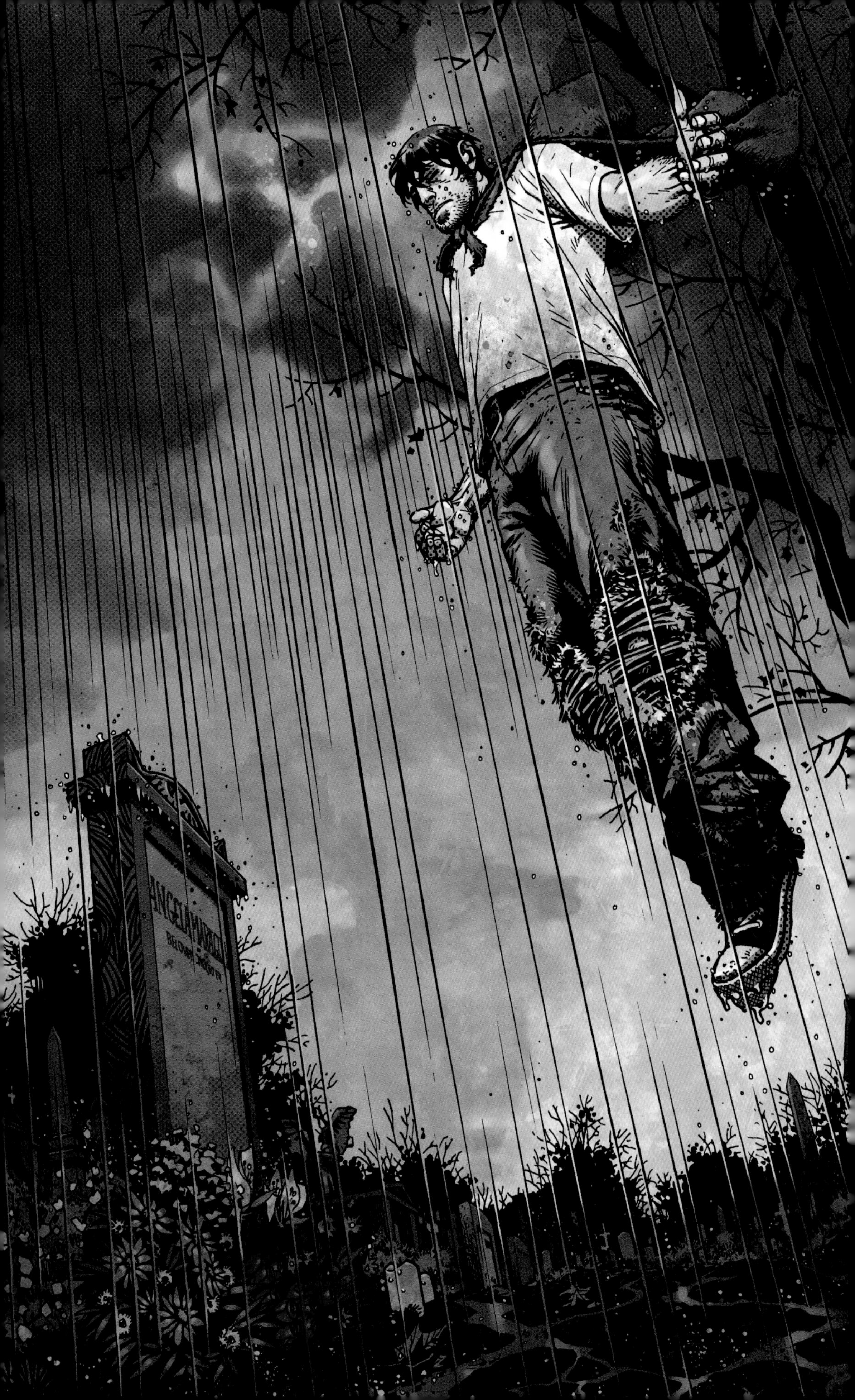

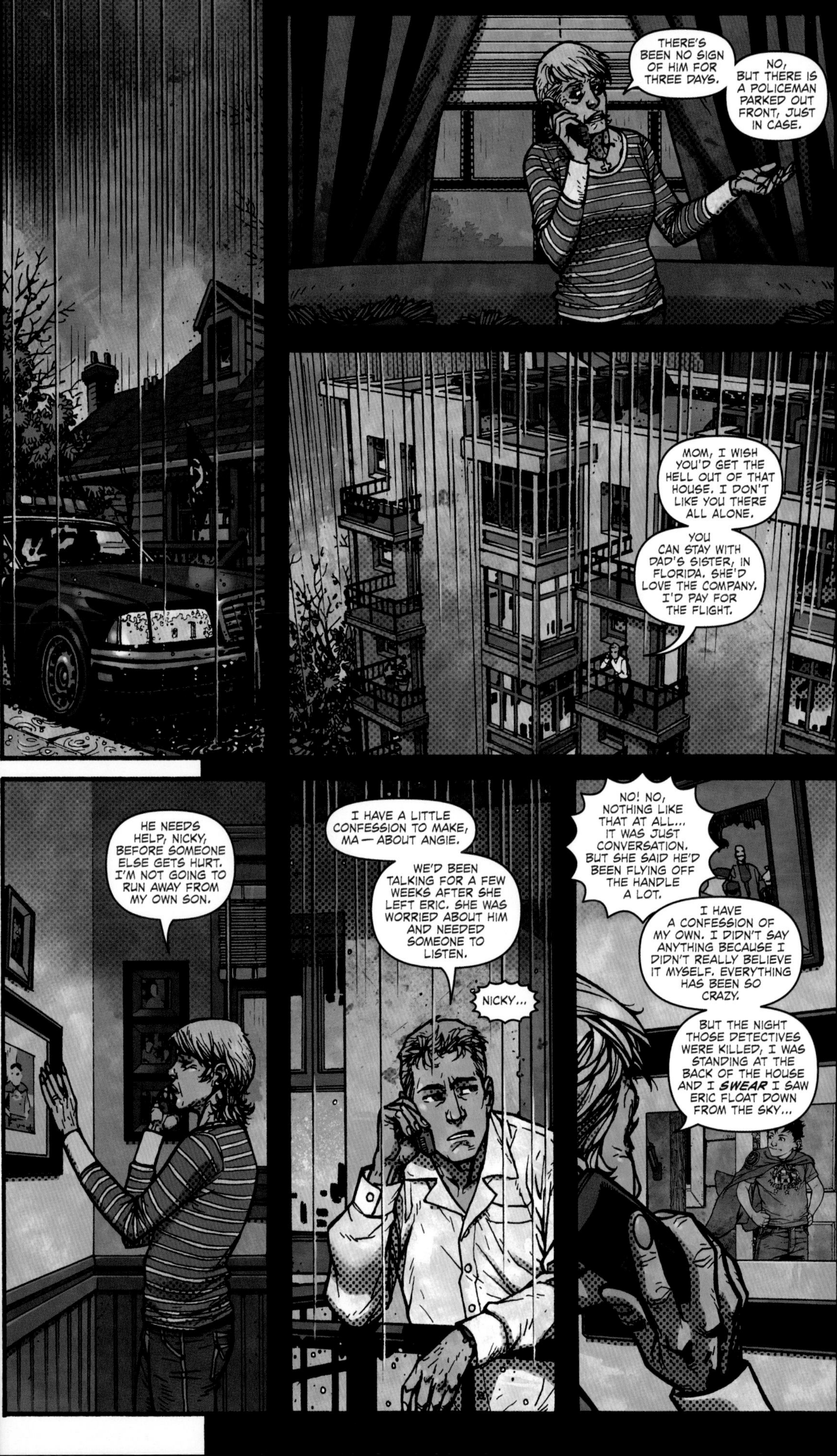

THERE'S BEEN NO SIGN OF HIM FOR THREE DAYS.
NO, BUT THERE IS A POLICEMAN PARKED OUT FRONT, JUST IN CASE.
MOM, I WISH YOU'D GET THE HELL OUT OF THAT HOUSE. I DON'T LIKE YOU THERE ALL ALONE.
YOU CAN STAY WITH DAD'S SISTER, IN FLORIDA. SHE'D LOVE THE COMPANY. I'D PAY FOR THE FLIGHT.
HE NEEDS HELP, NICKY, BEFORE SOMEONE ELSE GETS HURT. I'M NOT GOING TO RUN AWAY FROM MY OWN SON.
I HAVE A LITTLE CONFESSION TO MAKE, MA — ABOUT ANGIE.
WE'D BEEN TALKING FOR A FEW WEEKS AFTER SHE LEFT ERIC. SHE WAS WORRIED ABOUT HIM AND NEEDED SOMEONE TO LISTEN.
NICKY...
NO! NO, NOTHING LIKE THAT AT ALL... IT WAS JUST CONVERSATION. BUT SHE SAID HE'D BEEN FLYING OFF THE HANDLE A LOT.
I HAVE A CONFESSION OF MY OWN. I DIDN'T SAY ANYTHING BECAUSE I DIDN'T REALLY BELIEVE IT MYSELF. EVERYTHING HAS BEEN SO CRAZY.
BUT THE NIGHT THOSE DETECTIVES WERE KILLED, I WAS STANDING AT THE BACK OF THE HOUSE AND I SWEAR I SAW ERIC FLOAT DOWN FROM THE SKY...

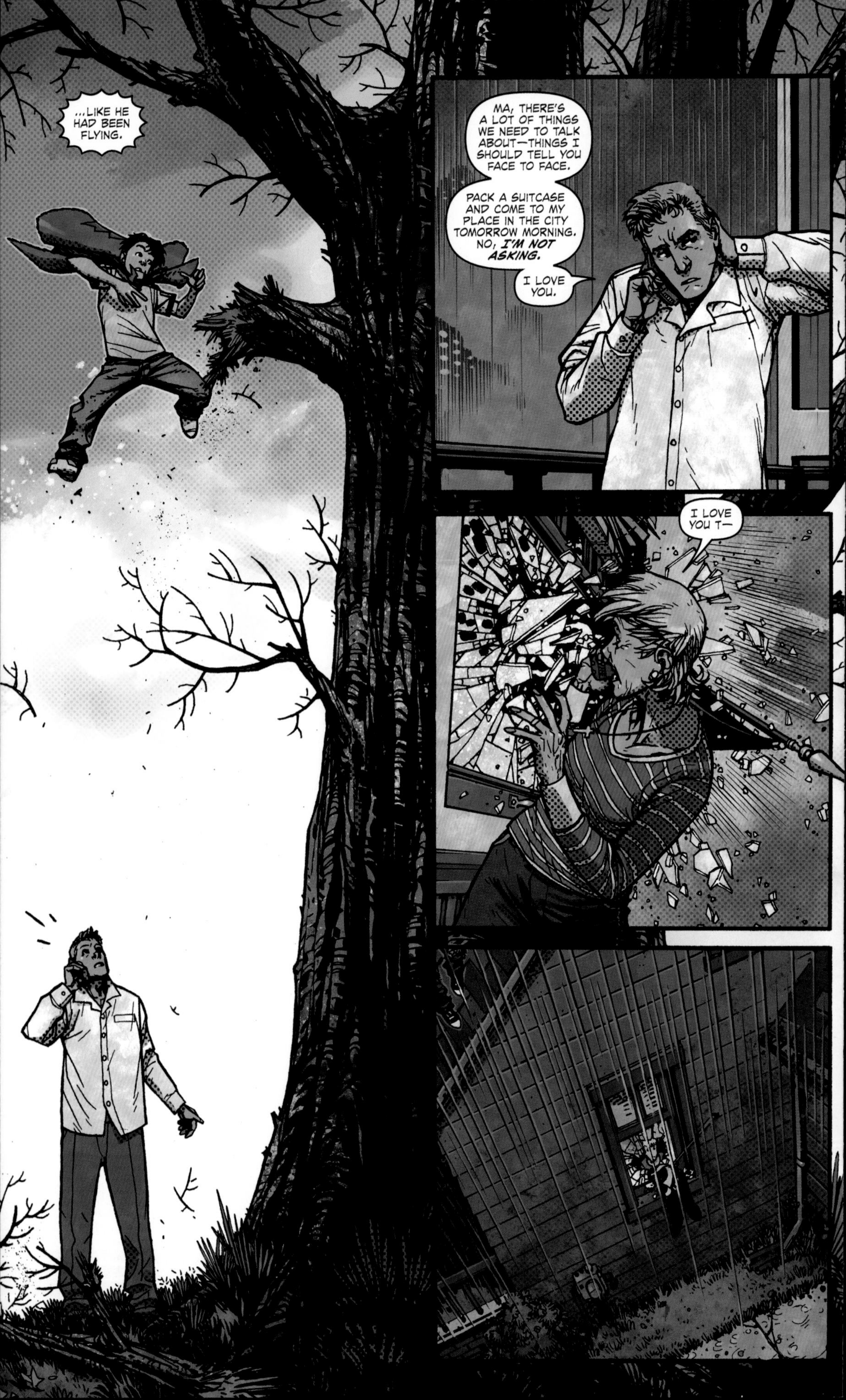
...LIKE HE HAD BEEN FLYING.
MA, THERE'S A LOT OF THINGS WE NEED TO TALK ABOUT—THINGS I SHOULD TELL YOU FACE TO FACE.
PACK A SUITCASE AND COME TO MY PLACE IN THE CITY TOMORROW MORNING. NO, I'M NOT ASKING.
I LOVE YOU.
I LOVE YOU T—

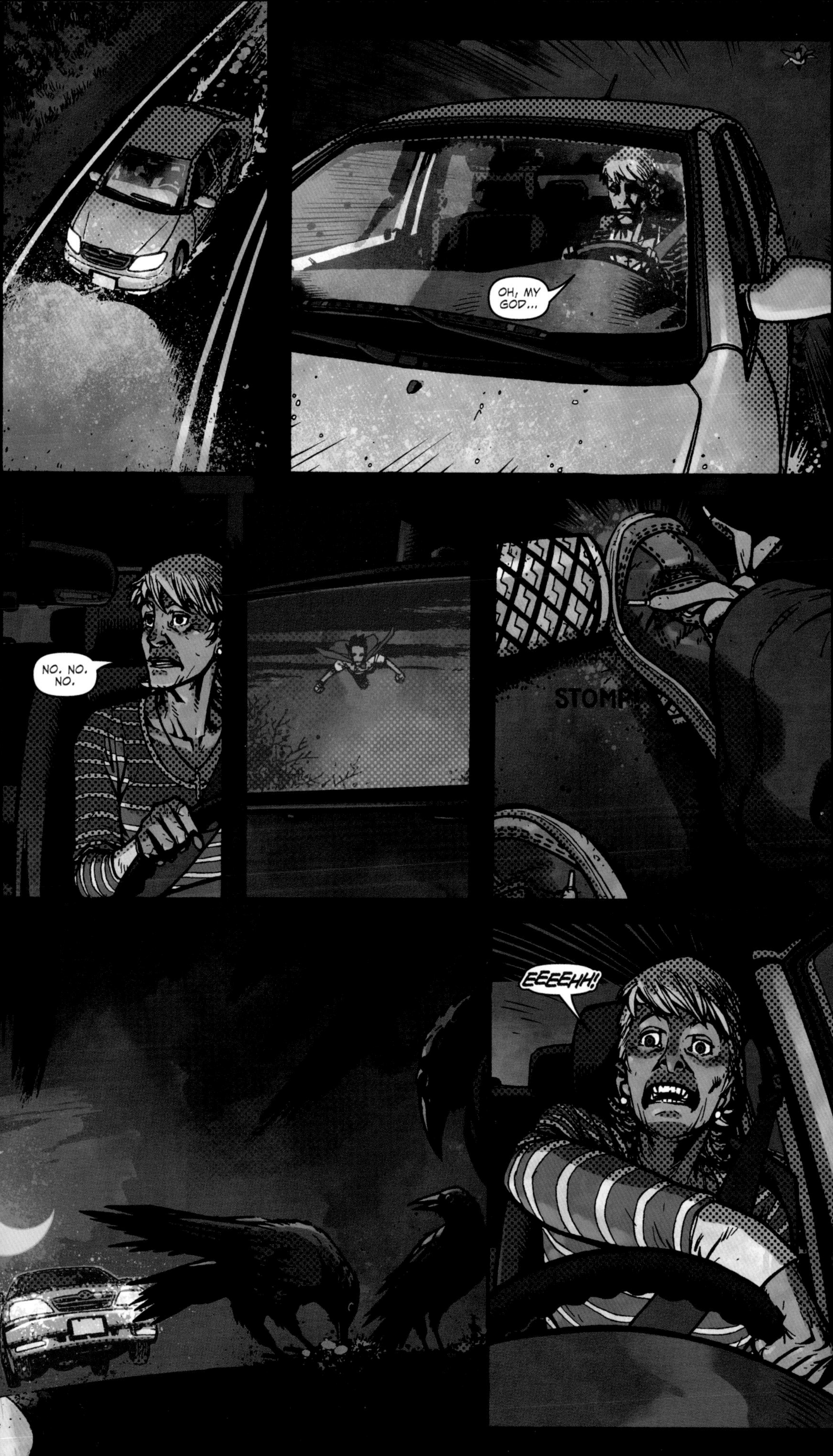
OH, MY GOD...
NO. NO. NO.
STOMP
EEEEHH!

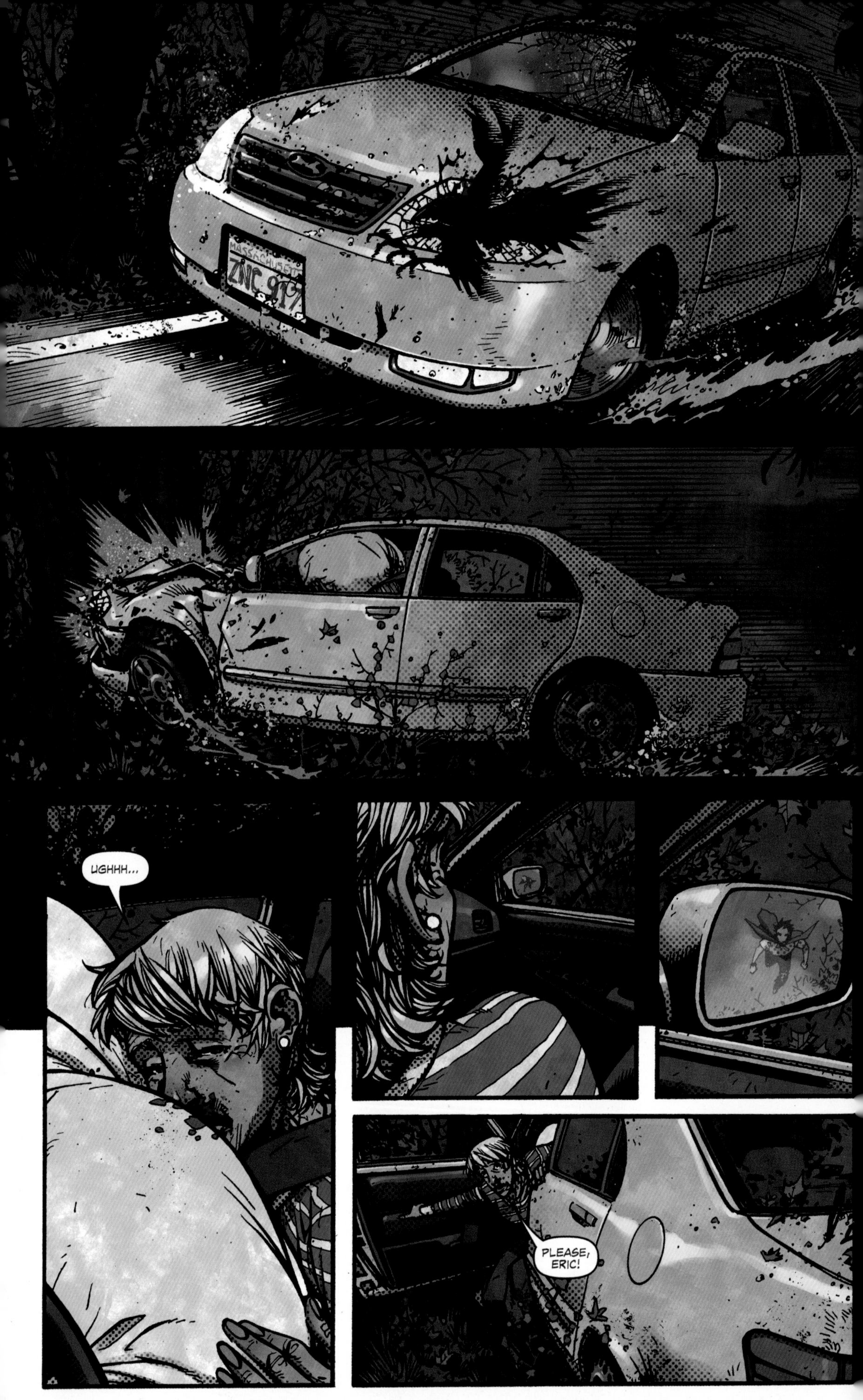
MASSACHUSETTS
ZNC 91
UGHHH...
PLEASE, ERIC!

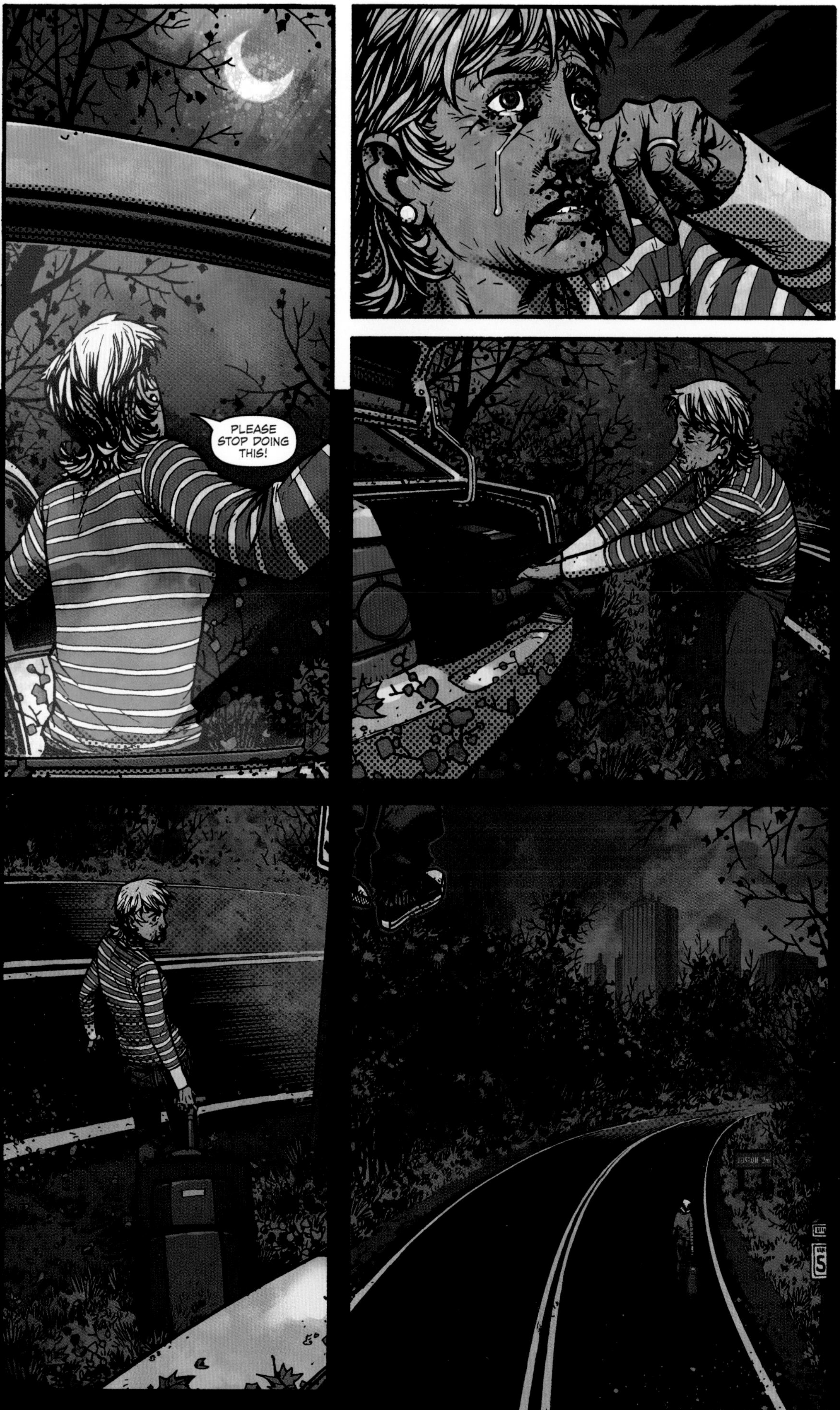
PLEASE STOP DOING THIS!

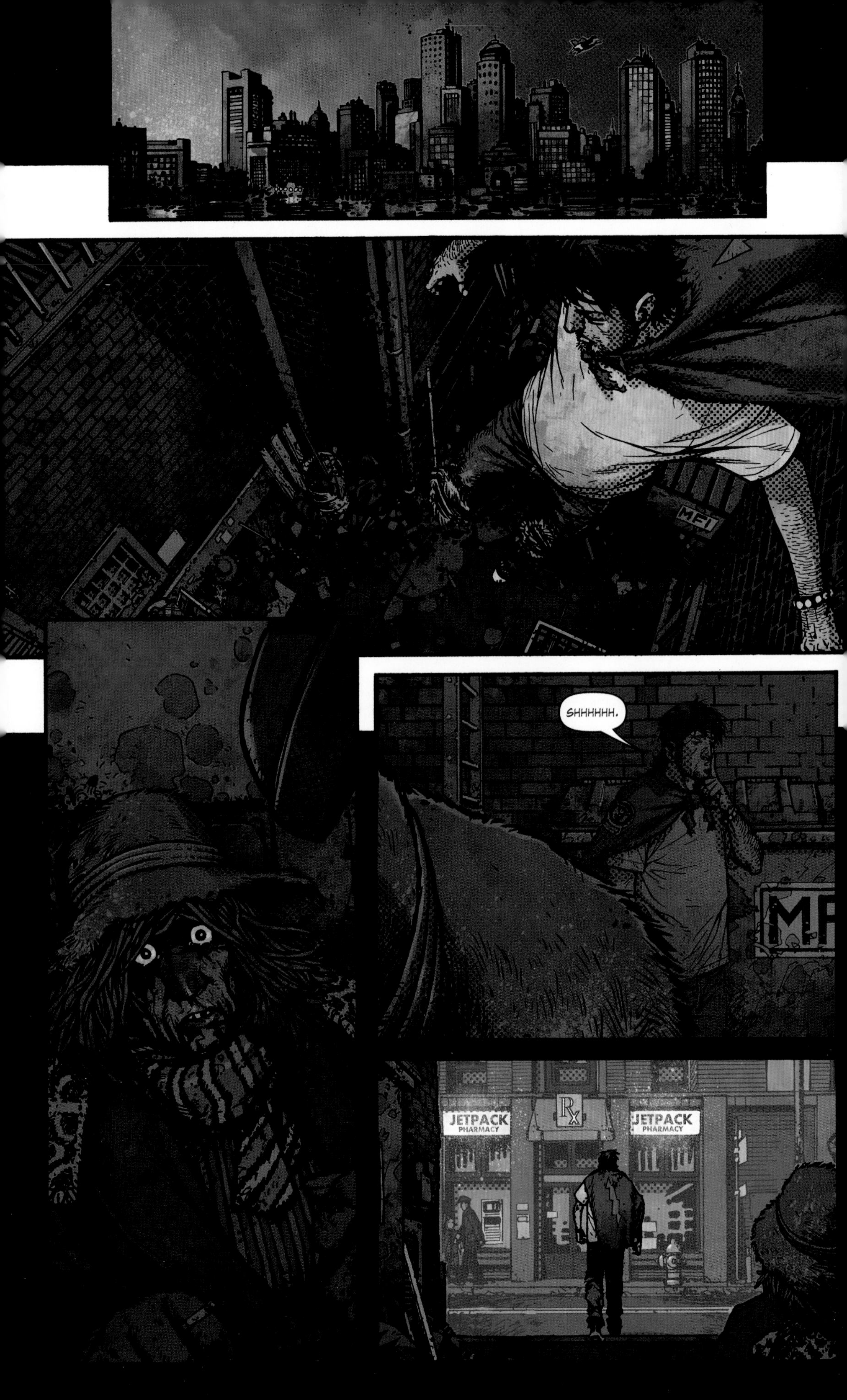
SHHHHHH.
JETPACK
PHARMACY

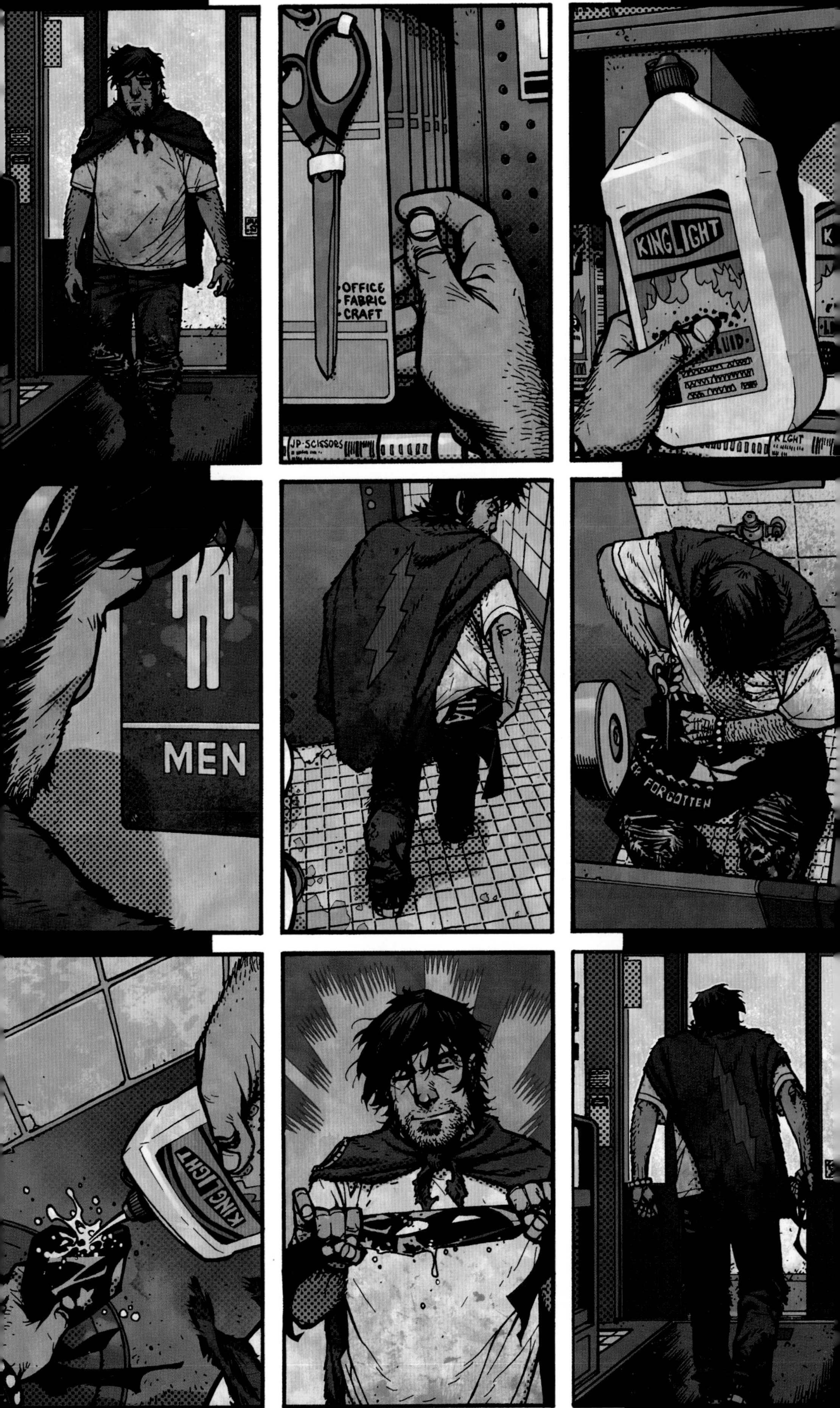

OFFICE
FABRIC
CRAFT
JP-SCISSORS
KING LIGHT
MEN
FORGOTTEN
KING LIGHT

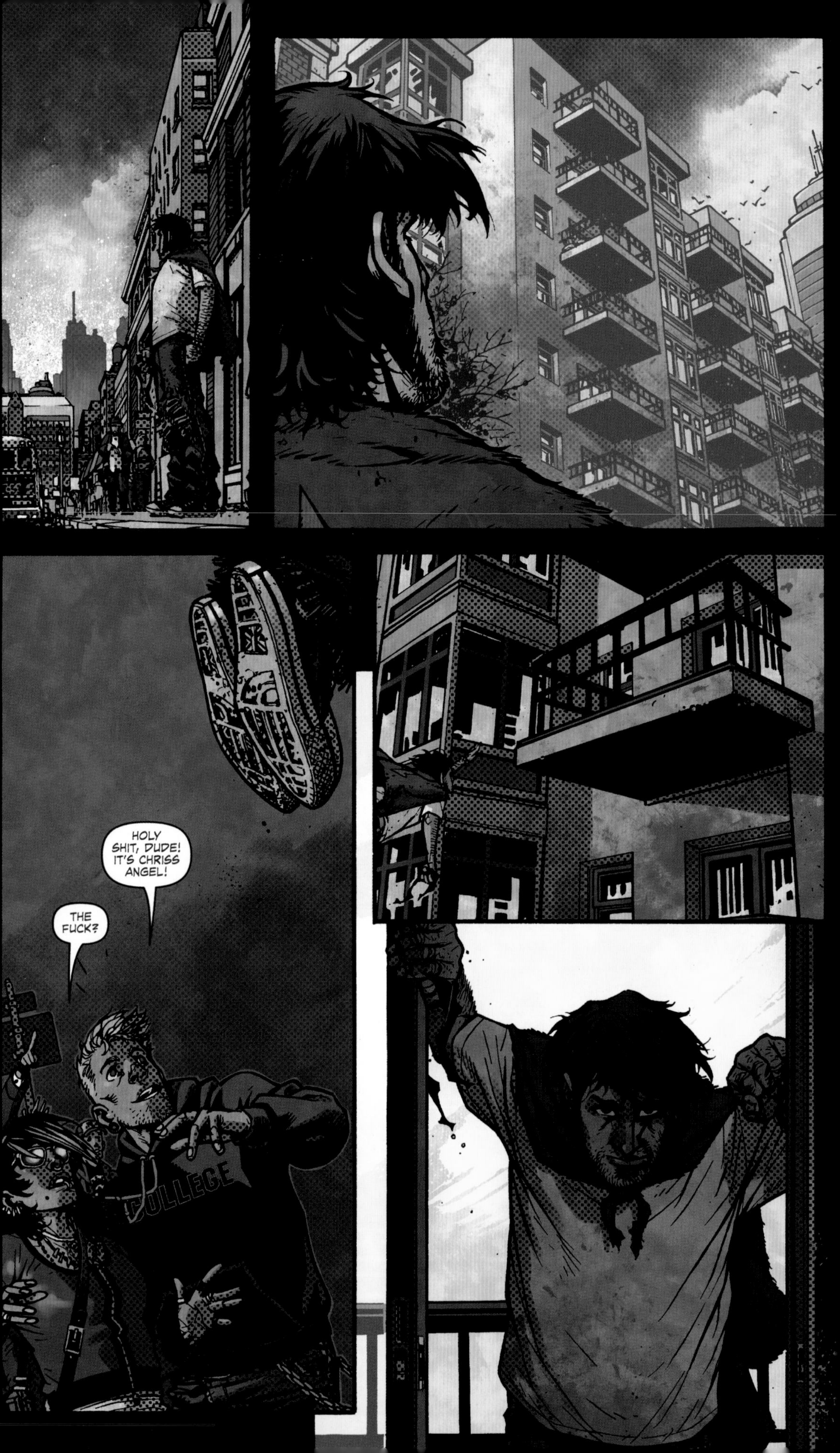
HOLY SHIT, DUDE! IT'S CHRISS ANGEL!
THE FUCK?
COLLEGE

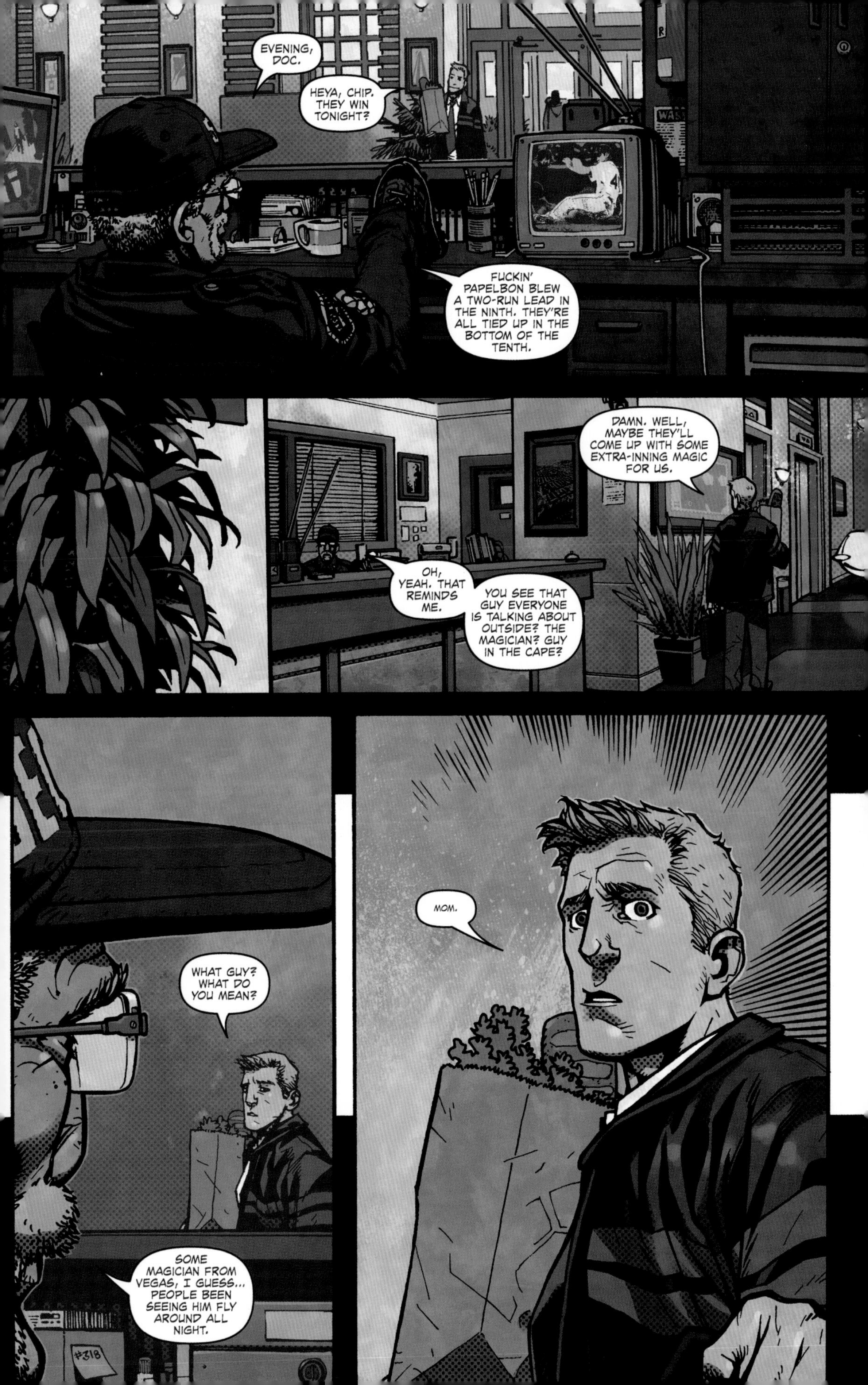
EVENING, DOC.
HEYA, CHIP. THEY WIN TONIGHT?
FUCKIN' PAPELBON BLEW A TWO-RUN LEAD IN THE NINTH. THEY'RE ALL TIED UP IN THE BOTTOM OF THE TENTH.
DAMN. WELL, MAYBE THEY'LL COME UP WITH SOME EXTRA-INNING MAGIC FOR US.
OH, YEAH. THAT REMINDS ME.
YOU SEE THAT GUY EVERYONE IS TALKING ABOUT OUTSIDE? THE MAGICIAN? GUY IN THE CAPE?
WHAT GUY? WHAT DO YOU MEAN?
SOME MAGICIAN FROM VEGAS, I GUESS... PEOPLE BEEN SEEING HIM FLY AROUND ALL NIGHT.
MOM.

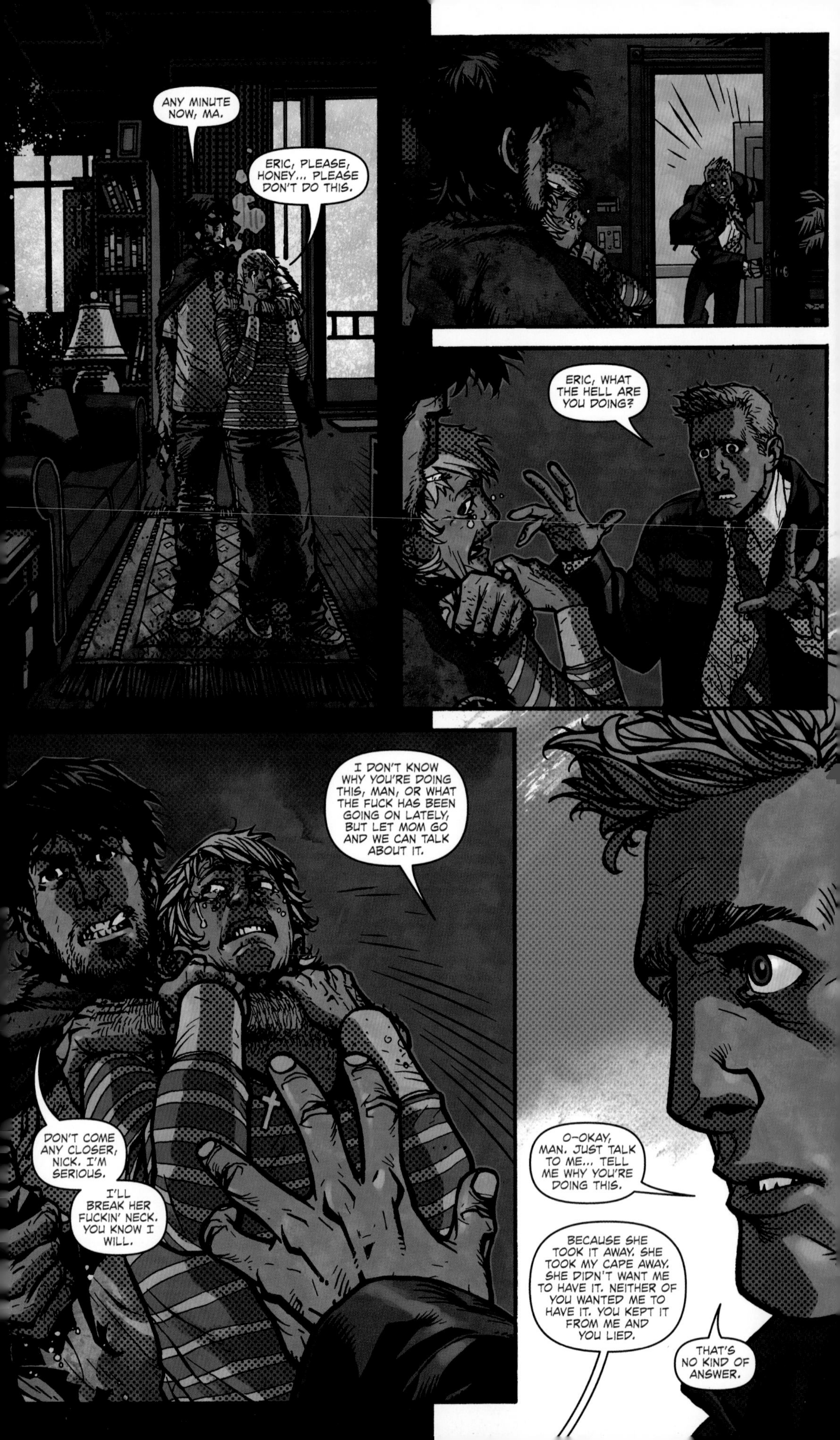
ANY MINUTE NOW, MA.
ERIC, PLEASE, HONEY... PLEASE DON'T DO THIS.
ERIC, WHAT THE HELL ARE YOU DOING?
I DON'T KNOW WHY YOU'RE DOING THIS, MAN, OR WHAT THE FUCK HAS BEEN GOING ON LATELY, BUT LET MOM GO AND WE CAN TALK ABOUT IT.
DON'T COME ANY CLOSER, NICK. I'M SERIOUS.
I'LL BREAK HER FUCKIN' NECK. YOU KNOW I WILL.
O-OKAY, MAN. JUST TALK TO ME... TELL ME WHY YOU'RE DOING THIS.
BECAUSE SHE TOOK IT AWAY. SHE TOOK MY CAPE AWAY. SHE DIDN'T WANT ME TO HAVE IT. NEITHER OF YOU WANTED ME TO HAVE IT. YOU KEPT IT FROM ME AND YOU LIED.
THAT'S NO KIND OF ANSWER.

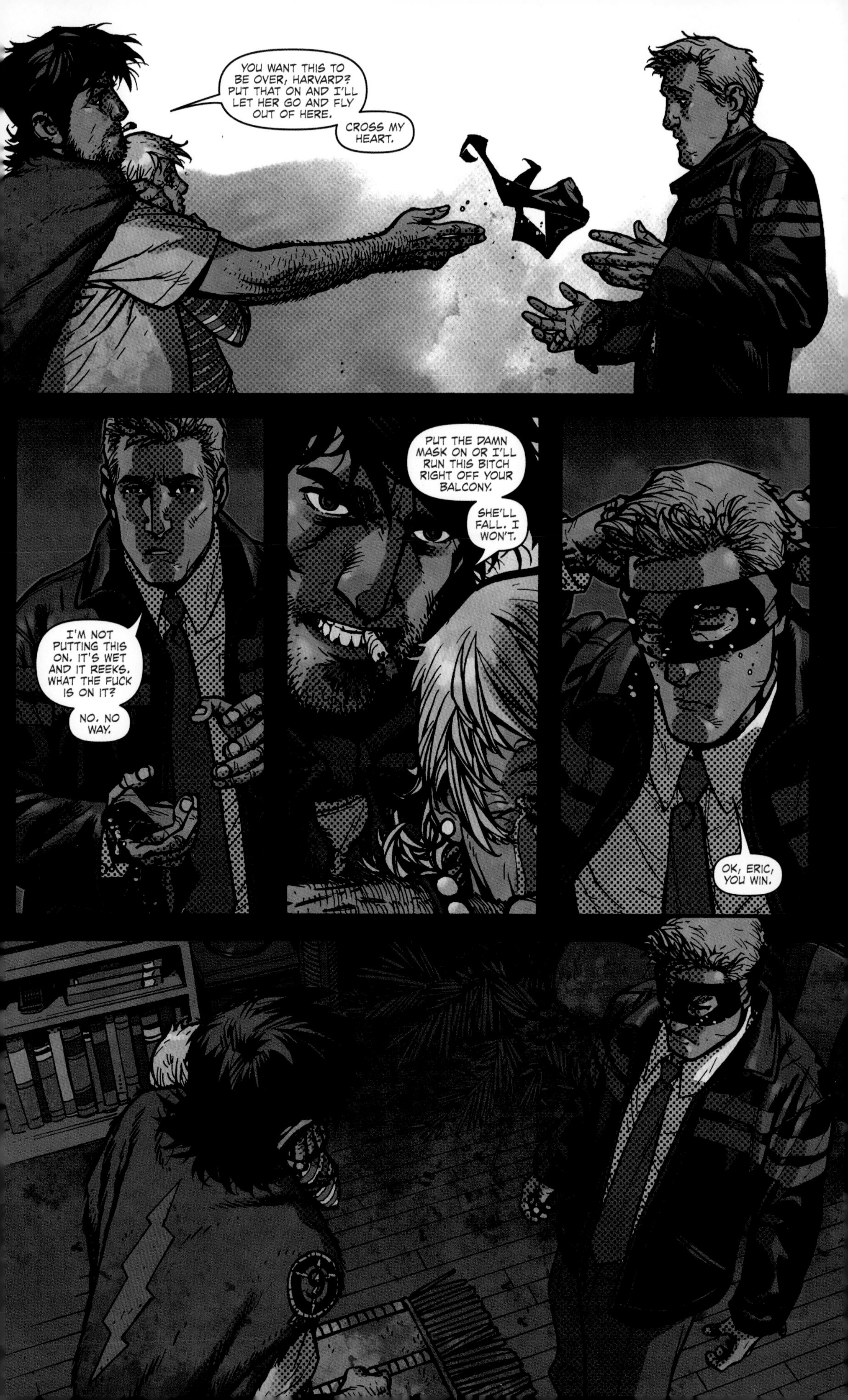
YOU WANT THIS TO BE OVER, HARVARD? PUT THAT ON AND I'LL LET HER GO AND FLY OUT OF HERE.
CROSS MY HEART.
I'M NOT PUTTING THIS ON. IT'S WET AND IT REEKS. WHAT THE FUCK IS ON IT?
NO. NO WAY.
PUT THE DAMN MASK ON OR I'LL RUN THIS BITCH RIGHT OFF YOUR BALCONY.
SHE'LL FALL. I WON'T.
OK, ERIC, YOU WIN.

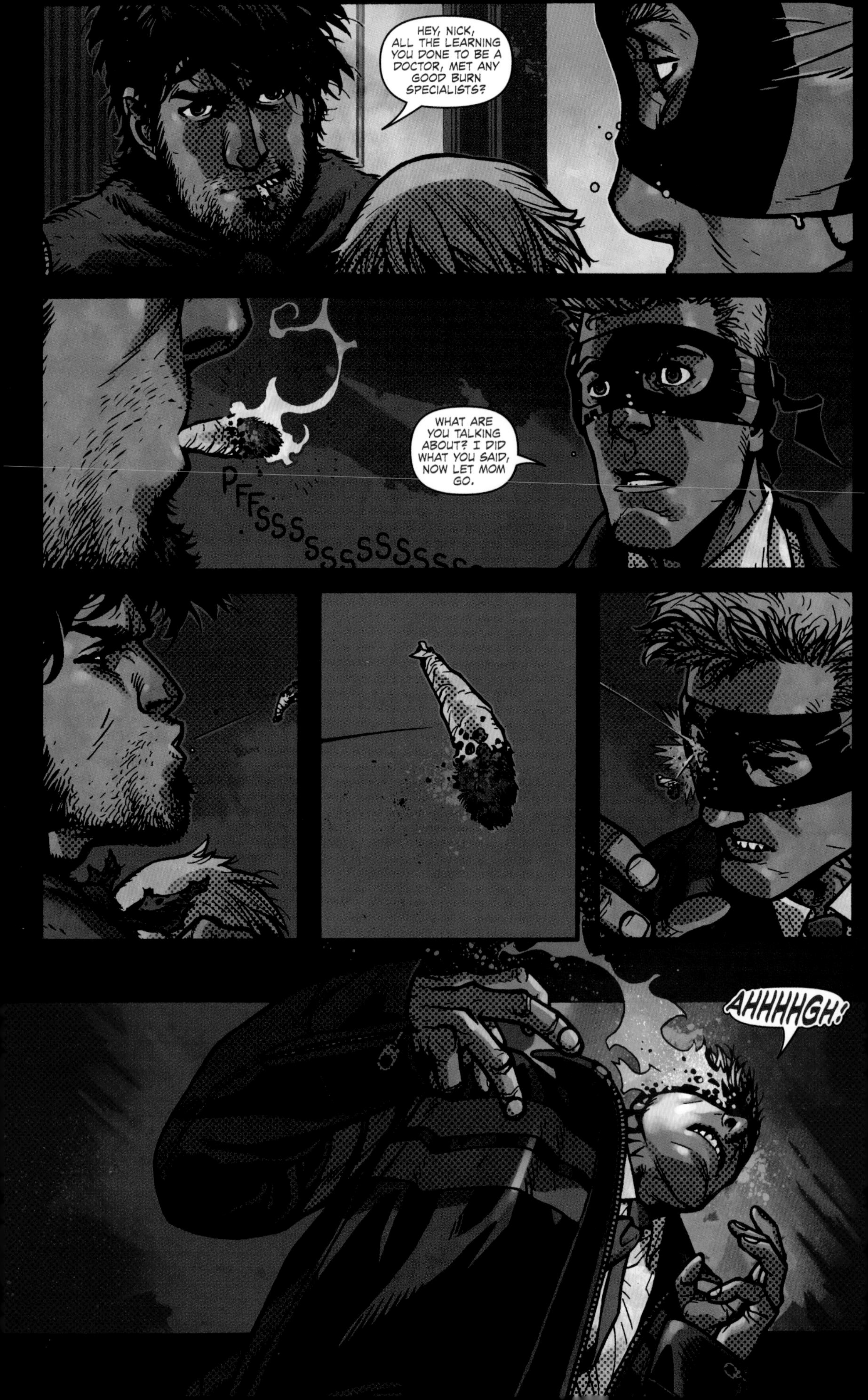
HEY, NICK, ALL THE LEARNING YOU DONE TO BE A DOCTOR, MET ANY GOOD BURN SPECIALISTS?
WHAT ARE YOU TALKING ABOUT? I DID WHAT YOU SAID, NOW LET MOM GO.
PFFSSSSSSSSSSSS
AHHHHGH!

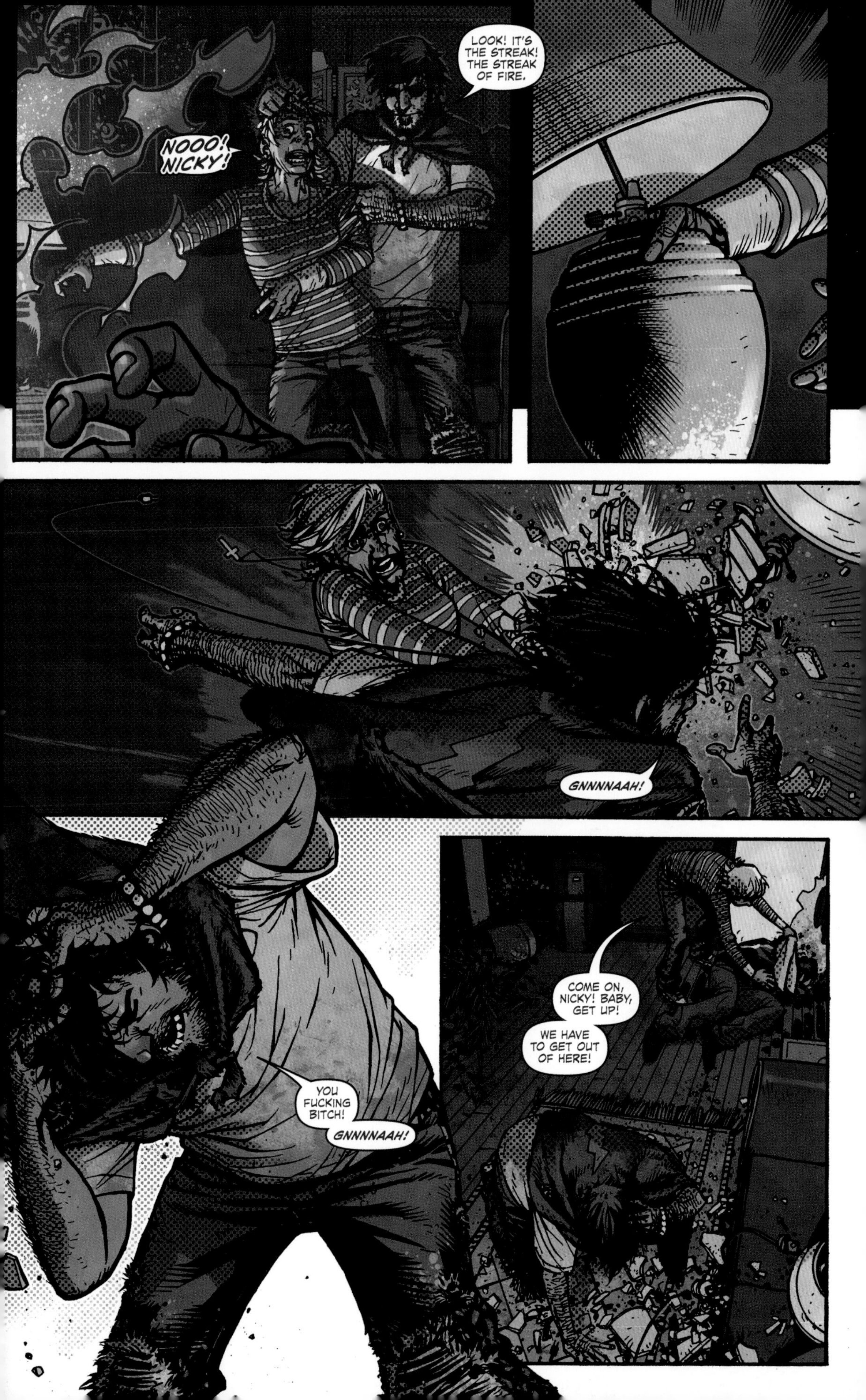
NOOO! NICKY!
LOOK! IT'S THE STREAK! THE STREAK OF FIRE.
GNNNNAAH!
YOU FUCKING BITCH!
GNNNNAAH!
COME ON, NICKY! BABY, GET UP!
WE HAVE TO GET OUT OF HERE!

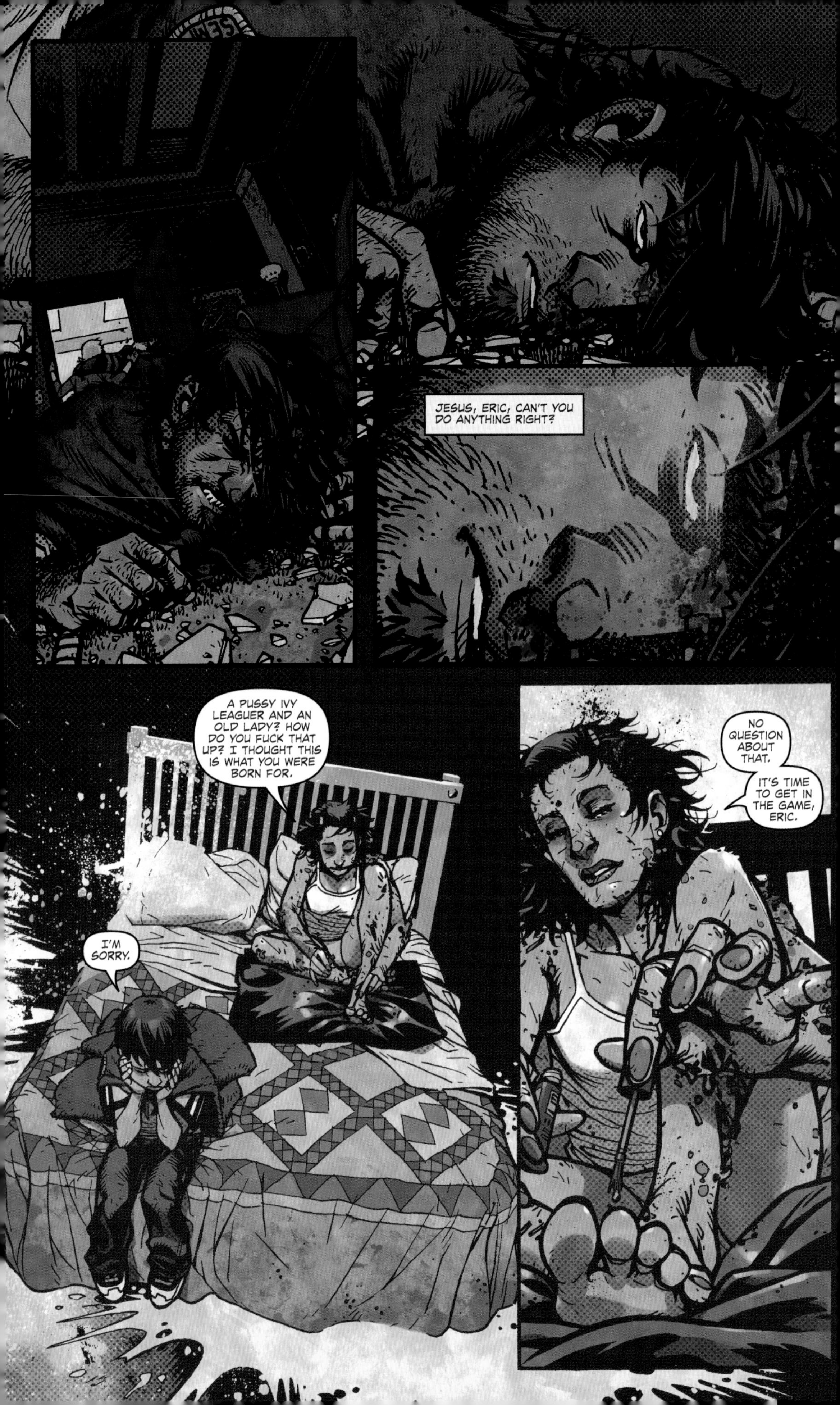
JESUS, ERIC, CAN'T YOU DO ANYTHING RIGHT?
A PUSSY IVY LEAGUER AND AN OLD LADY? HOW DO YOU FUCK THAT UP? I THOUGHT THIS IS WHAT YOU WERE BORN FOR.
I'M SORRY.
NO QUESTION ABOUT THAT.
IT'S TIME TO GET IN THE GAME, ERIC.

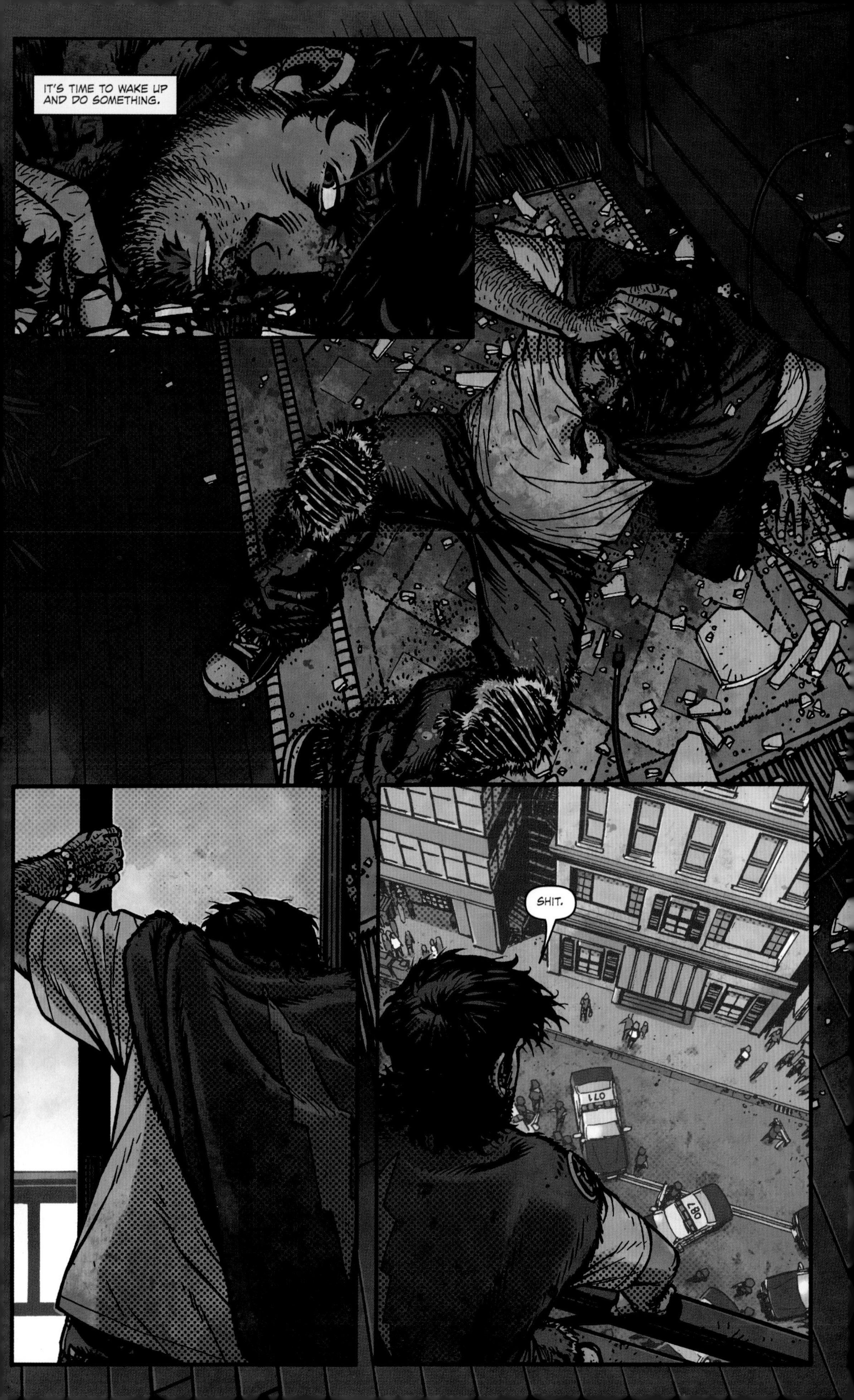
IT'S TIME TO WAKE UP AND DO SOMETHING.
SHIT.

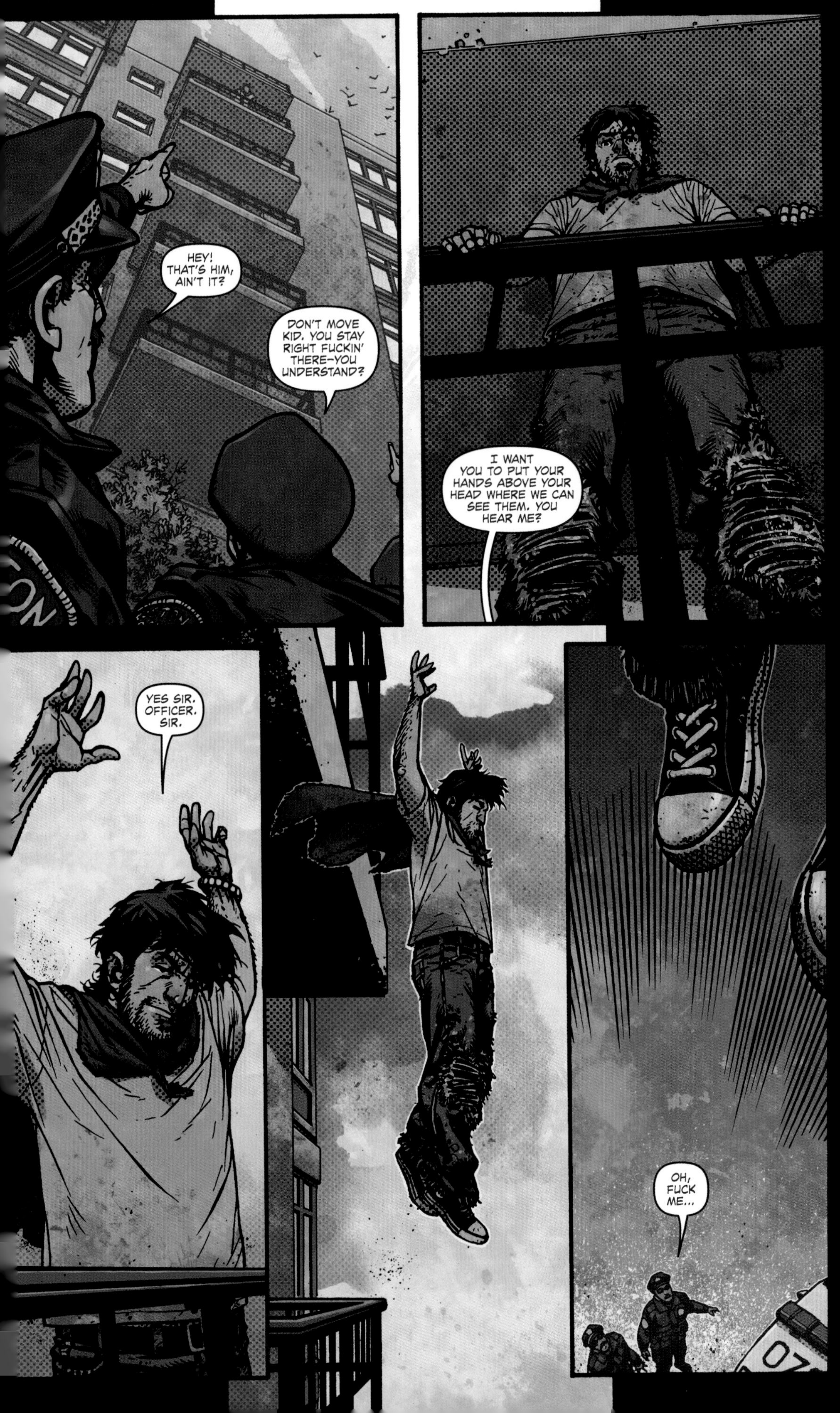
HEY! THAT'S HIM, AIN'T IT?
DON'T MOVE KID. YOU STAY RIGHT FUCKIN' THERE--YOU UNDERSTAND?
I WANT YOU TO PUT YOUR HANDS ABOVE YOUR HEAD WHERE WE CAN SEE THEM. YOU HEAR ME?
YES SIR. OFFICER. SIR.
OH, FUCK ME...

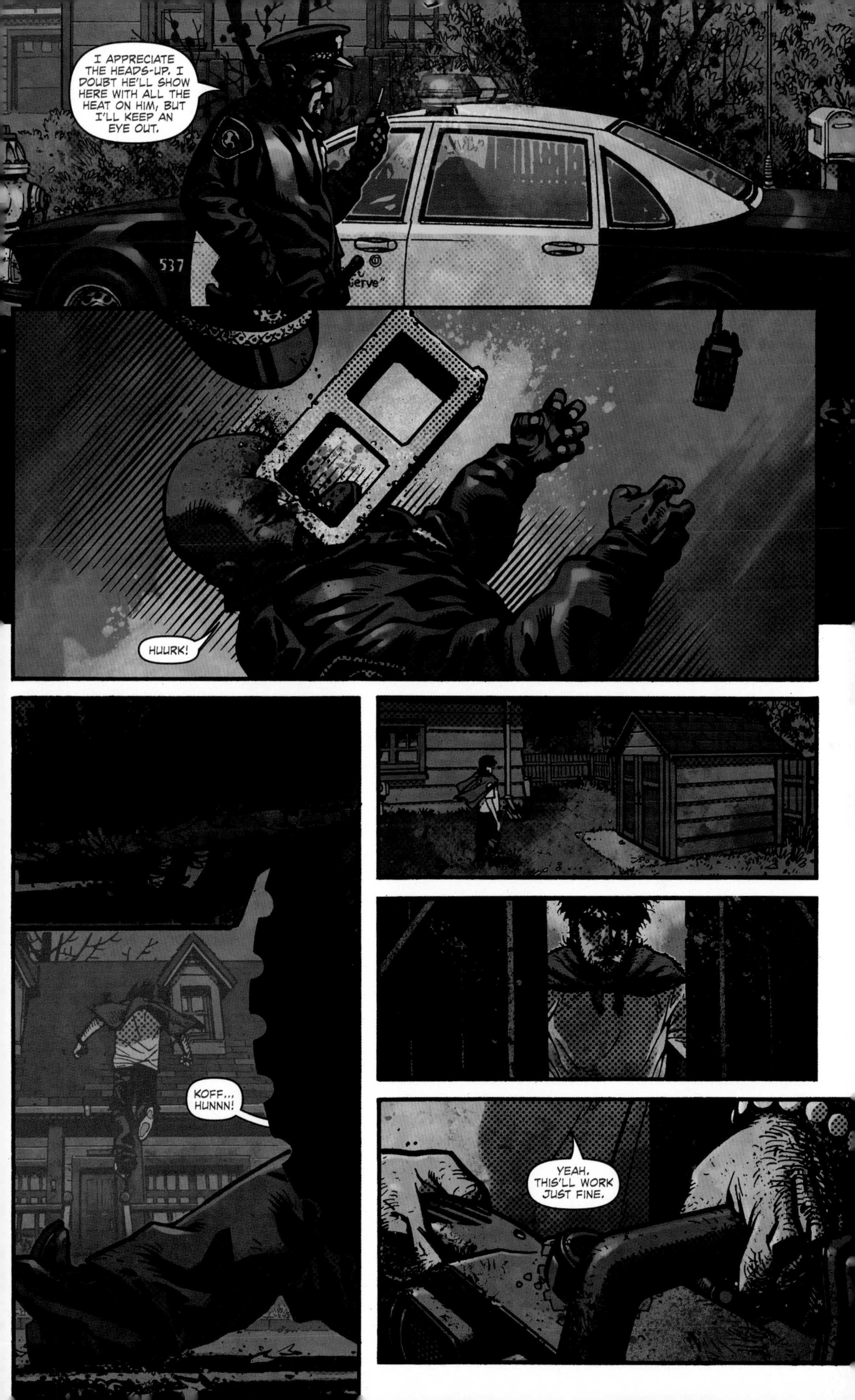
I APPRECIATE THE HEADS-UP. I DOUBT HE'LL SHOW HERE WITH ALL THE HEAT ON HIM, BUT I'LL KEEP AN EYE OUT.
537
HUURK!
KOFF... HUNNN!
YEAH, THIS'LL WORK JUST FINE.

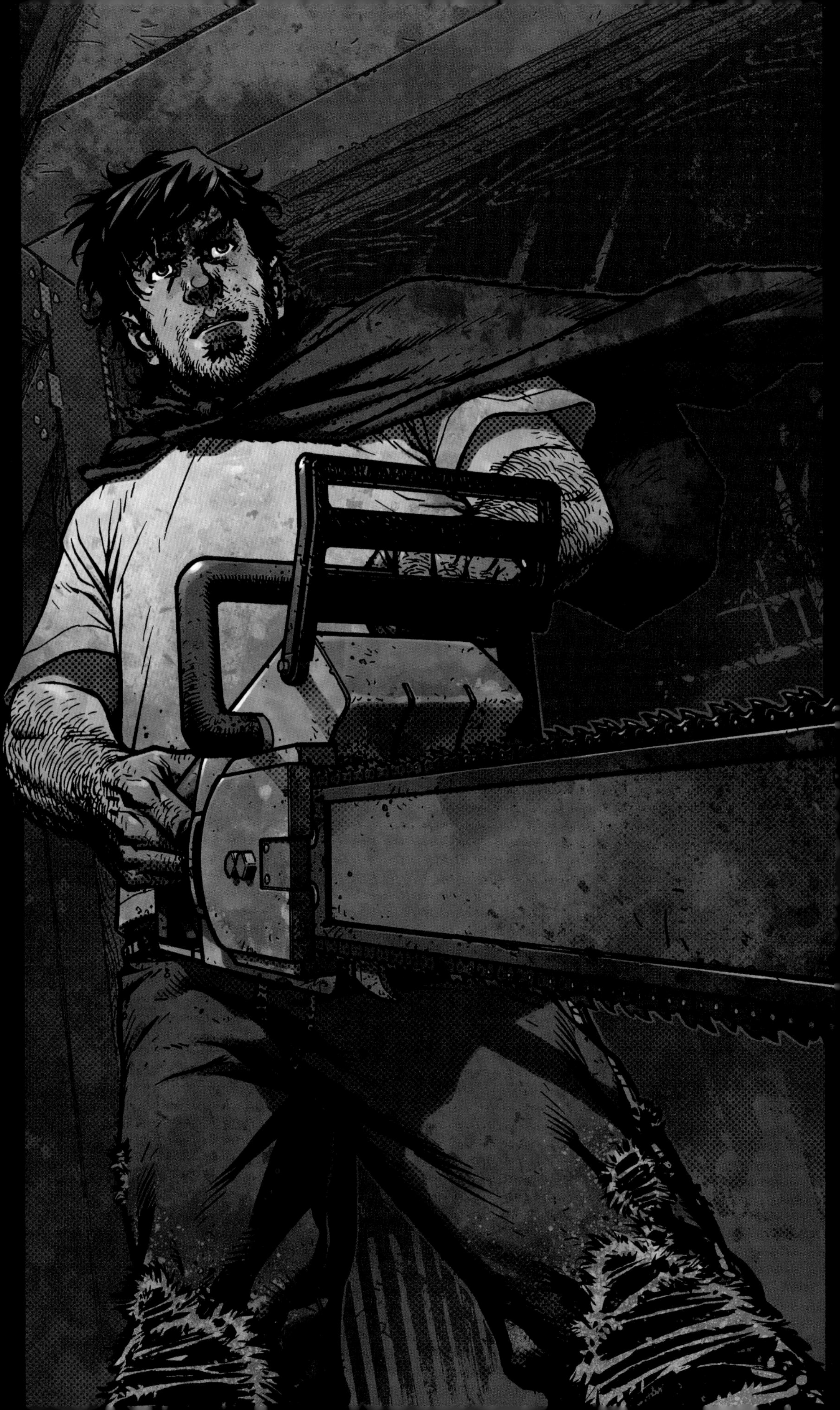

$$\text{"}F_g = G\,\frac{m_1 m_2}{r^2}\text{"}$$
—Sir Isaac Newton

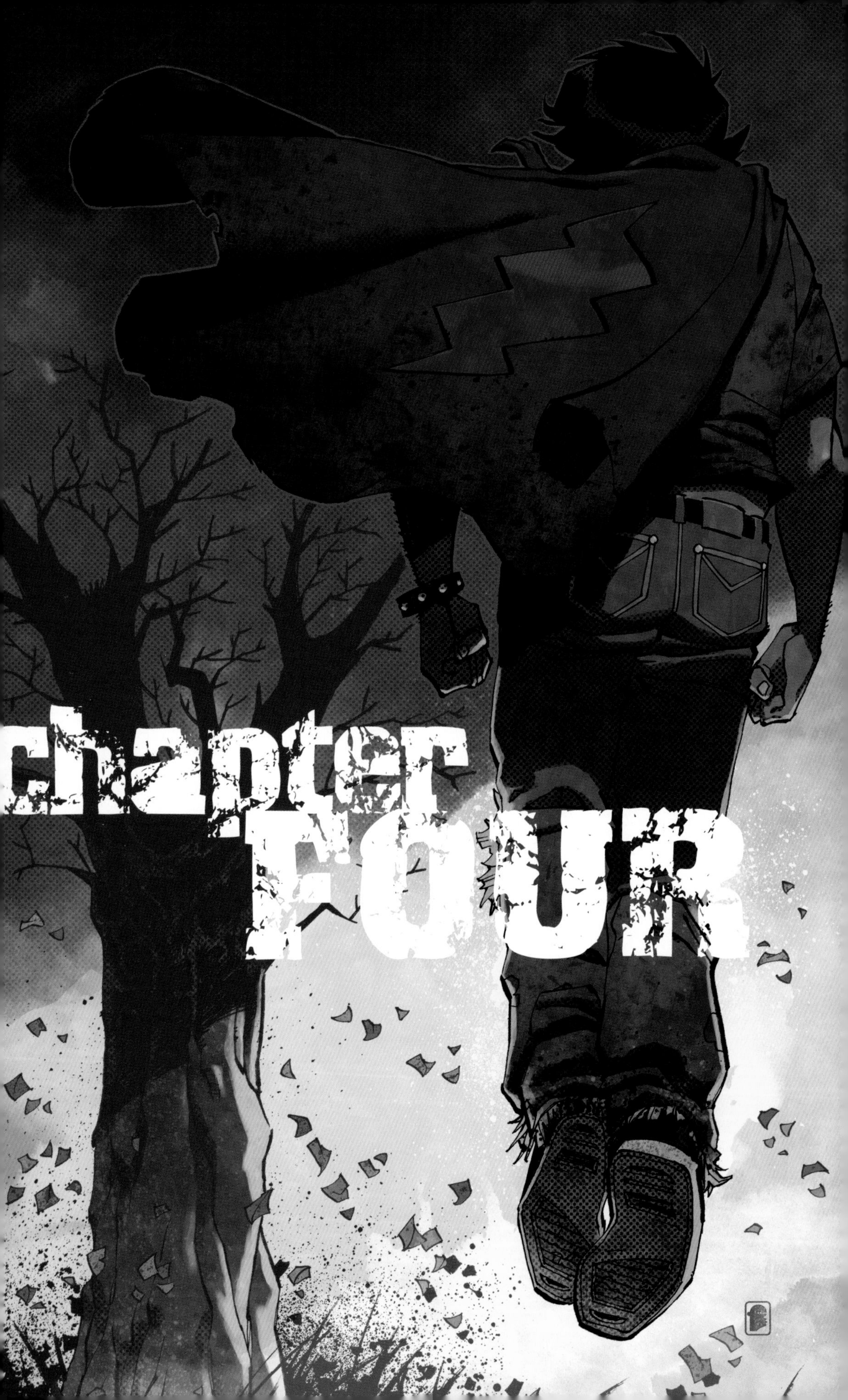
chapter
FOUR

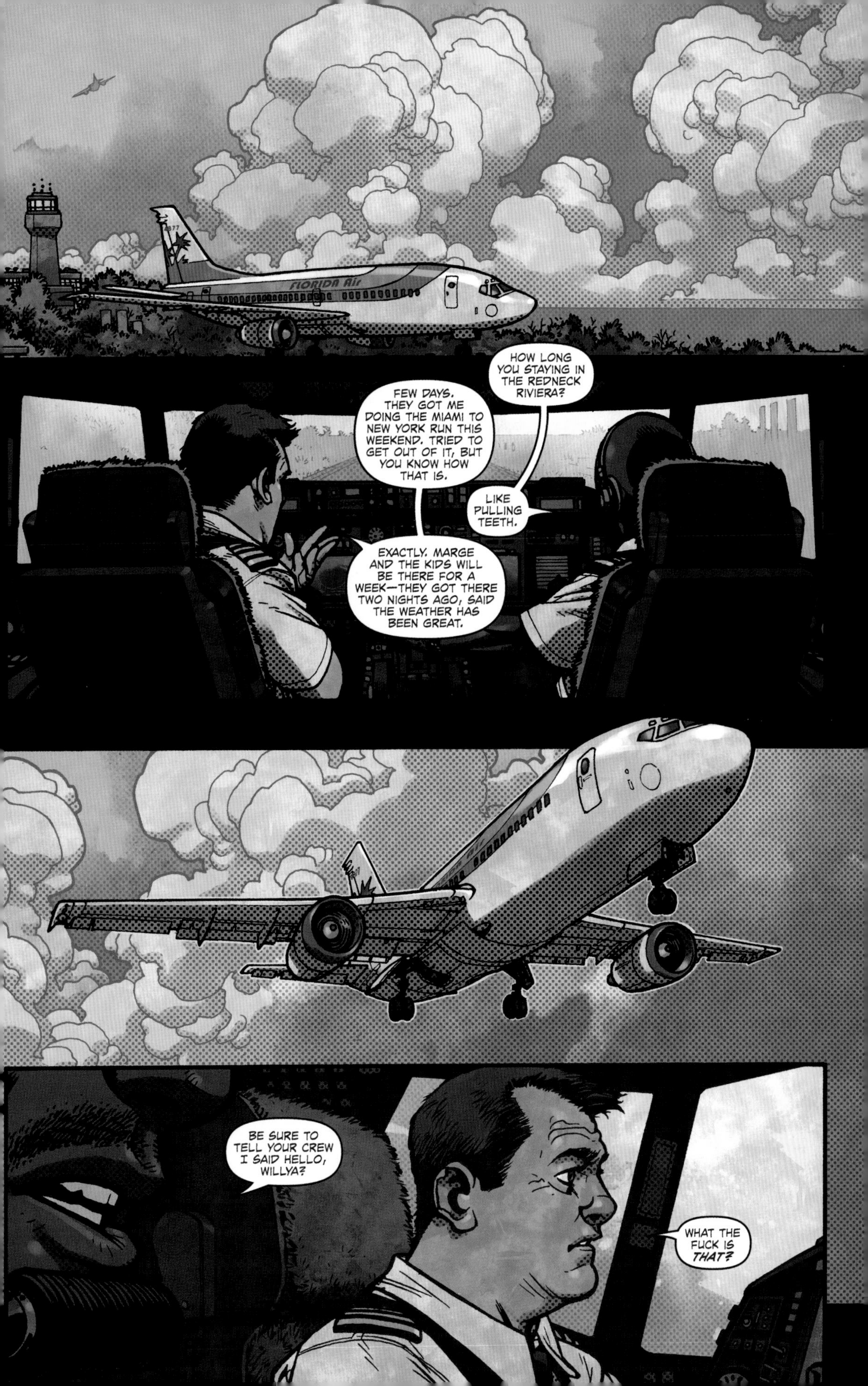
FLORIDA Air
HOW LONG YOU STAYING IN THE REDNECK RIVIERA?
FEW DAYS. THEY GOT ME DOING THE MIAMI TO NEW YORK RUN THIS WEEKEND. TRIED TO GET OUT OF IT, BUT YOU KNOW HOW THAT IS.
LIKE PULLING TEETH.
EXACTLY. MARGE AND THE KIDS WILL BE THERE FOR A WEEK—THEY GOT THERE TWO NIGHTS AGO, SAID THE WEATHER HAS BEEN GREAT.
BE SURE TO TELL YOUR CREW I SAID HELLO, WILLYA?
WHAT THE FUCK IS *THAT?*

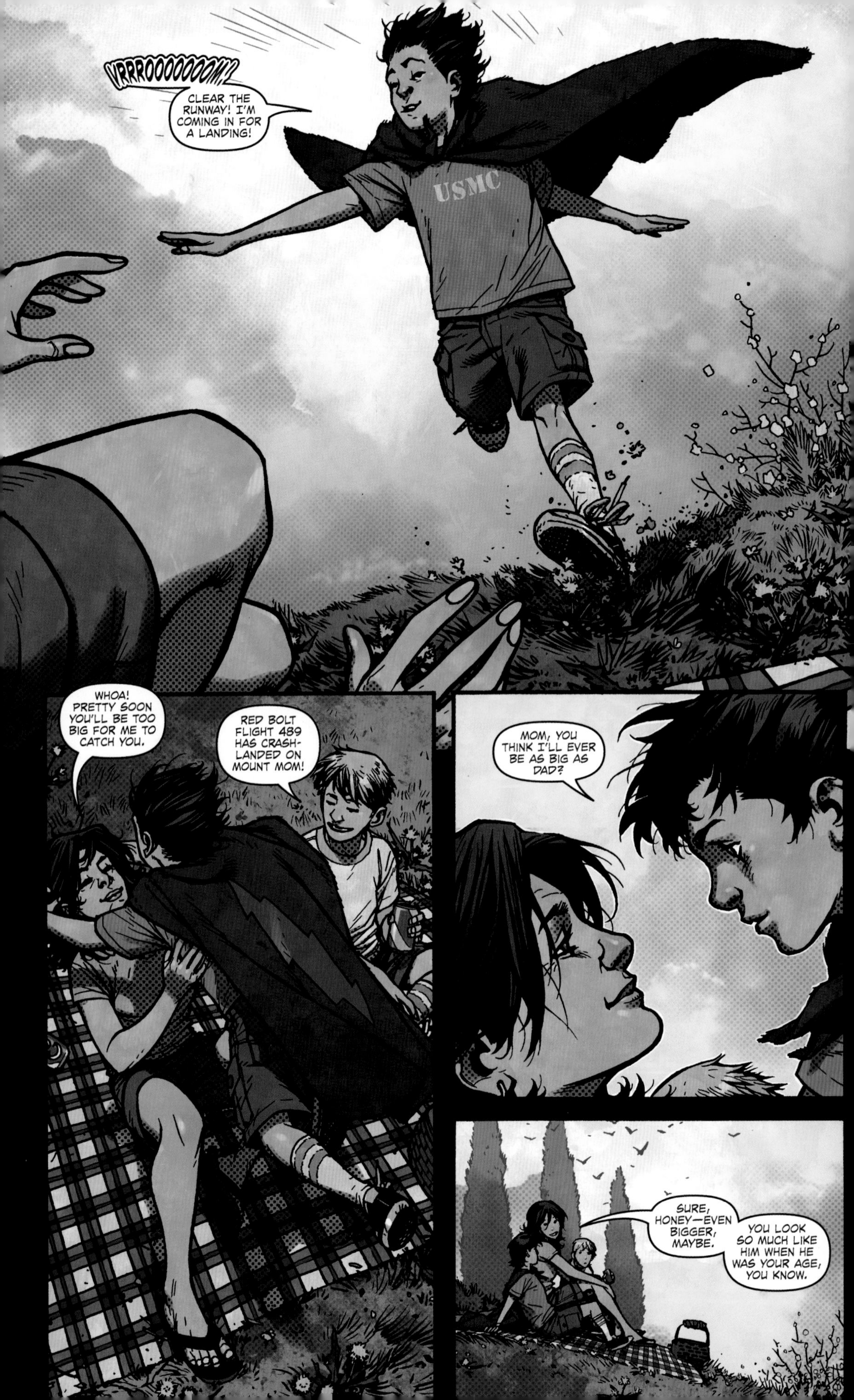
VRRROOOOOOOM!!
CLEAR THE RUNWAY! I'M COMING IN FOR A LANDING!
WHOA! PRETTY SOON YOU'LL BE TOO BIG FOR ME TO CATCH YOU.
RED BOLT FLIGHT 489 HAS CRASH-LANDED ON MOUNT MOM!
MOM, YOU THINK I'LL EVER BE AS BIG AS DAD?
SURE, HONEY—EVEN BIGGER, MAYBE.
YOU LOOK SO MUCH LIKE HIM WHEN HE WAS YOUR AGE, YOU KNOW.
USMC

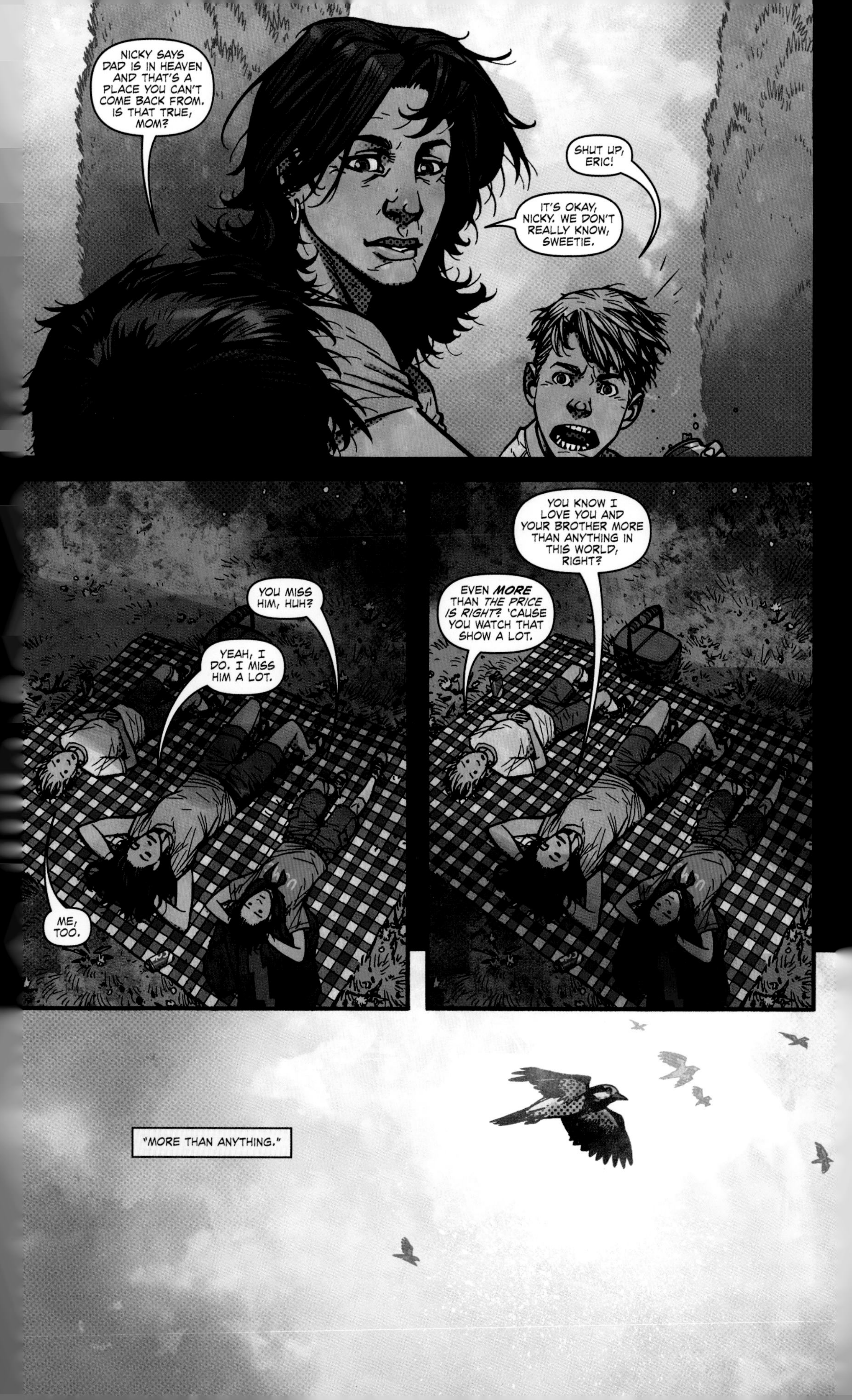
NICKY SAYS DAD IS IN HEAVEN AND THAT'S A PLACE YOU CAN'T COME BACK FROM. IS THAT TRUE, MOM?
SHUT UP, ERIC!
IT'S OKAY, NICKY. WE DON'T REALLY KNOW, SWEETIE.
YOU MISS HIM, HUH?
YEAH, I DO. I MISS HIM A LOT.
ME, TOO.
YOU KNOW I LOVE YOU AND YOUR BROTHER MORE THAN ANYTHING IN THIS WORLD, RIGHT?
EVEN MORE THAN THE PRICE IS RIGHT? 'CAUSE YOU WATCH THAT SHOW A LOT.
"MORE THAN ANYTHING."

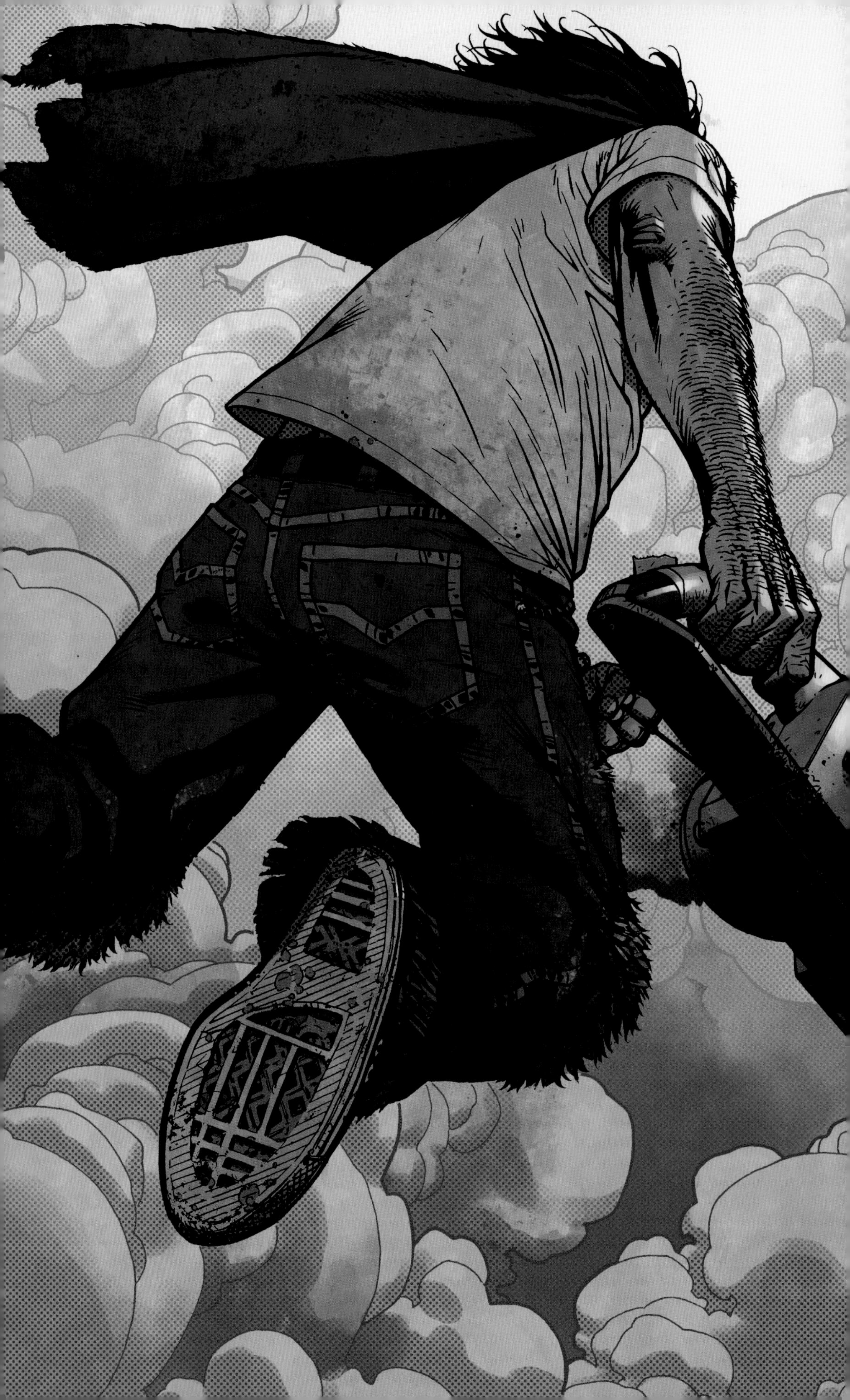

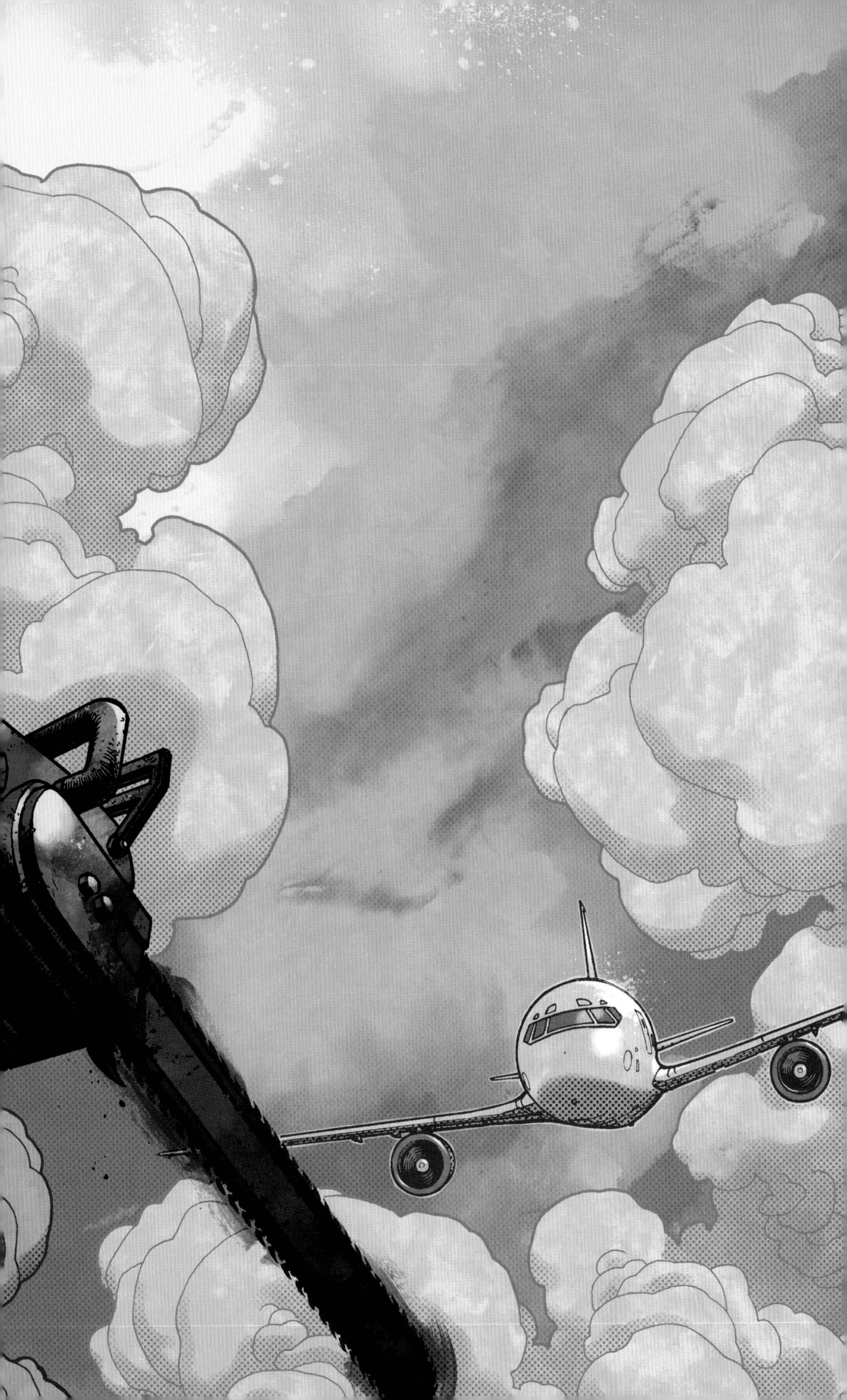

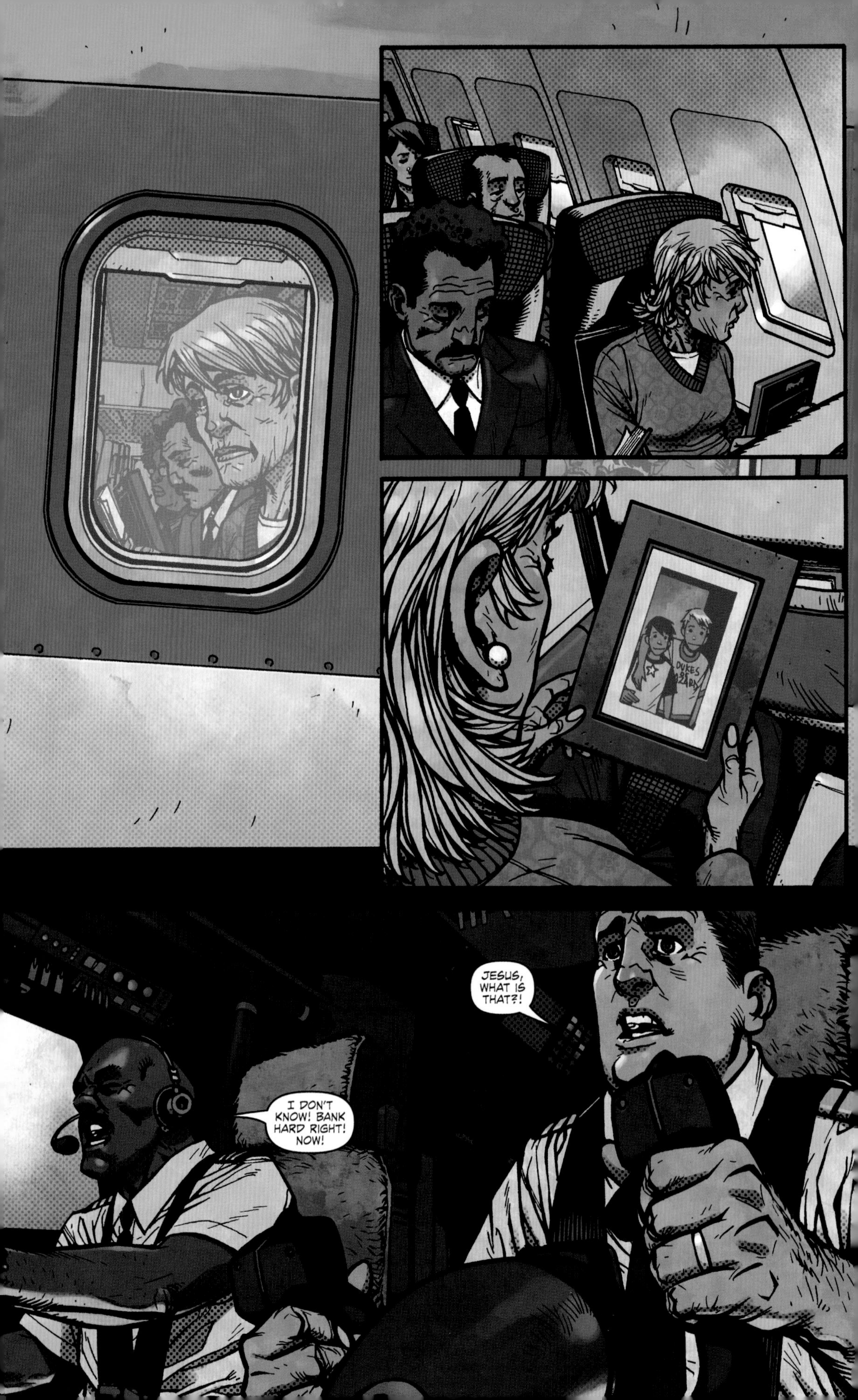
DUKES OF HAZZARD
JESUS, WHAT IS THAT?!
I DON'T KNOW! BANK HARD RIGHT! NOW!

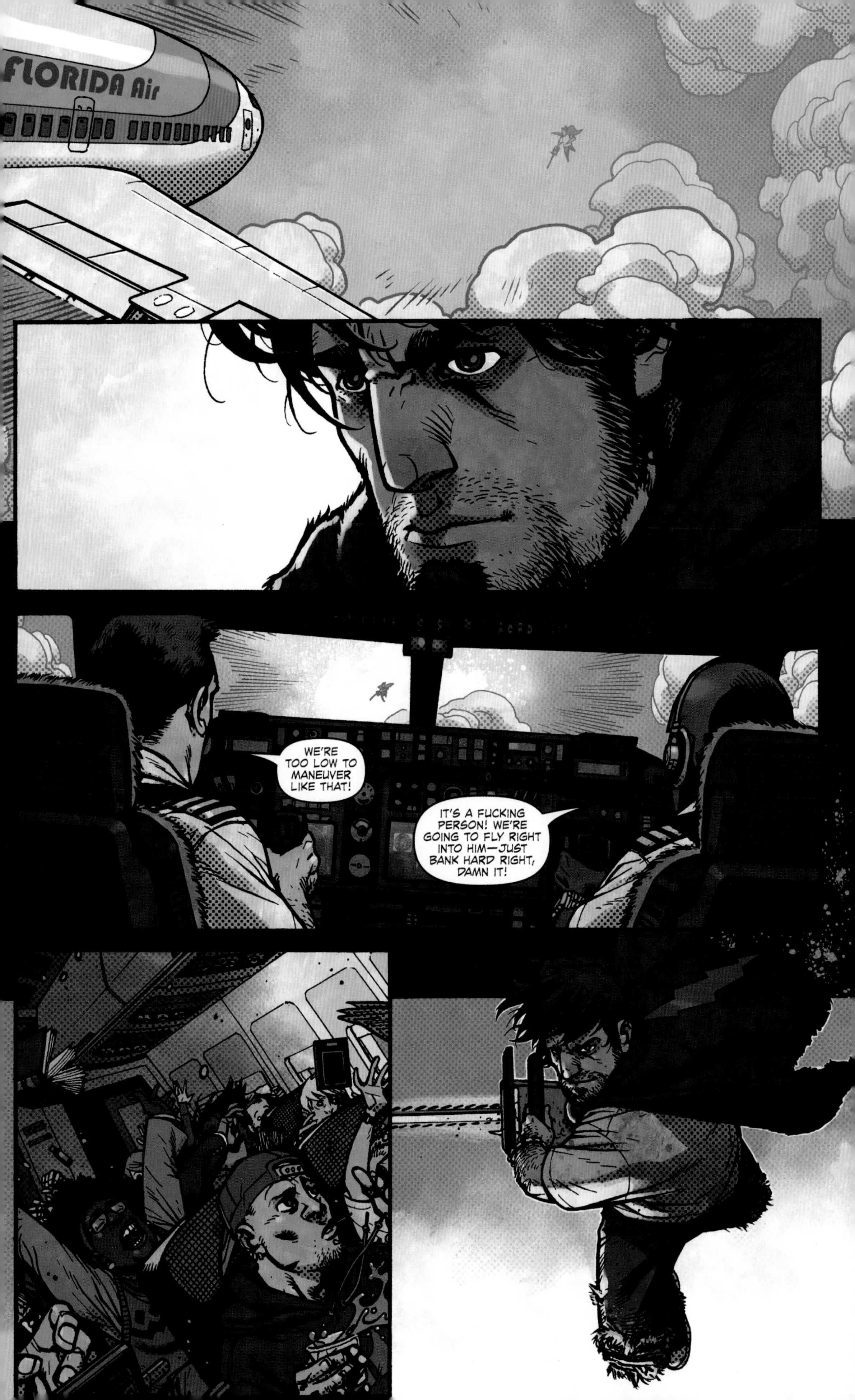
FLORIDA Air
WE'RE TOO LOW TO MANEUVER LIKE THAT!
IT'S A FUCKING PERSON! WE'RE GOING TO FLY RIGHT INTO HIM—JUST BANK HARD RIGHT, DAMN IT!

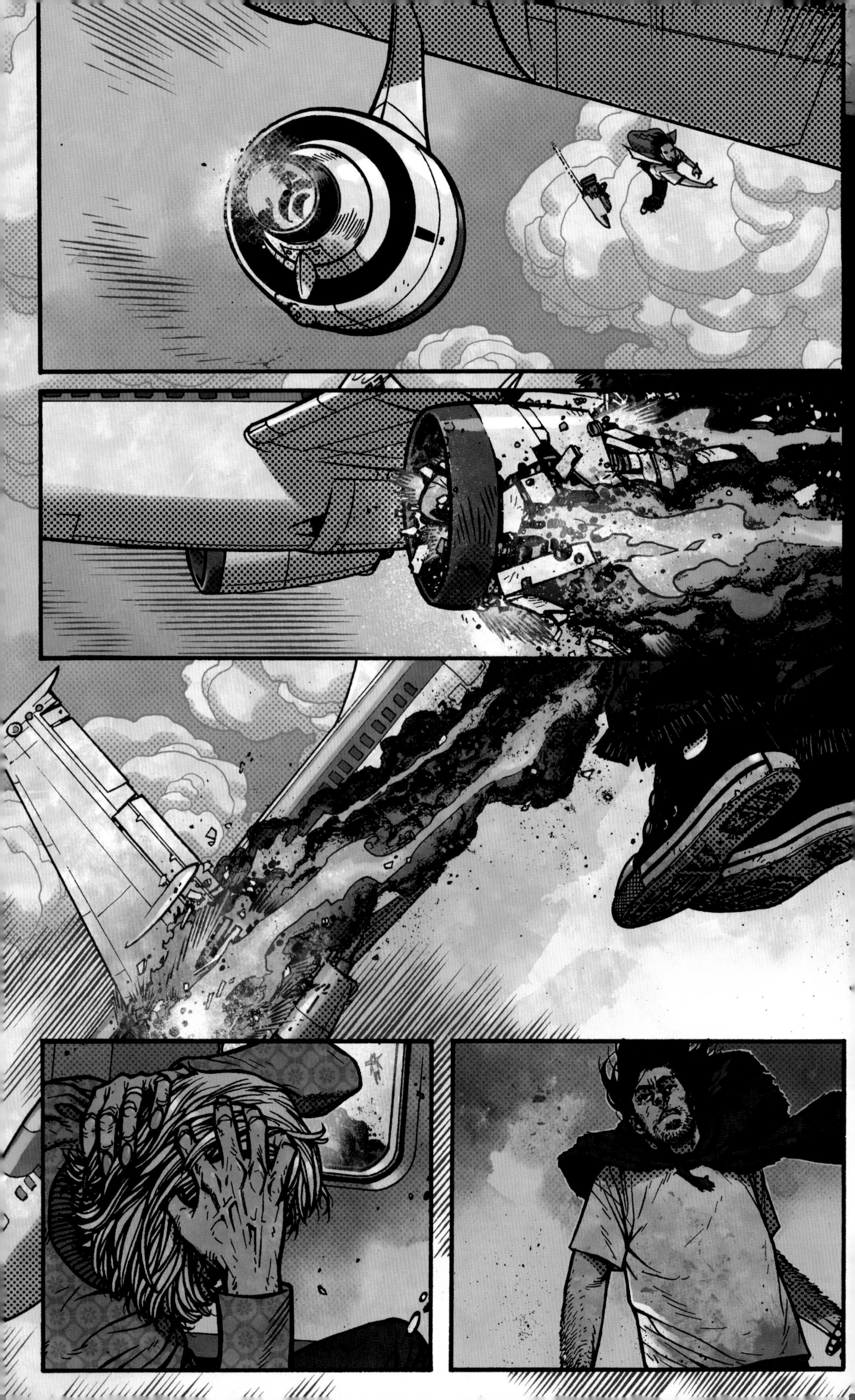

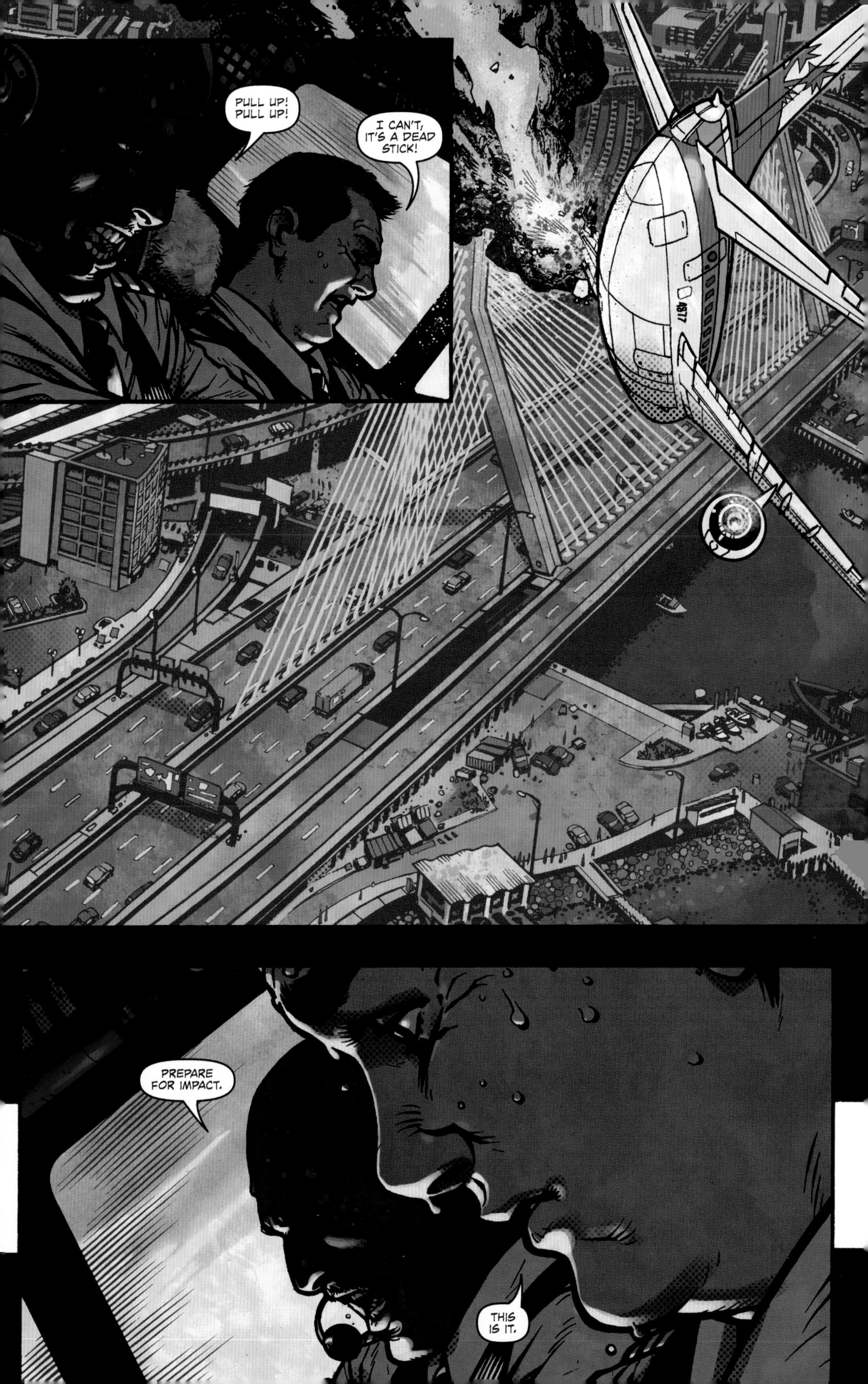
PULL UP! PULL UP!
I CAN'T, IT'S A DEAD STICK!
PREPARE FOR IMPACT.
THIS IS IT.

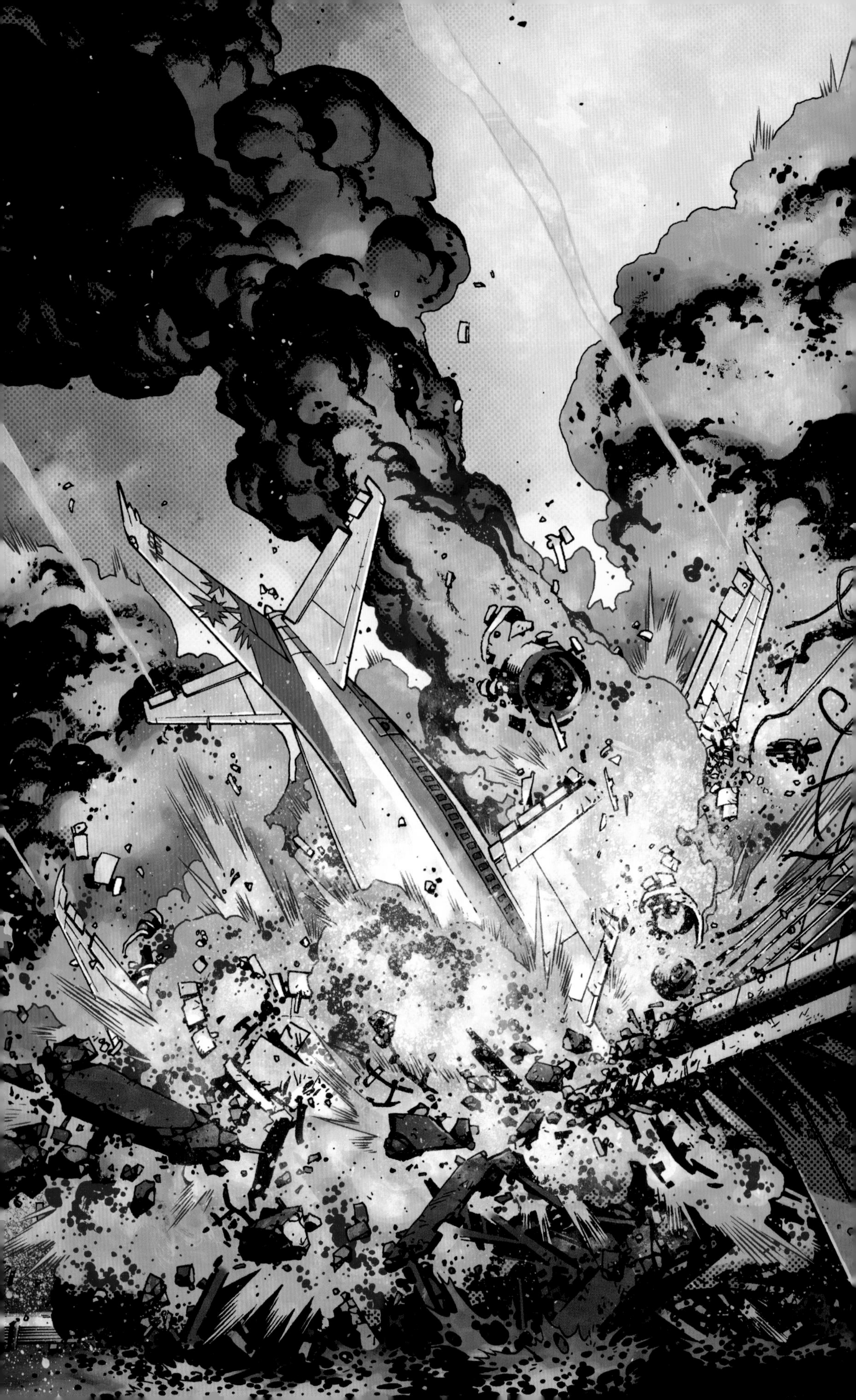

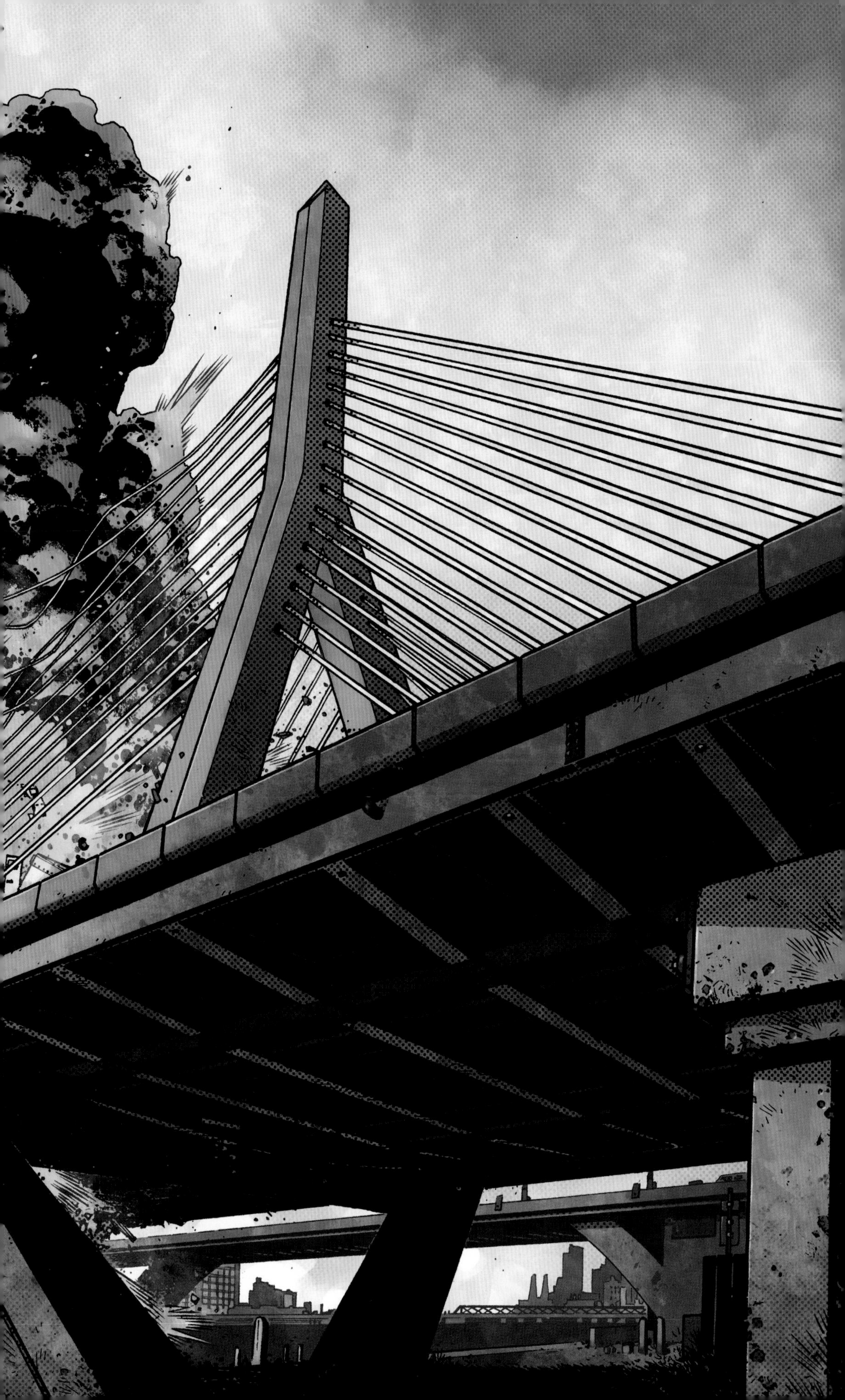

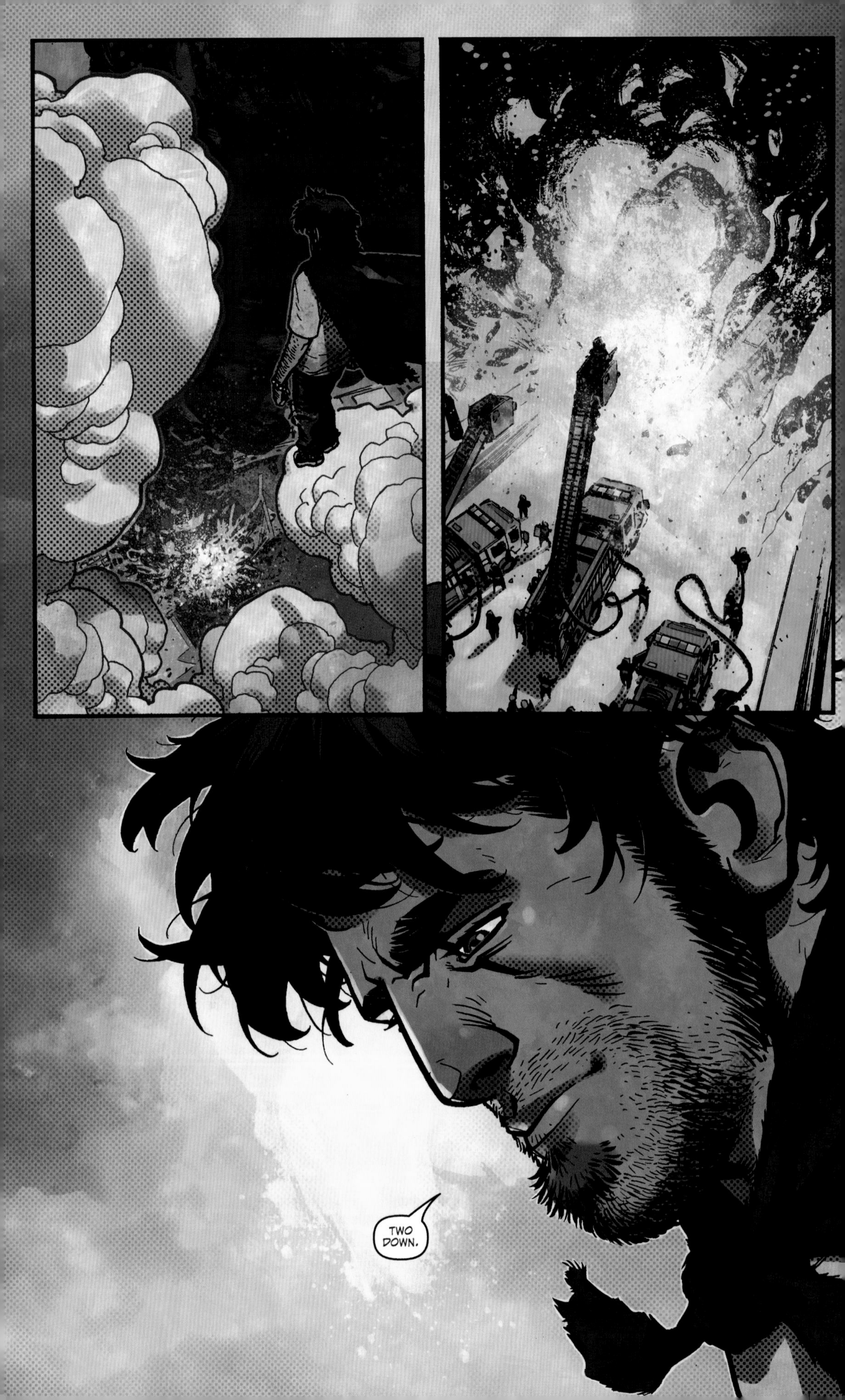
TWO DOWN.

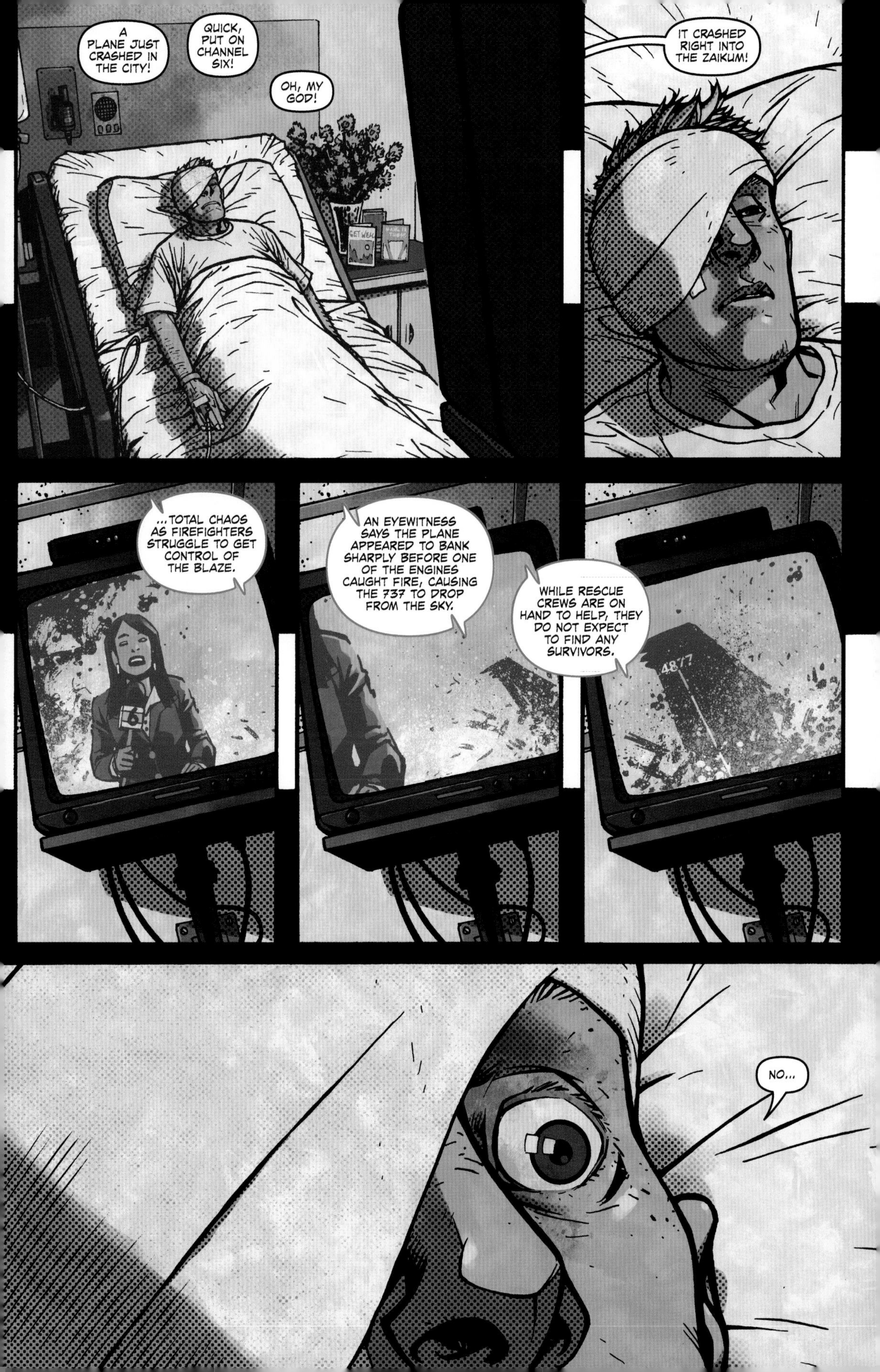
A PLANE JUST CRASHED IN THE CITY!
QUICK, PUT ON CHANNEL SIX!
OH, MY GOD!
IT CRASHED RIGHT INTO THE ZAIKUM!
...TOTAL CHAOS AS FIREFIGHTERS STRUGGLE TO GET CONTROL OF THE BLAZE.
AN EYEWITNESS SAYS THE PLANE APPEARED TO BANK SHARPLY BEFORE ONE OF THE ENGINES CAUGHT FIRE, CAUSING THE 737 TO DROP FROM THE SKY.
WHILE RESCUE CREWS ARE ON HAND TO HELP, THEY DO NOT EXPECT TO FIND ANY SURVIVORS.
NO...

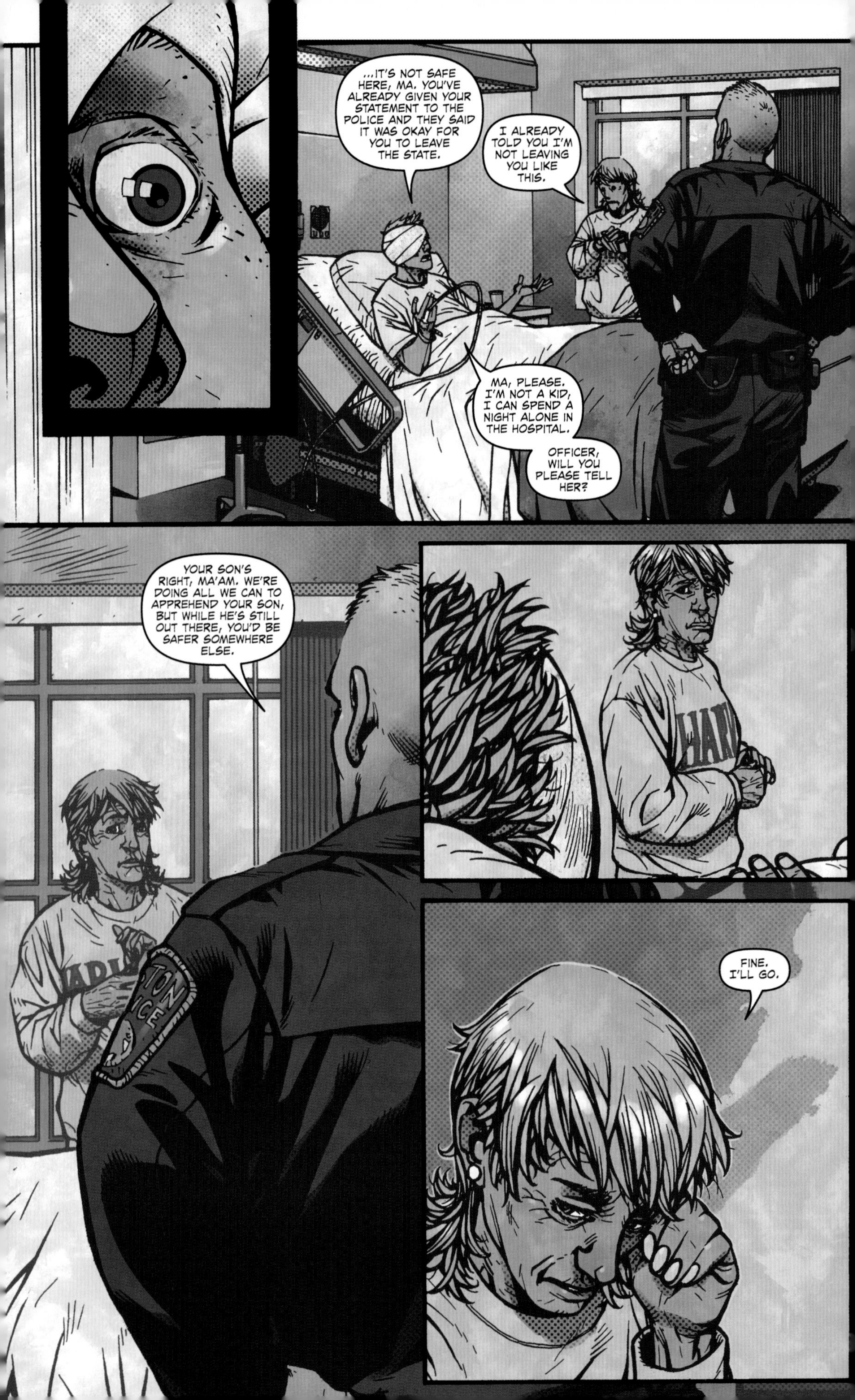
...IT'S NOT SAFE HERE, MA. YOU'VE ALREADY GIVEN YOUR STATEMENT TO THE POLICE AND THEY SAID IT WAS OKAY FOR YOU TO LEAVE THE STATE.
I ALREADY TOLD YOU I'M NOT LEAVING YOU LIKE THIS.
MA, PLEASE. I'M NOT A KID, I CAN SPEND A NIGHT ALONE IN THE HOSPITAL.
OFFICER, WILL YOU PLEASE TELL HER?
YOUR SON'S RIGHT, MA'AM. WE'RE DOING ALL WE CAN TO APPREHEND YOUR SON, BUT WHILE HE'S STILL OUT THERE, YOU'D BE SAFER SOMEWHERE ELSE.
FINE. I'LL GO.

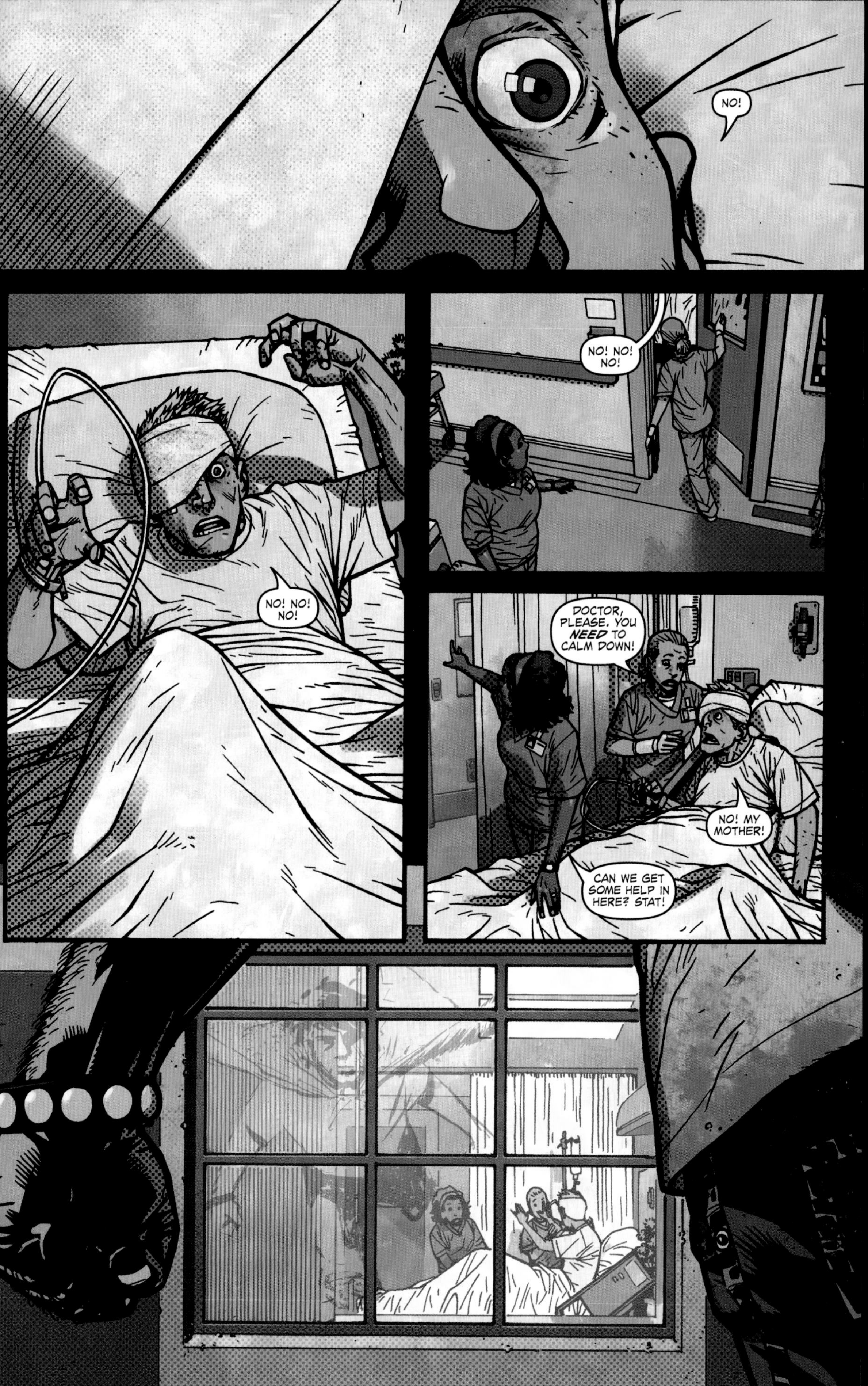
NO!
NO! NO! NO!
NO! NO! NO!
DOCTOR, PLEASE. YOU *NEED* TO CALM DOWN!
NO! MY MOTHER!
CAN WE GET SOME HELP IN HERE? STAT!

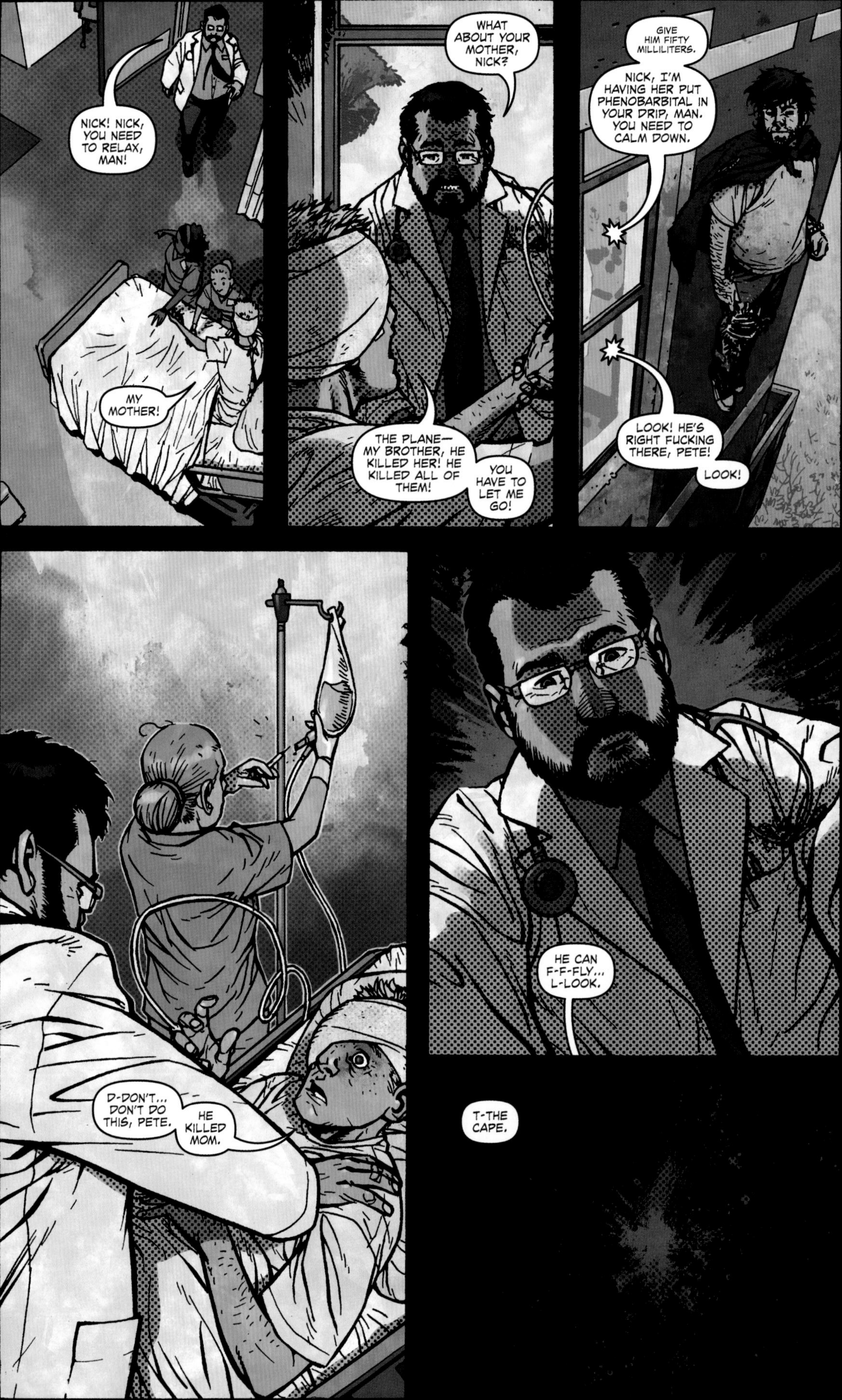

NICK! NICK, YOU NEED TO RELAX, MAN!
MY MOTHER!
WHAT ABOUT YOUR MOTHER, NICK?
THE PLANE— MY BROTHER, HE KILLED HER! HE KILLED ALL OF THEM!
YOU HAVE TO LET ME GO!
GIVE HIM FIFTY MILLILITERS.
NICK, I'M HAVING HER PUT PHENOBARBITAL IN YOUR DRIP, MAN. YOU NEED TO CALM DOWN.
LOOK! HE'S RIGHT FUCKING THERE, PETE!
LOOK!
D-DON'T... DON'T DO THIS, PETE.
HE KILLED MOM.
HE CAN F-F-FLY... L-LOOK.
T-THE CAPE.

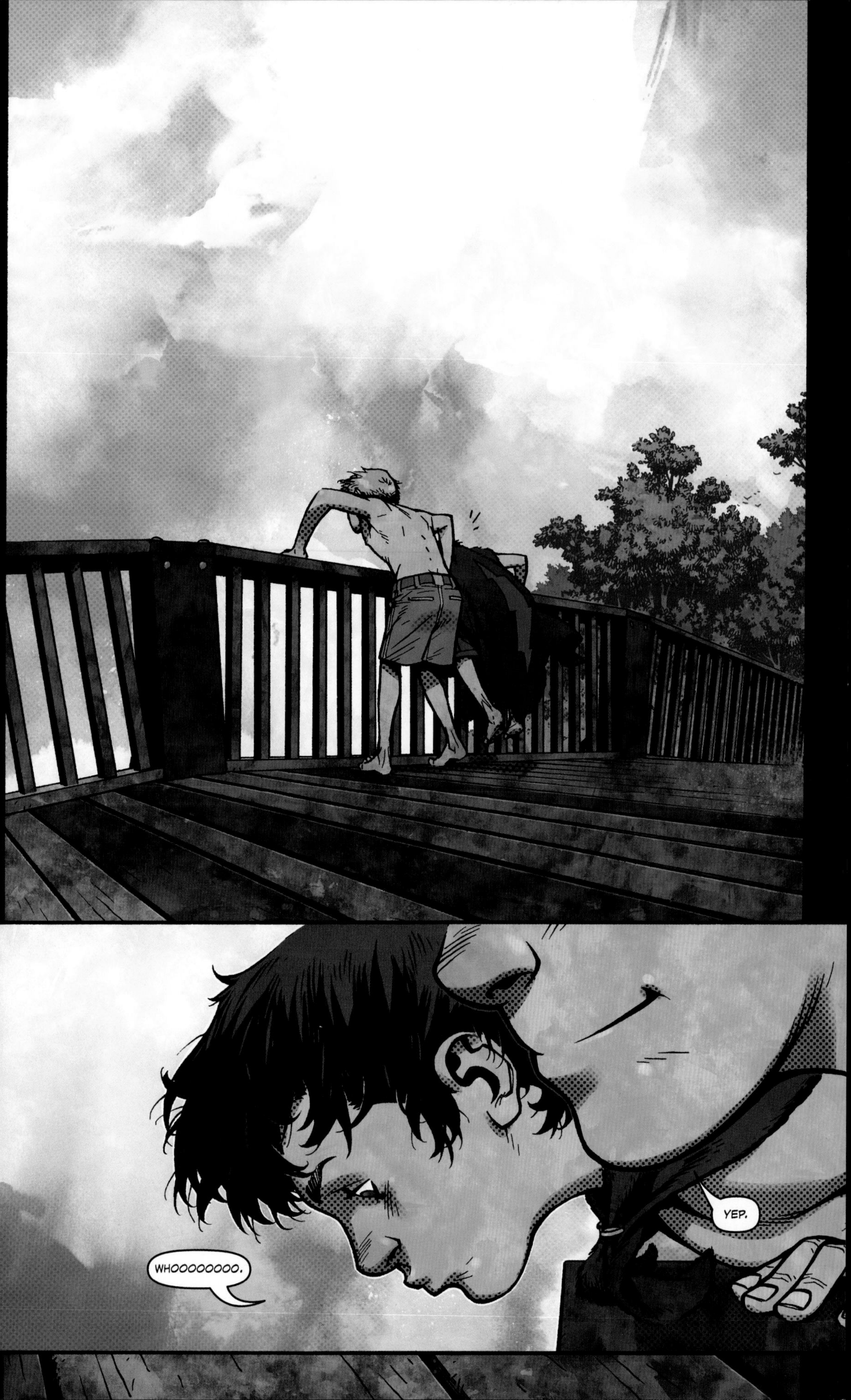
YEP.
WHOOOOOOOO.

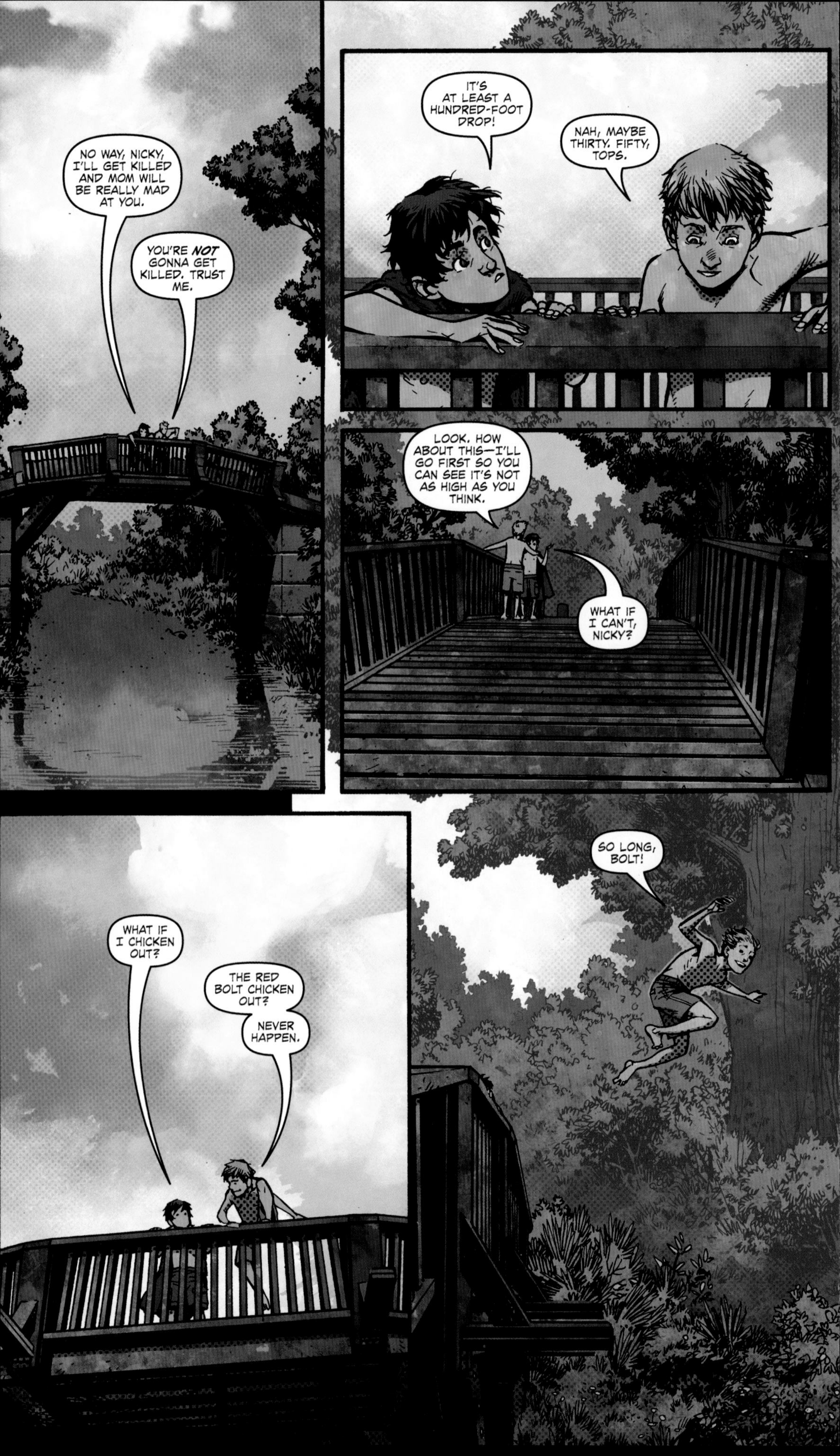
NO WAY, NICKY, I'LL GET KILLED AND MOM WILL BE REALLY MAD AT YOU.
YOU'RE **NOT** GONNA GET KILLED. TRUST ME.
IT'S AT LEAST A HUNDRED-FOOT DROP!
NAH, MAYBE THIRTY. FIFTY, TOPS.
LOOK. HOW ABOUT THIS—I'LL GO FIRST SO YOU CAN SEE IT'S NOT AS HIGH AS YOU THINK.
WHAT IF I CAN'T, NICKY?
WHAT IF I CHICKEN OUT?
THE RED BOLT CHICKEN OUT?
NEVER HAPPEN.
SO LONG, BOLT!

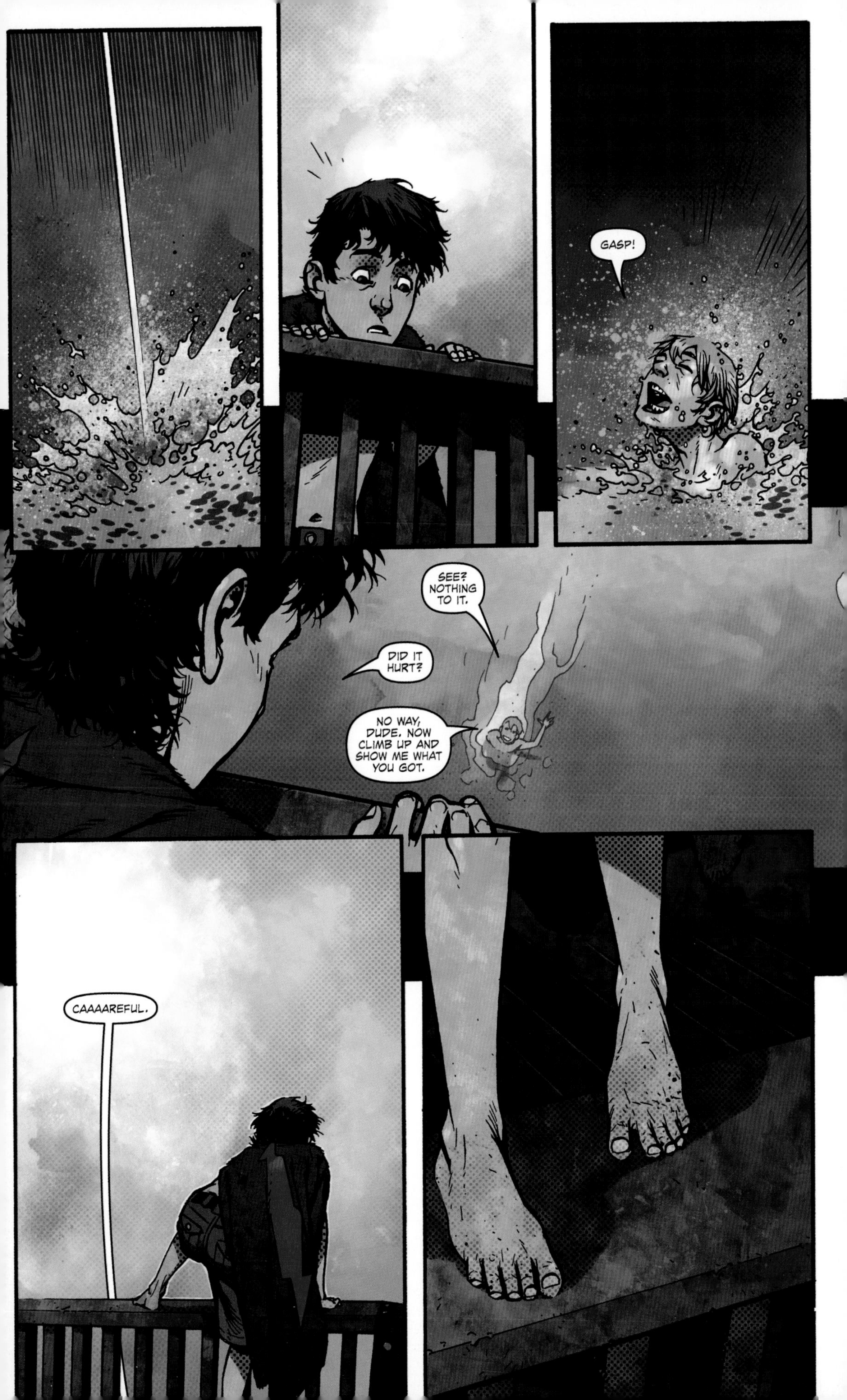
GASP!
SEE? NOTHING TO IT.
DID IT HURT?
NO WAY, DUDE. NOW CLIMB UP AND SHOW ME WHAT YOU GOT.
CAAAAREFUL.

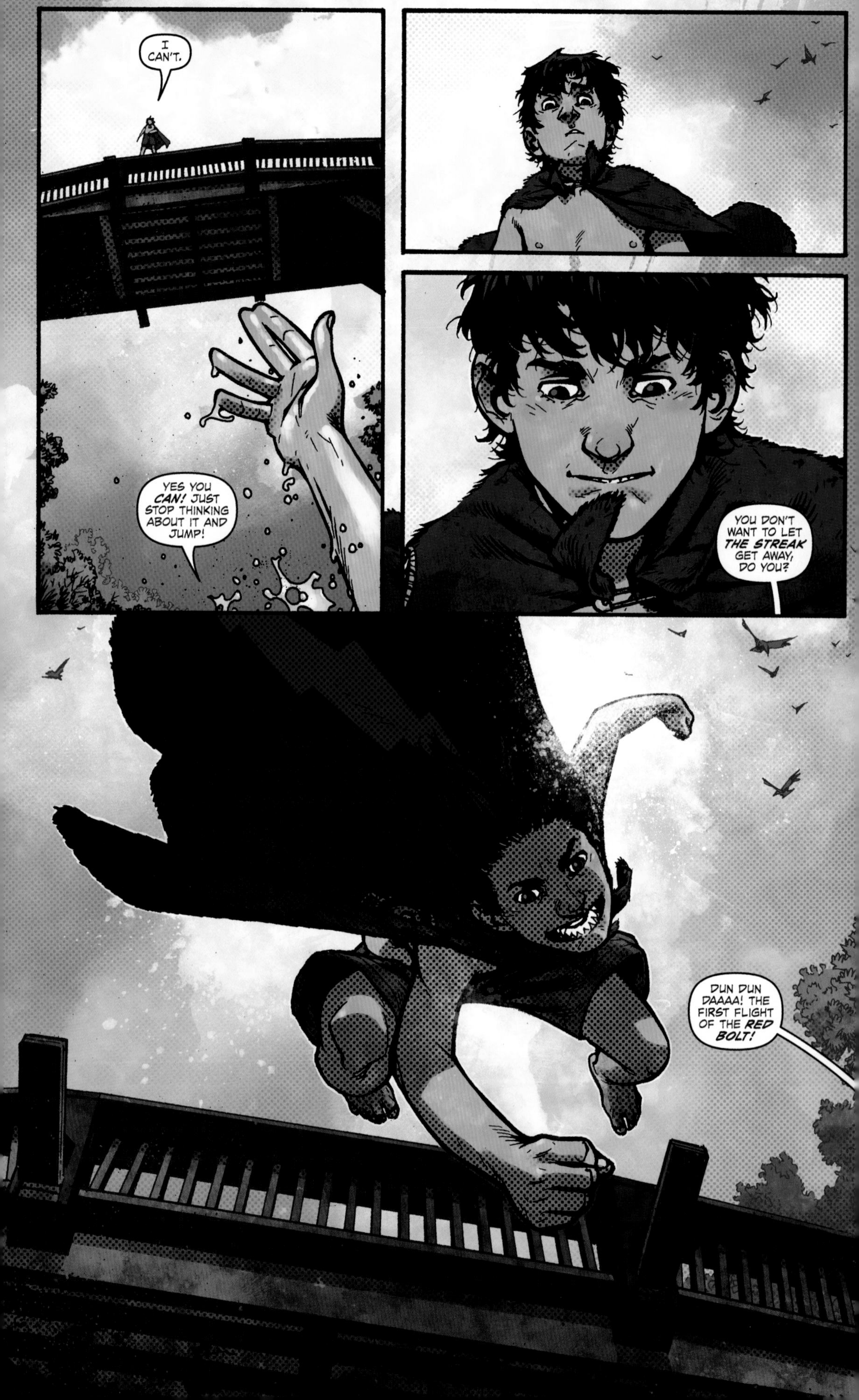
I CAN'T.
YES YOU CAN! JUST STOP THINKING ABOUT IT AND JUMP!
YOU DON'T WANT TO LET THE STREAK GET AWAY, DO YOU?
DUN DUN DAAAA! THE FIRST FLIGHT OF THE RED BOLT!

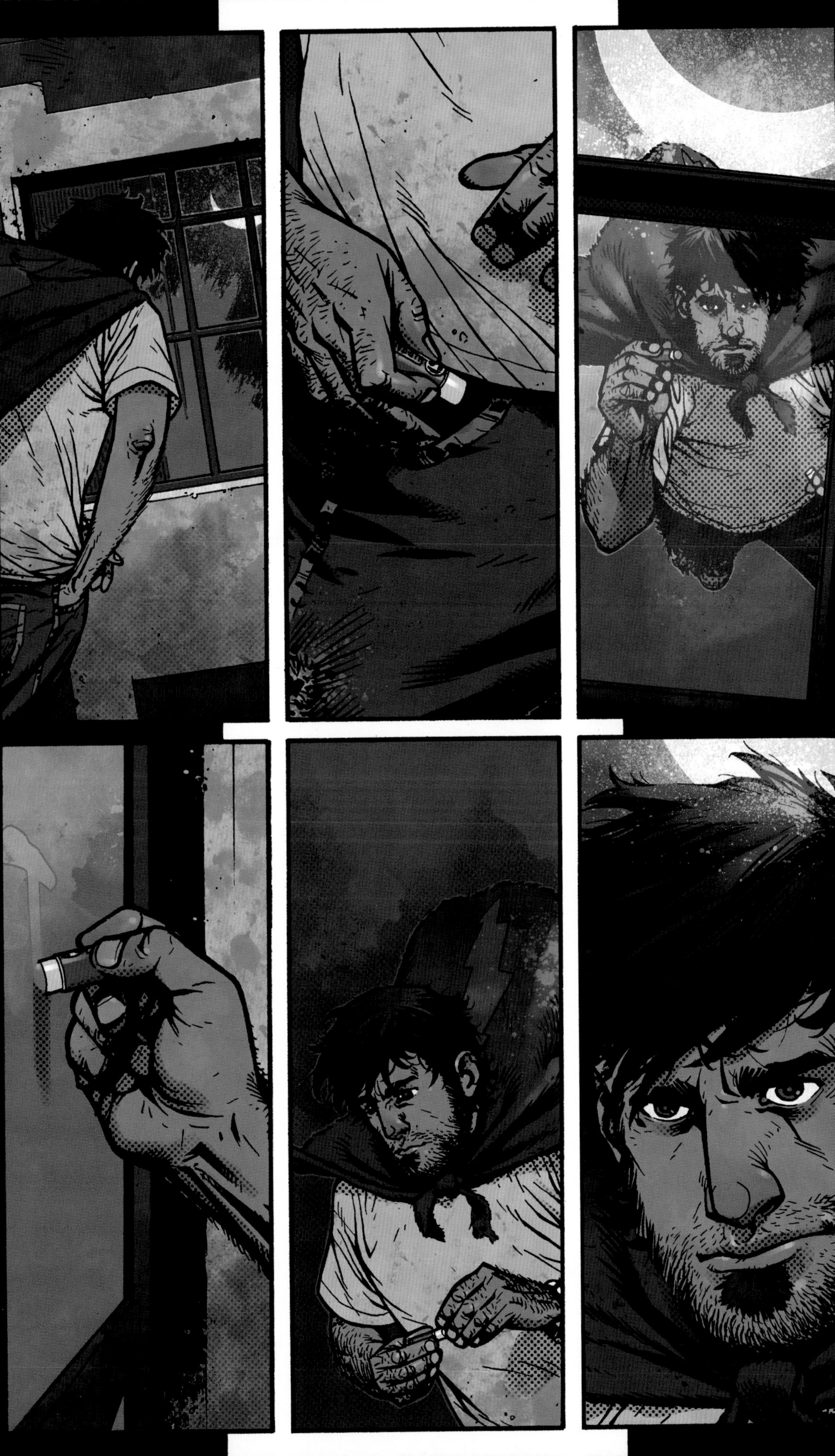

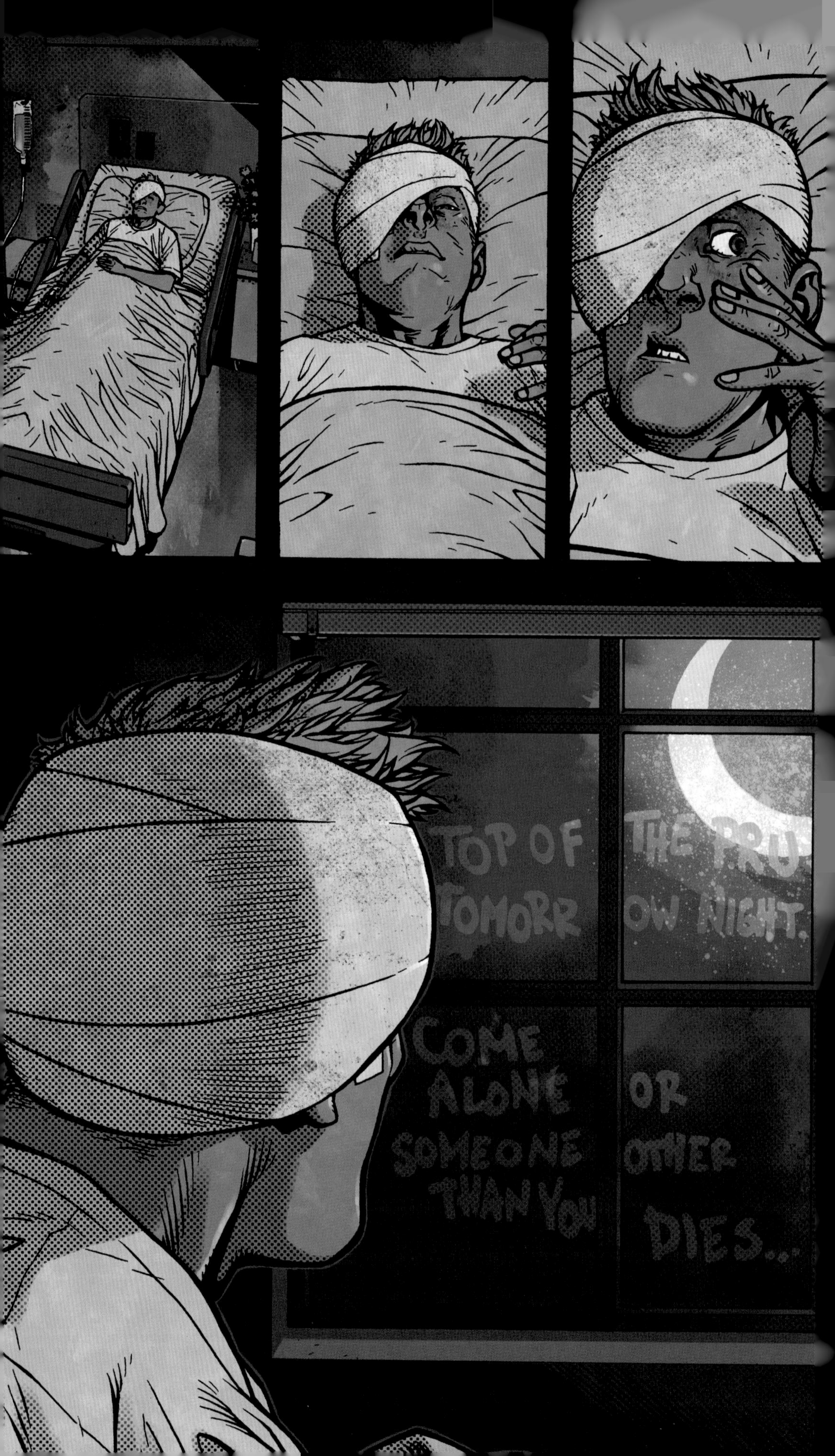
TOP OF THE PRU.
TOMORROW NIGHT.
COME ALONE OR SOMEONE OTHER THAN YOU DIES...

"Do not be dismayed to learn there is a bit of the
devil in you. There is a bit of the devil in us all."
—Authur Byron Cover

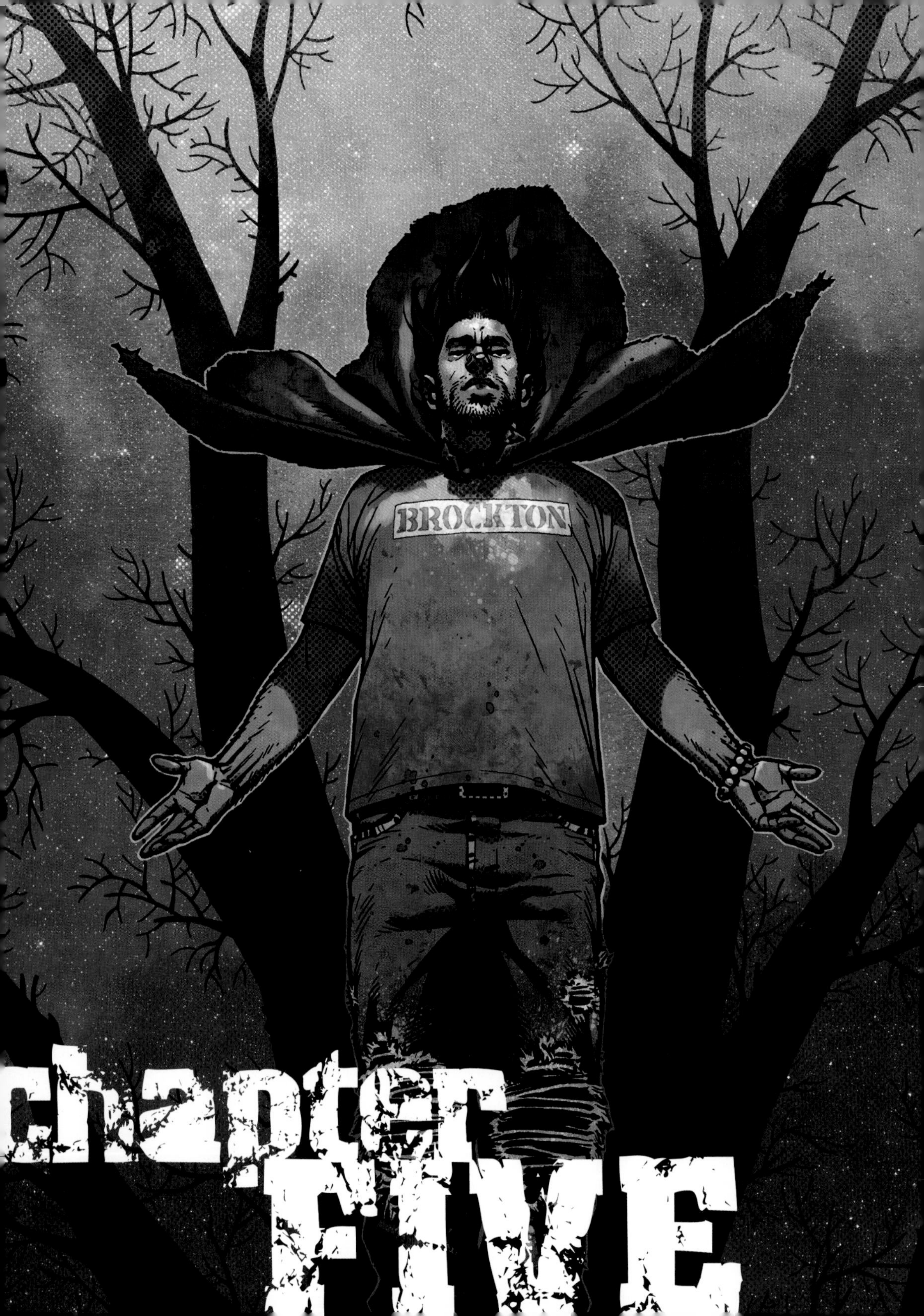
BROCKTON
chapter
FIVE

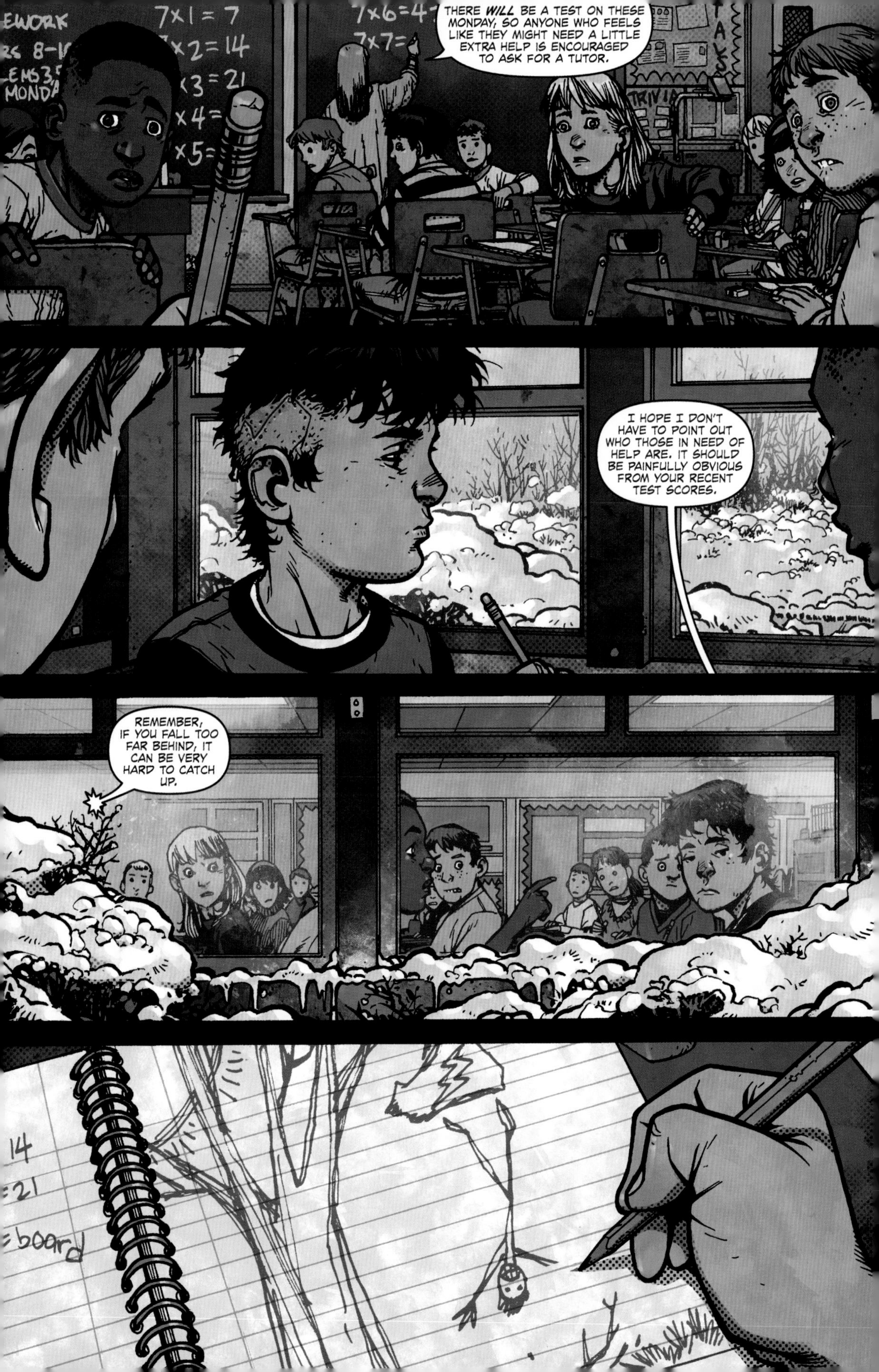
THERE WILL BE A TEST ON THESE MONDAY, SO ANYONE WHO FEELS LIKE THEY MIGHT NEED A LITTLE EXTRA HELP IS ENCOURAGED TO ASK FOR A TUTOR.
I HOPE I DON'T HAVE TO POINT OUT WHO THOSE IN NEED OF HELP ARE. IT SHOULD BE PAINFULLY OBVIOUS FROM YOUR RECENT TEST SCORES.
REMEMBER, IF YOU FALL TOO FAR BEHIND, IT CAN BE VERY HARD TO CATCH UP.

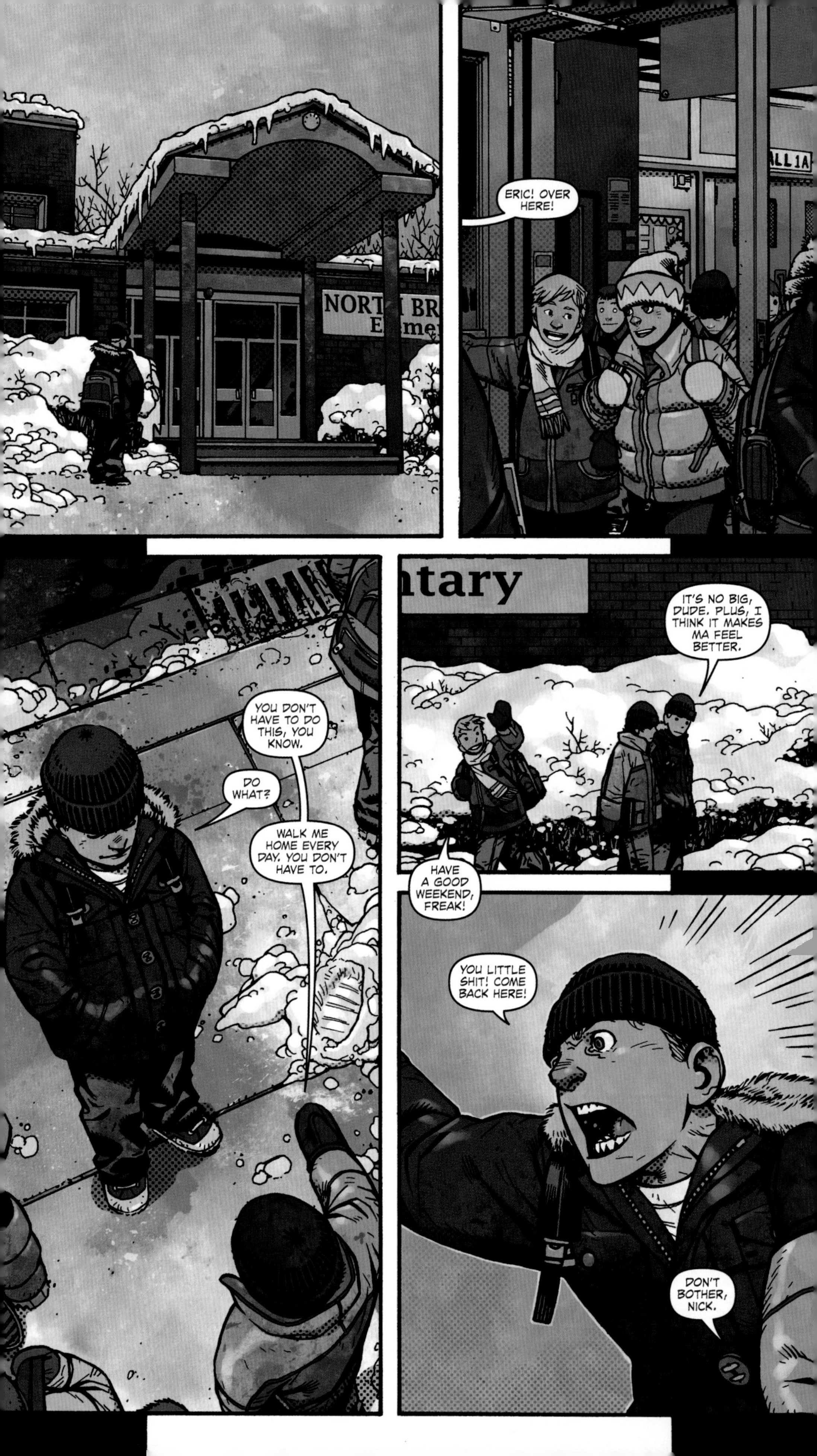

NORTH BR
ERIC! OVER HERE!
ntary
YOU DON'T HAVE TO DO THIS, YOU KNOW.
DO WHAT?
WALK ME HOME EVERY DAY. YOU DON'T HAVE TO.
IT'S NO BIG, DUDE. PLUS, I THINK IT MAKES MA FEEL BETTER.
HAVE A GOOD WEEKEND, FREAK!
YOU LITTLE SHIT! COME BACK HERE!
DON'T BOTHER, NICK.

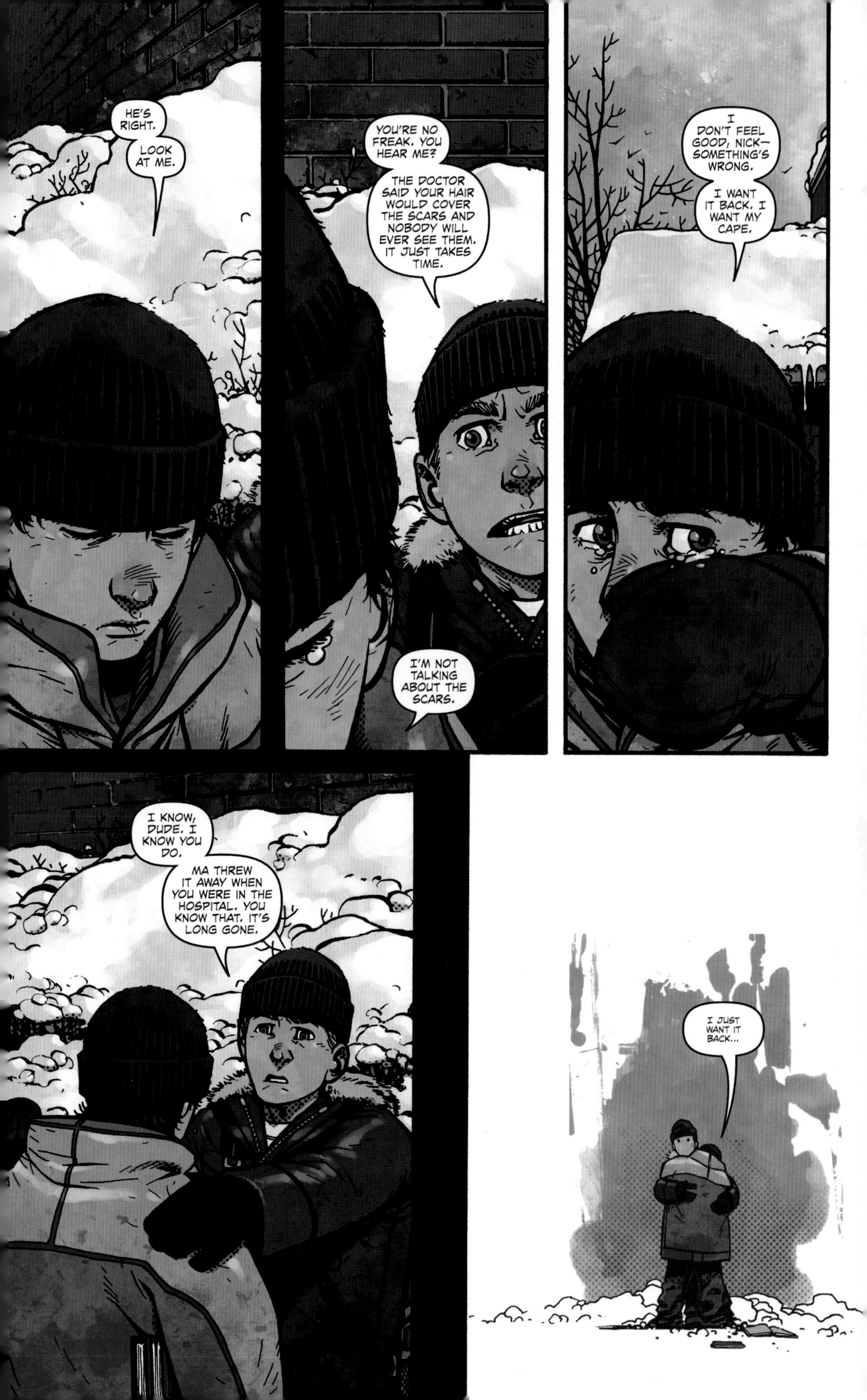
HE'S RIGHT.
LOOK AT ME.
YOU'RE NO FREAK. YOU HEAR ME?
THE DOCTOR SAID YOUR HAIR WOULD COVER THE SCARS AND NOBODY WILL EVER SEE THEM. IT JUST TAKES TIME.
I'M NOT TALKING ABOUT THE SCARS.
I DON'T FEEL GOOD, NICK— SOMETHING'S WRONG.
I WANT IT BACK. I WANT MY CAPE.
I KNOW, DUDE. I KNOW YOU DO.
MA THREW IT AWAY WHEN YOU WERE IN THE HOSPITAL. YOU KNOW THAT. IT'S LONG GONE.
I JUST WANT IT BACK...

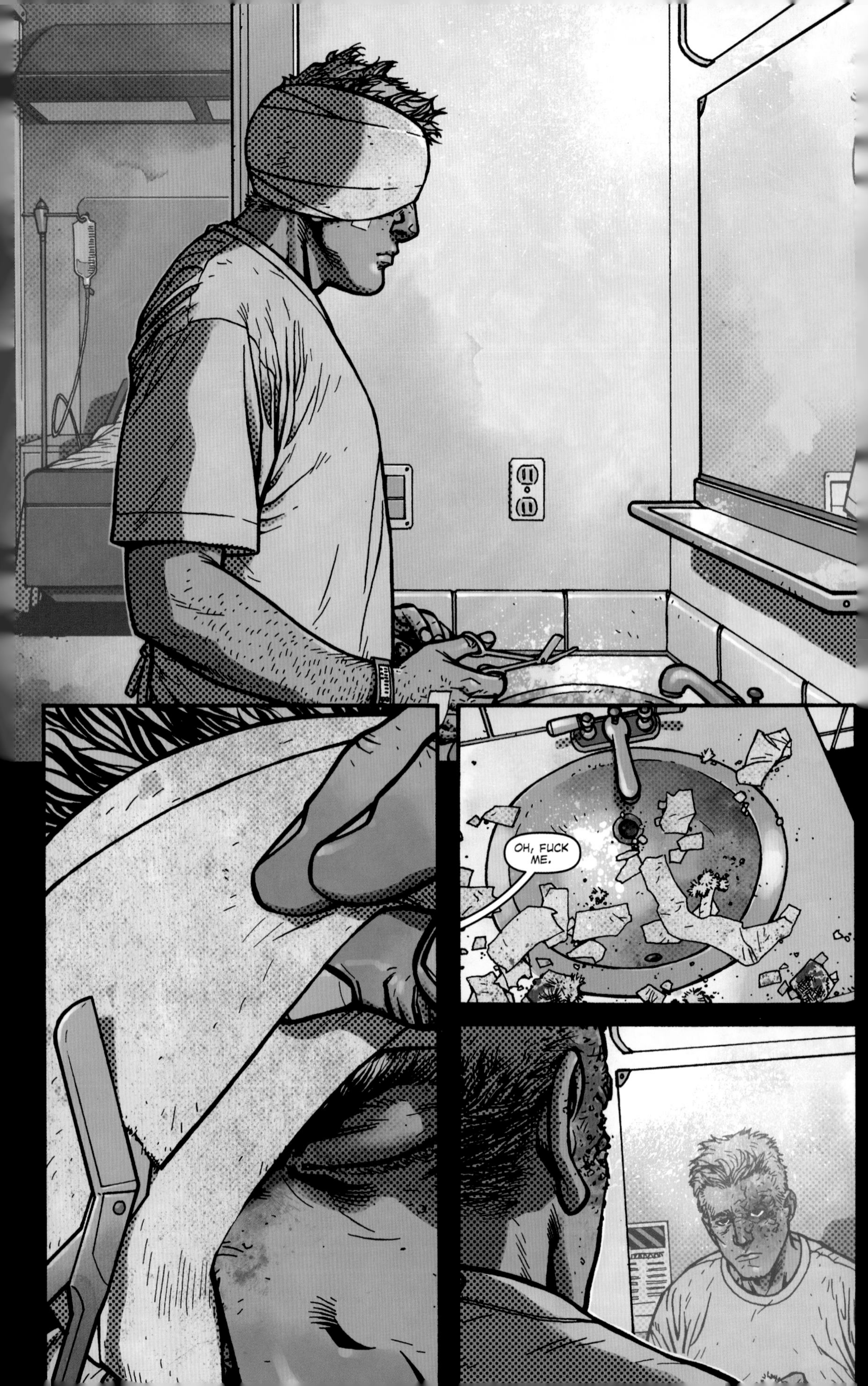
OH, FUCK ME.

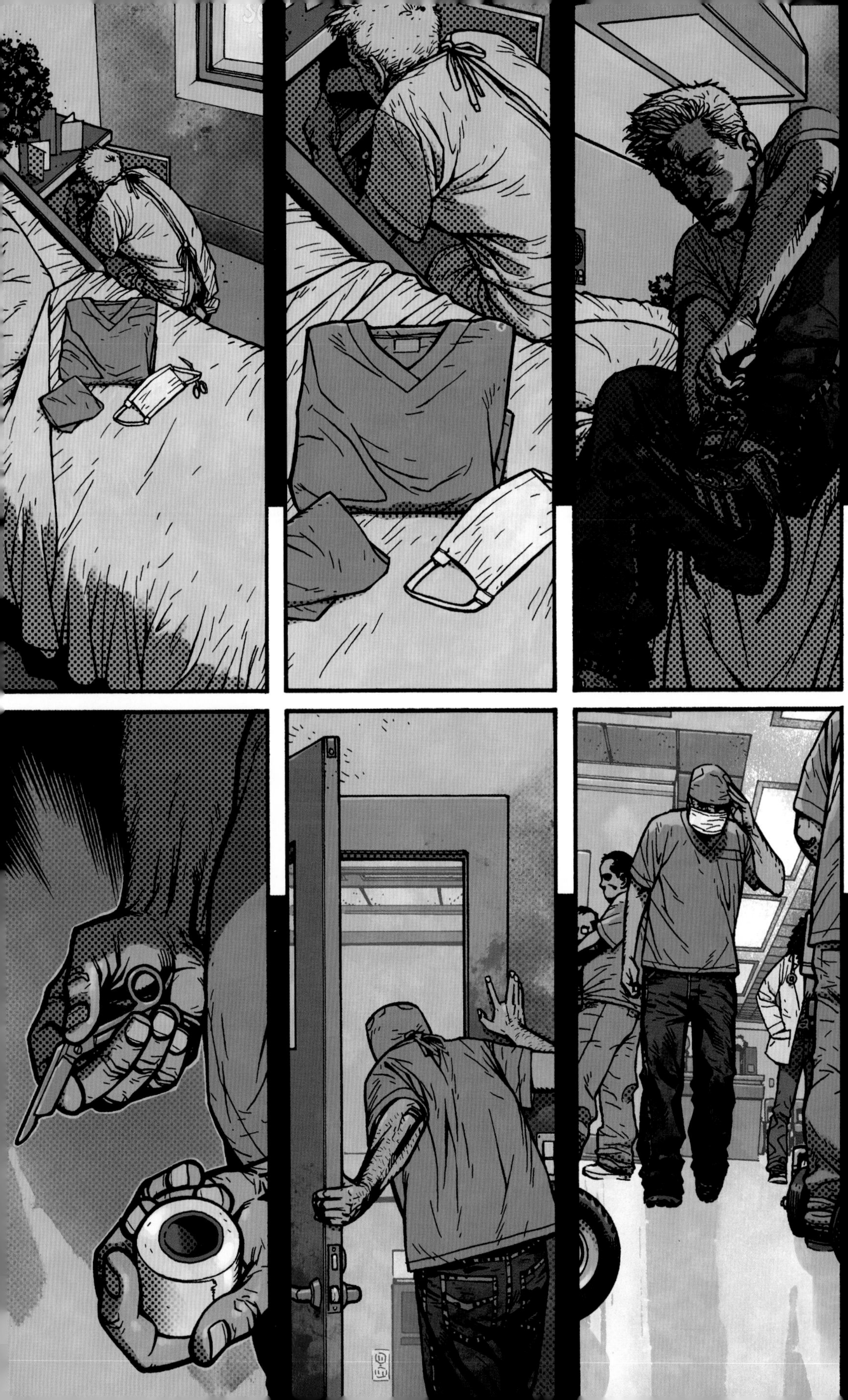

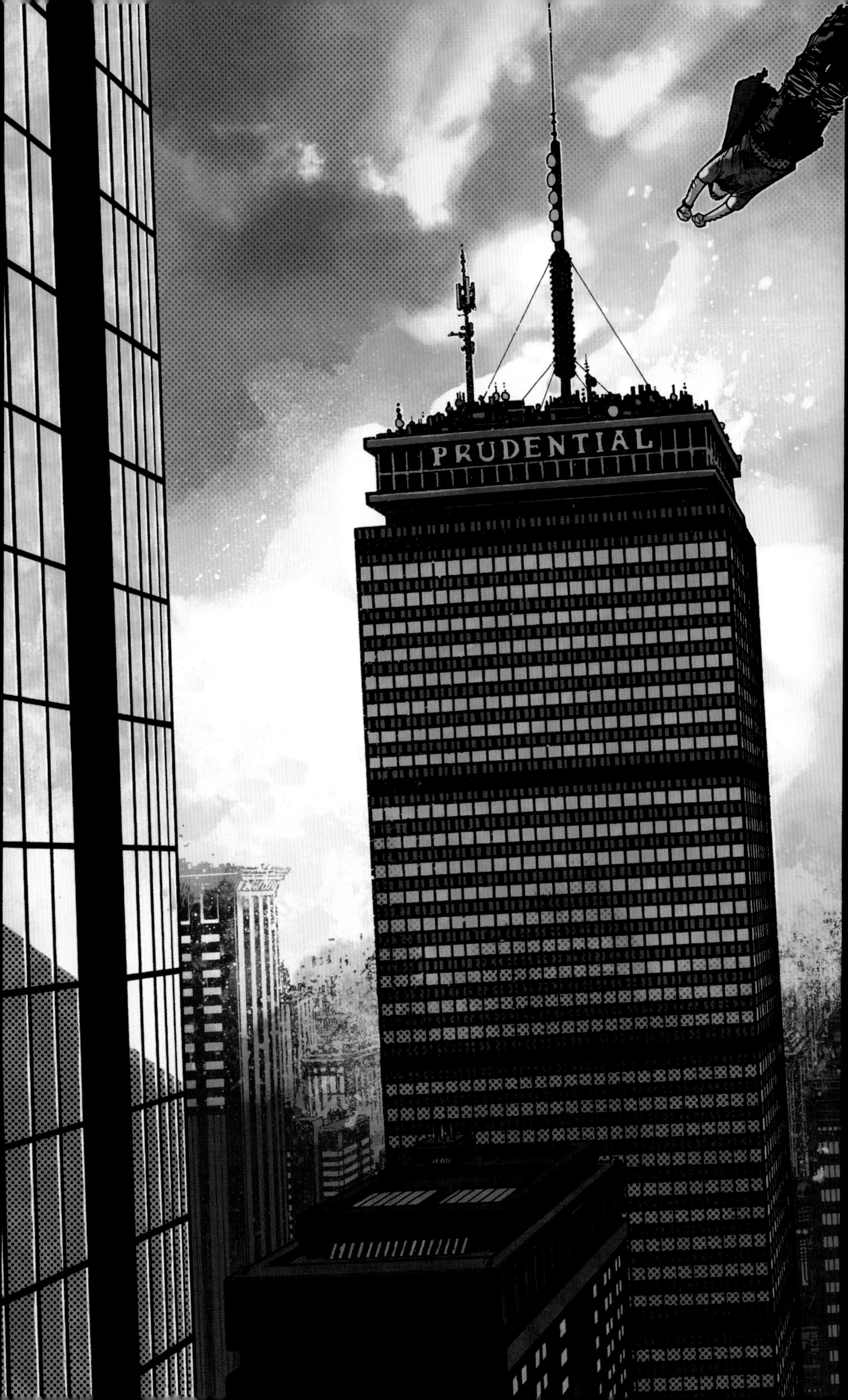
PRUDENTIAL

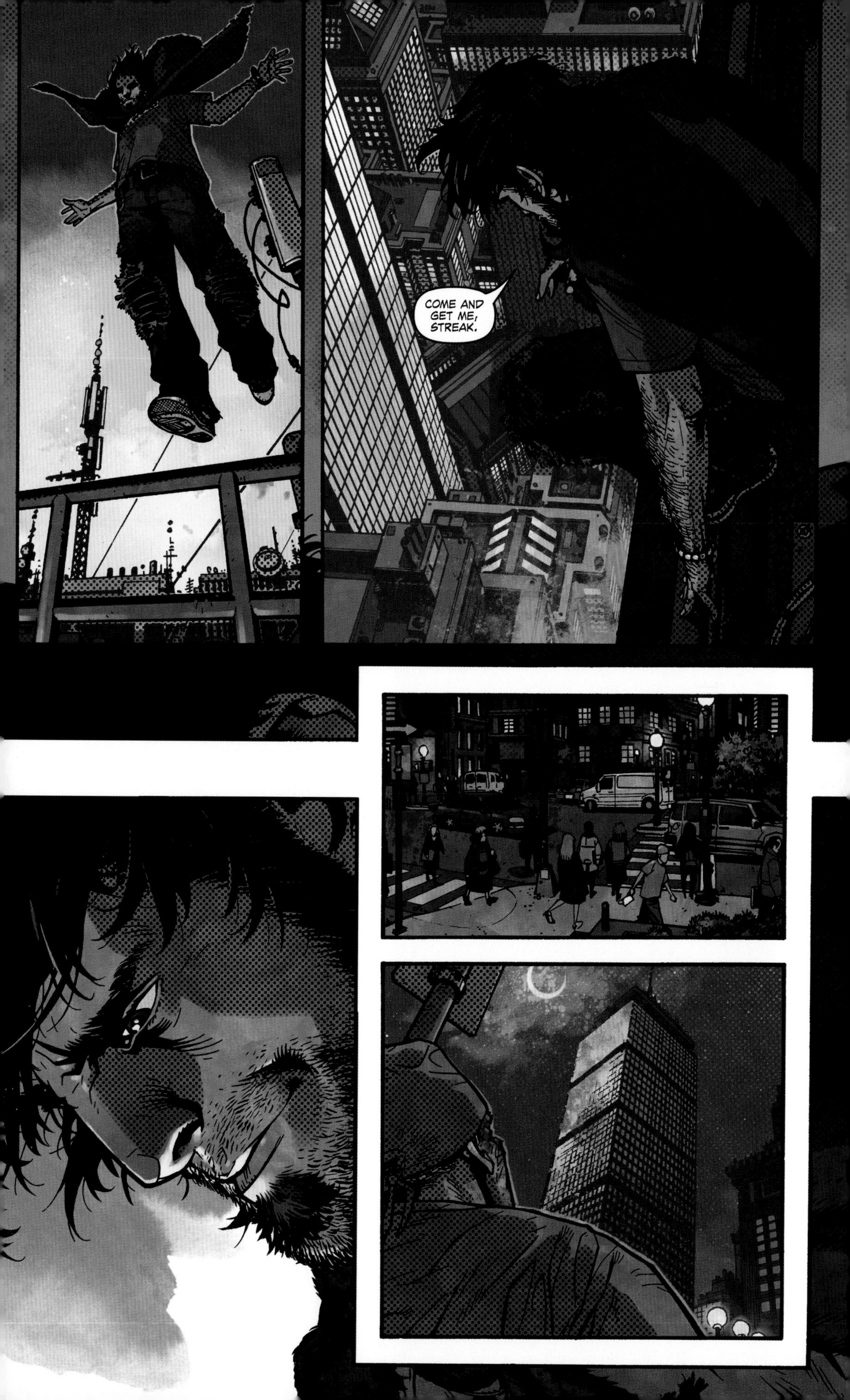
COME AND GET ME, STREAK.

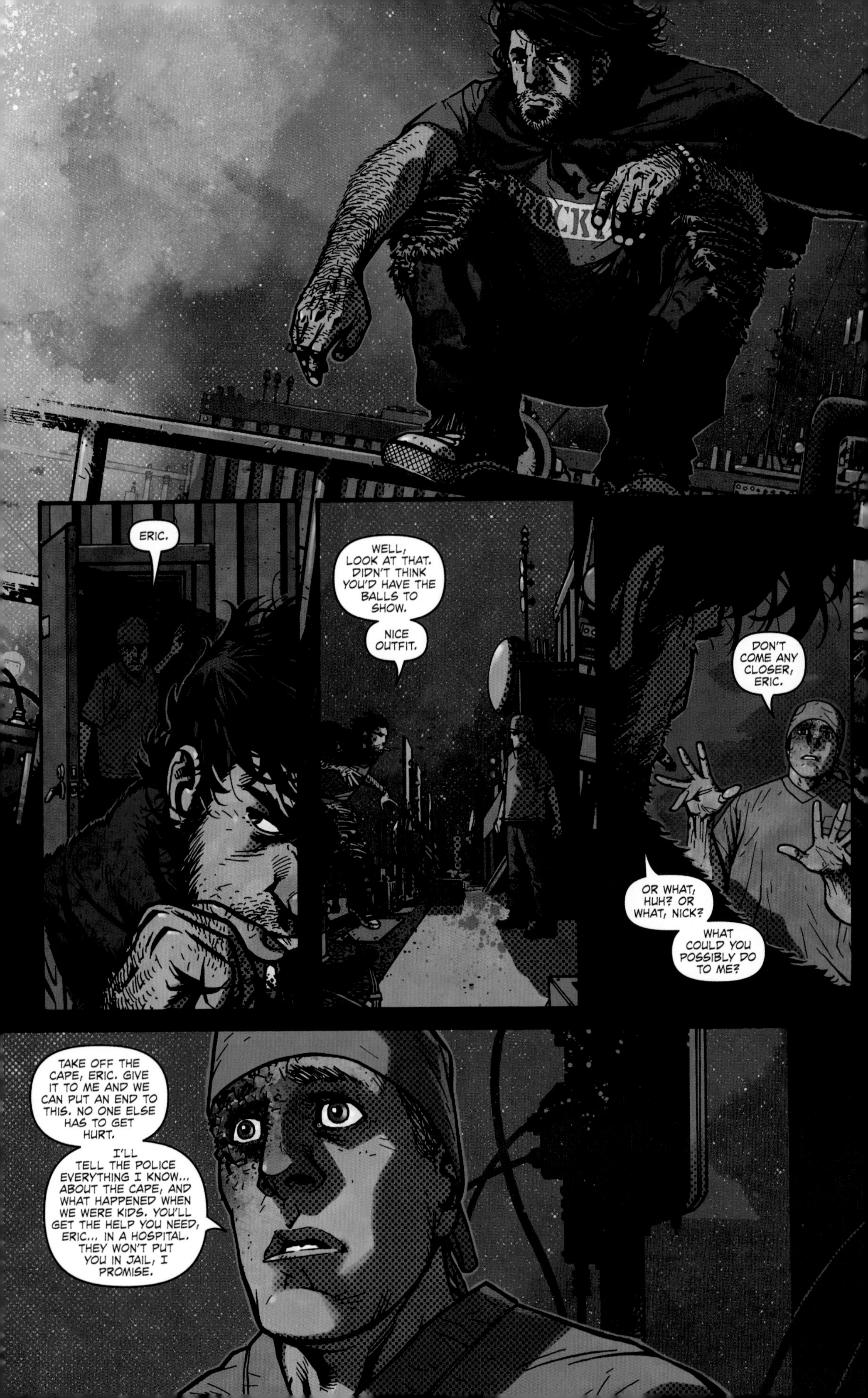

ERIC.
WELL, LOOK AT THAT. DIDN'T THINK YOU'D HAVE THE BALLS TO SHOW.
NICE OUTFIT.
DON'T COME ANY CLOSER, ERIC.
OR WHAT, HUH? OR WHAT, NICK?
WHAT COULD YOU POSSIBLY DO TO ME?
TAKE OFF THE CAPE, ERIC. GIVE IT TO ME AND WE CAN PUT AN END TO THIS. NO ONE ELSE HAS TO GET HURT.
I'LL TELL THE POLICE EVERYTHING I KNOW... ABOUT THE CAPE, AND WHAT HAPPENED WHEN WE WERE KIDS. YOU'LL GET THE HELP YOU NEED, ERIC... IN A HOSPITAL. THEY WON'T PUT YOU IN JAIL, I PROMISE.

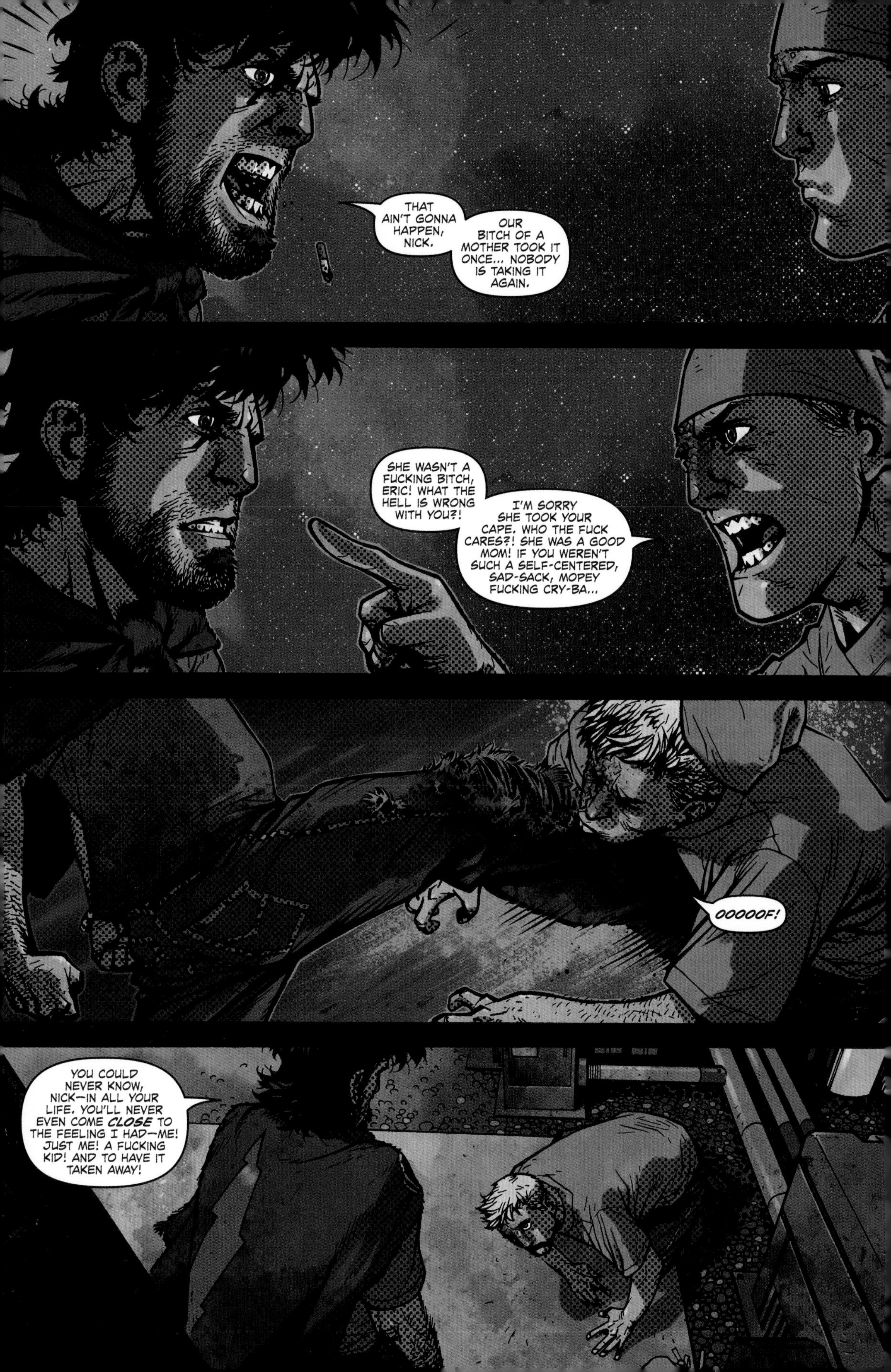
THAT AIN'T GONNA HAPPEN, NICK.
OUR BITCH OF A MOTHER TOOK IT ONCE... NOBODY IS TAKING IT AGAIN.
SHE WASN'T A FUCKING BITCH, ERIC! WHAT THE HELL IS WRONG WITH YOU?!
I'M SORRY SHE TOOK YOUR CAPE. WHO THE FUCK CARES?! SHE WAS A GOOD MOM! IF YOU WEREN'T SUCH A SELF-CENTERED, SAD-SACK, MOPEY FUCKING CRY-BA...
OOOOOF!
YOU COULD NEVER KNOW, NICK—IN ALL YOUR LIFE. YOU'LL NEVER EVEN COME *CLOSE* TO THE FEELING I HAD—ME! JUST ME! A FUCKING KID! AND TO HAVE IT TAKEN AWAY!

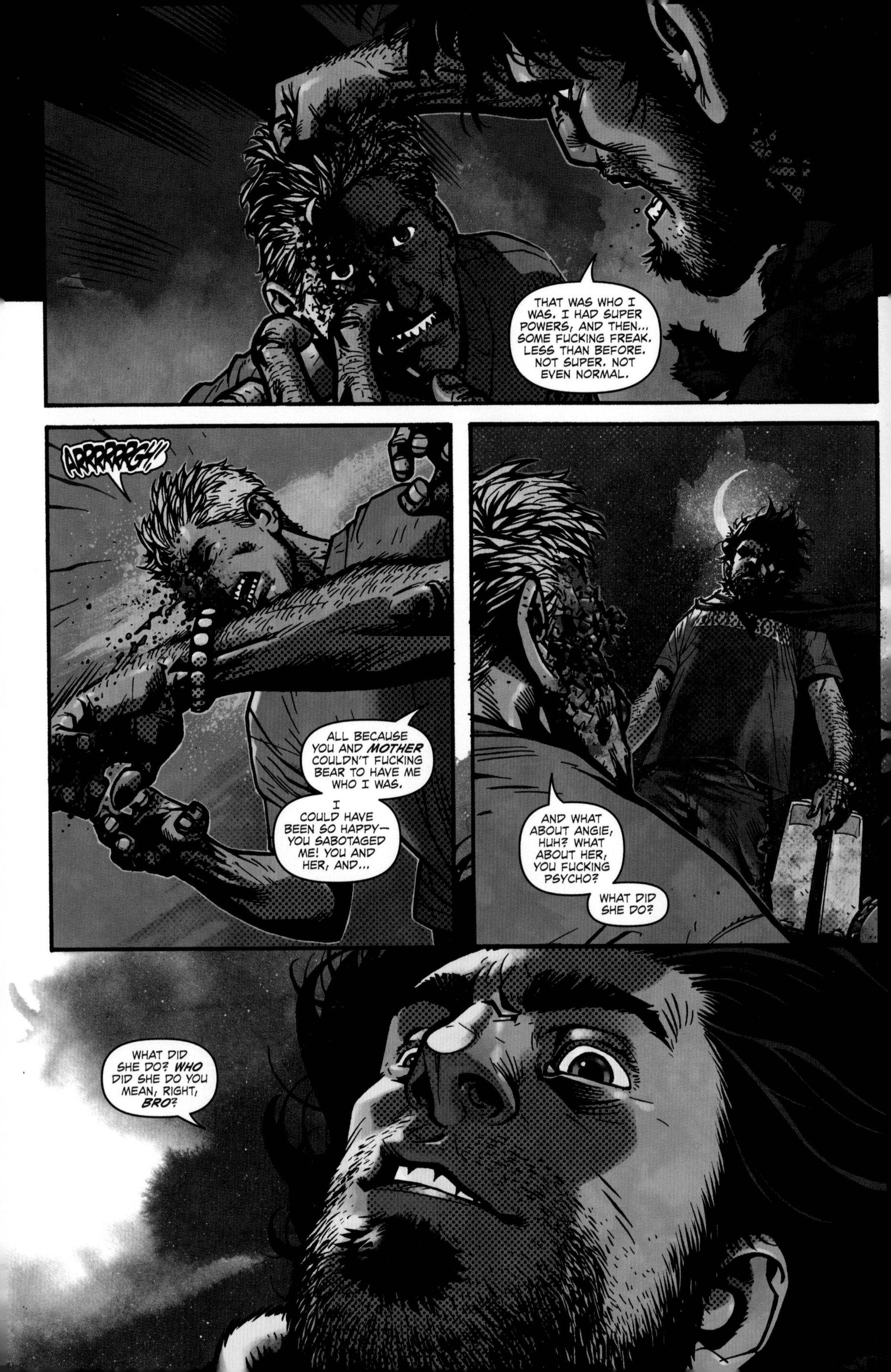
THAT WAS WHO I WAS. I HAD SUPER POWERS, AND THEN... SOME FUCKING FREAK. LESS THAN BEFORE. NOT SUPER. NOT EVEN NORMAL.
ARRRRRGH!!
ALL BECAUSE YOU AND MOTHER COULDN'T FUCKING BEAR TO HAVE ME WHO I WAS.
I COULD HAVE BEEN SO HAPPY— YOU SABOTAGED ME! YOU AND HER, AND...
AND WHAT ABOUT ANGIE, HUH? WHAT ABOUT HER, YOU FUCKING PSYCHO?
WHAT DID SHE DO?
WHAT DID SHE DO? WHO DID SHE DO YOU MEAN, RIGHT, BRO?

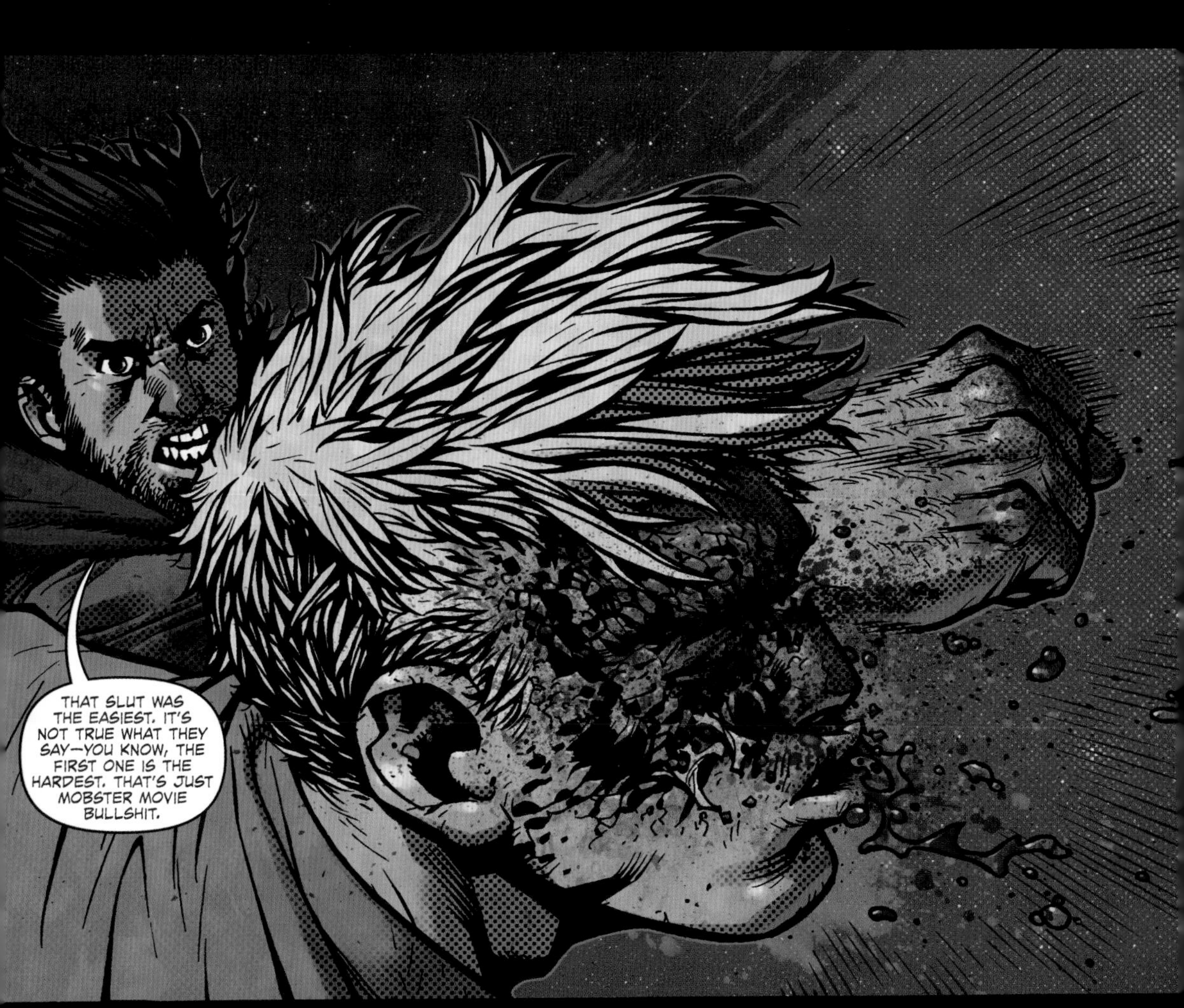
THAT SLUT WAS THE EASIEST. IT'S NOT TRUE WHAT THEY SAY—YOU KNOW, THE FIRST ONE IS THE HARDEST. THAT'S JUST MOBSTER MOVIE BULLSHIT.

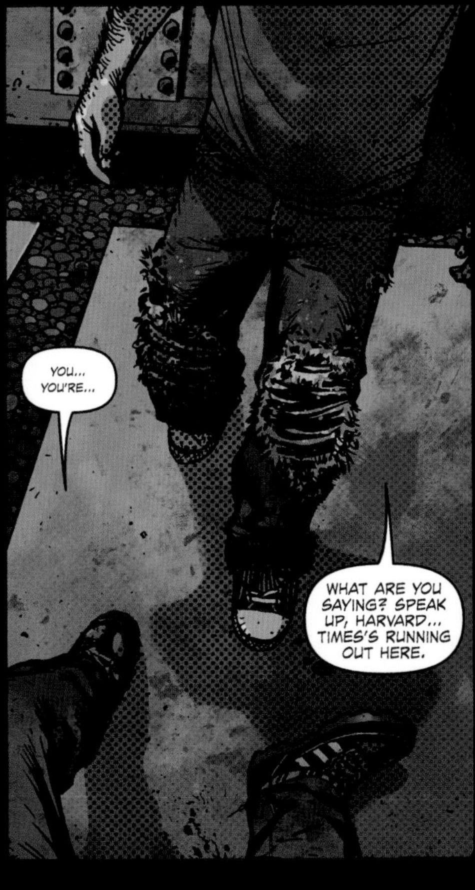
YOU... YOU'RE...
WHAT ARE YOU SAYING? SPEAK UP, HARVARD... TIMES'S RUNNING OUT HERE.

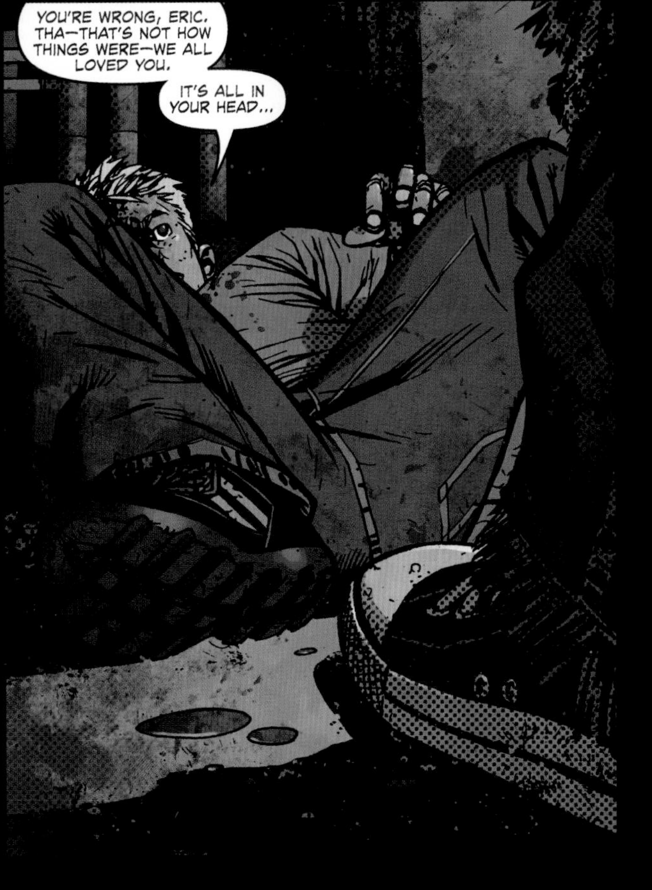
YOU'RE WRONG, ERIC. THA—THAT'S NOT HOW THINGS WERE—WE ALL LOVED YOU.
IT'S ALL IN YOUR HEAD...

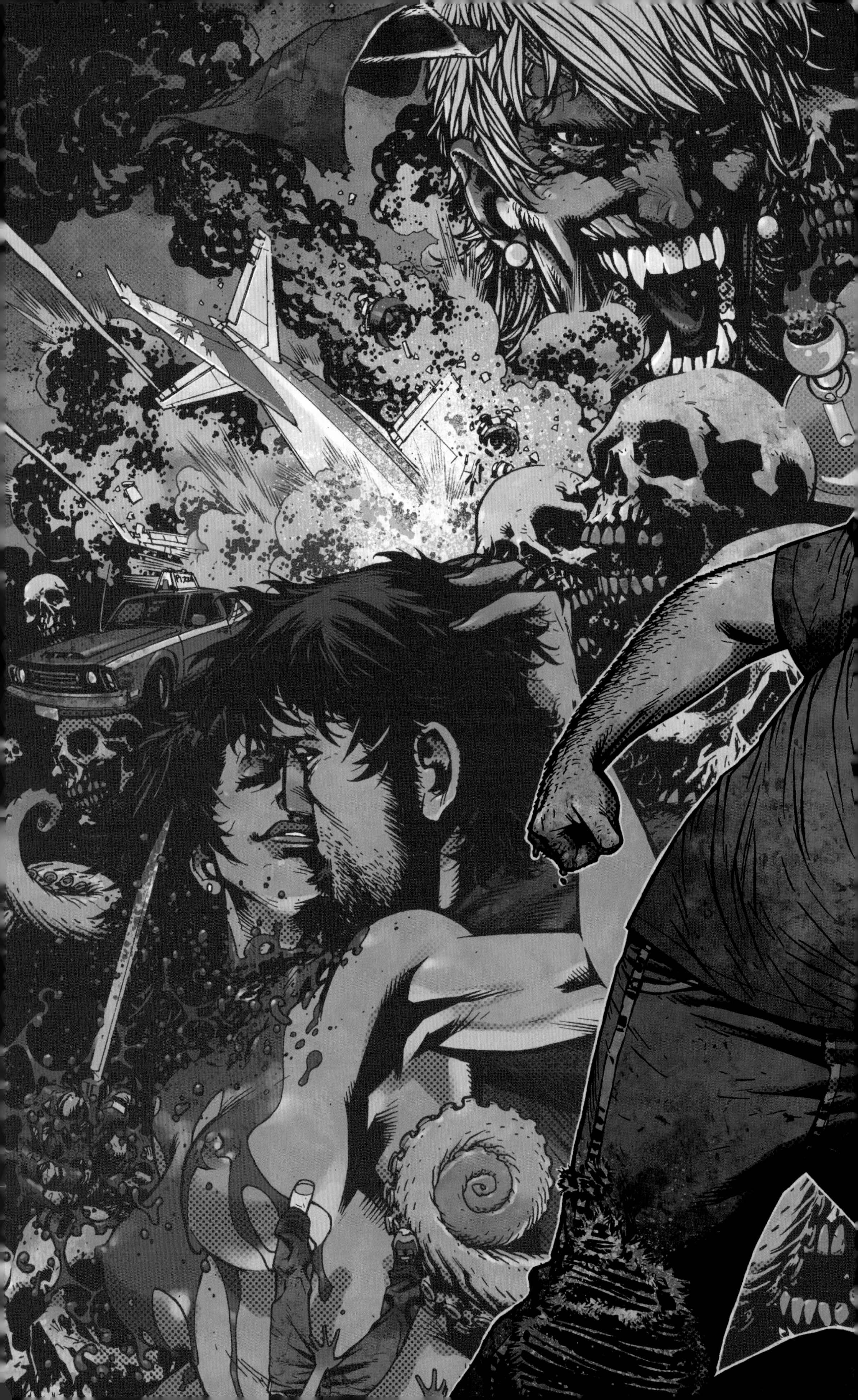

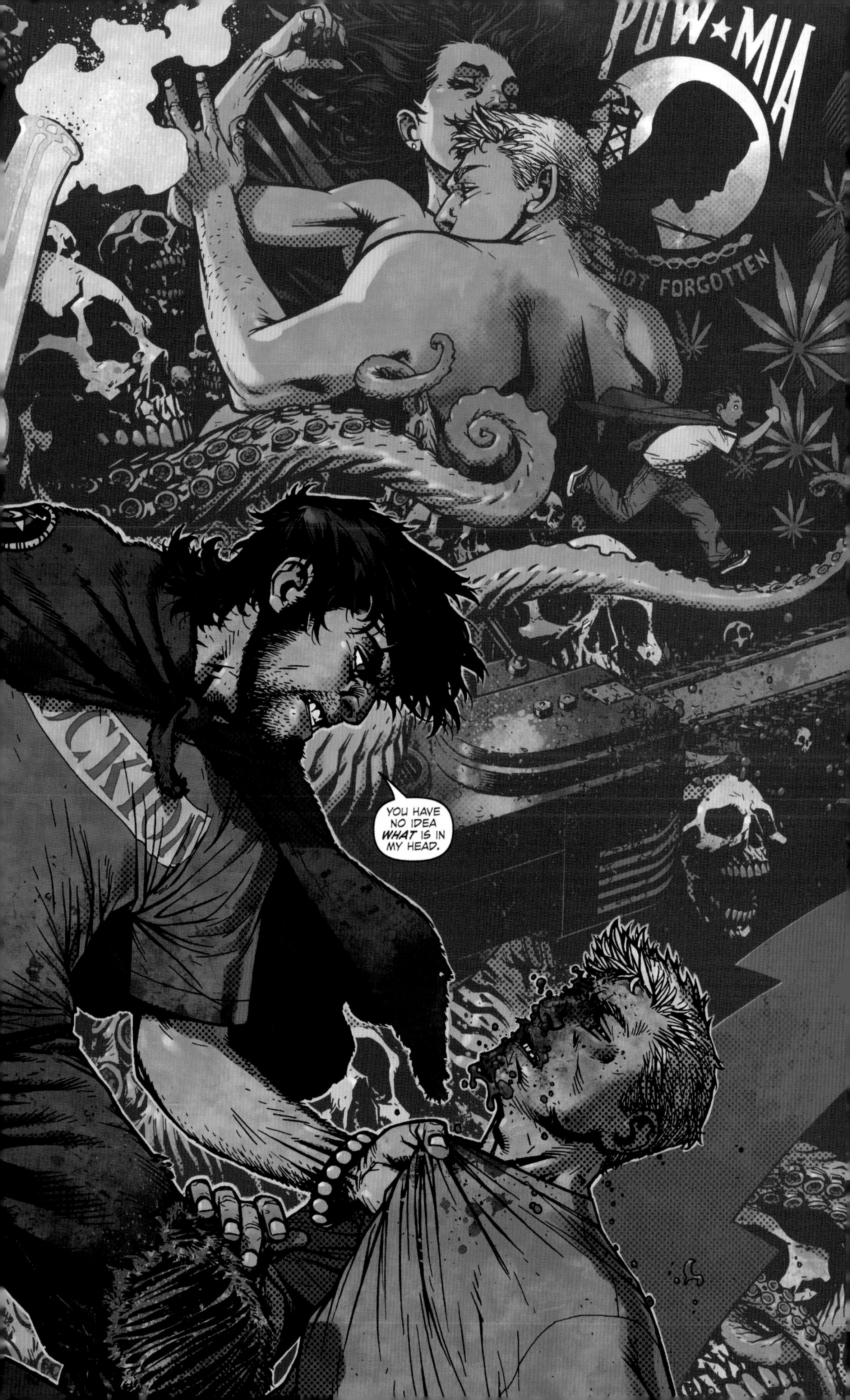
POW★MIA
NOT FORGOTTEN
YOU HAVE NO IDEA WHAT IS IN MY HEAD.

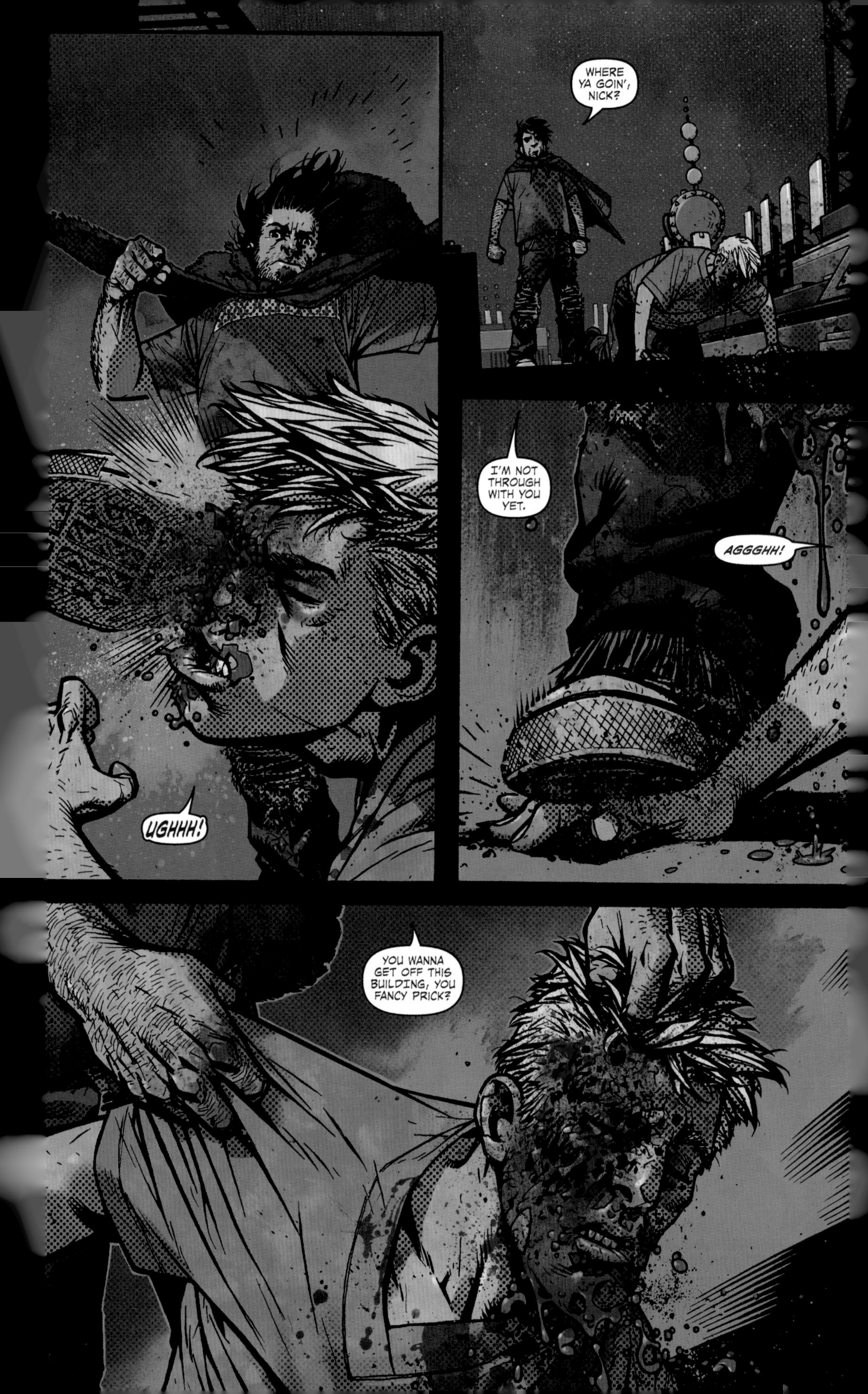
UGHHH!
WHERE YA GOIN', NICK?
I'M NOT THROUGH WITH YOU YET.
AGGGHH!
YOU WANNA GET OFF THIS BUILDING, YOU FANCY PRICK?

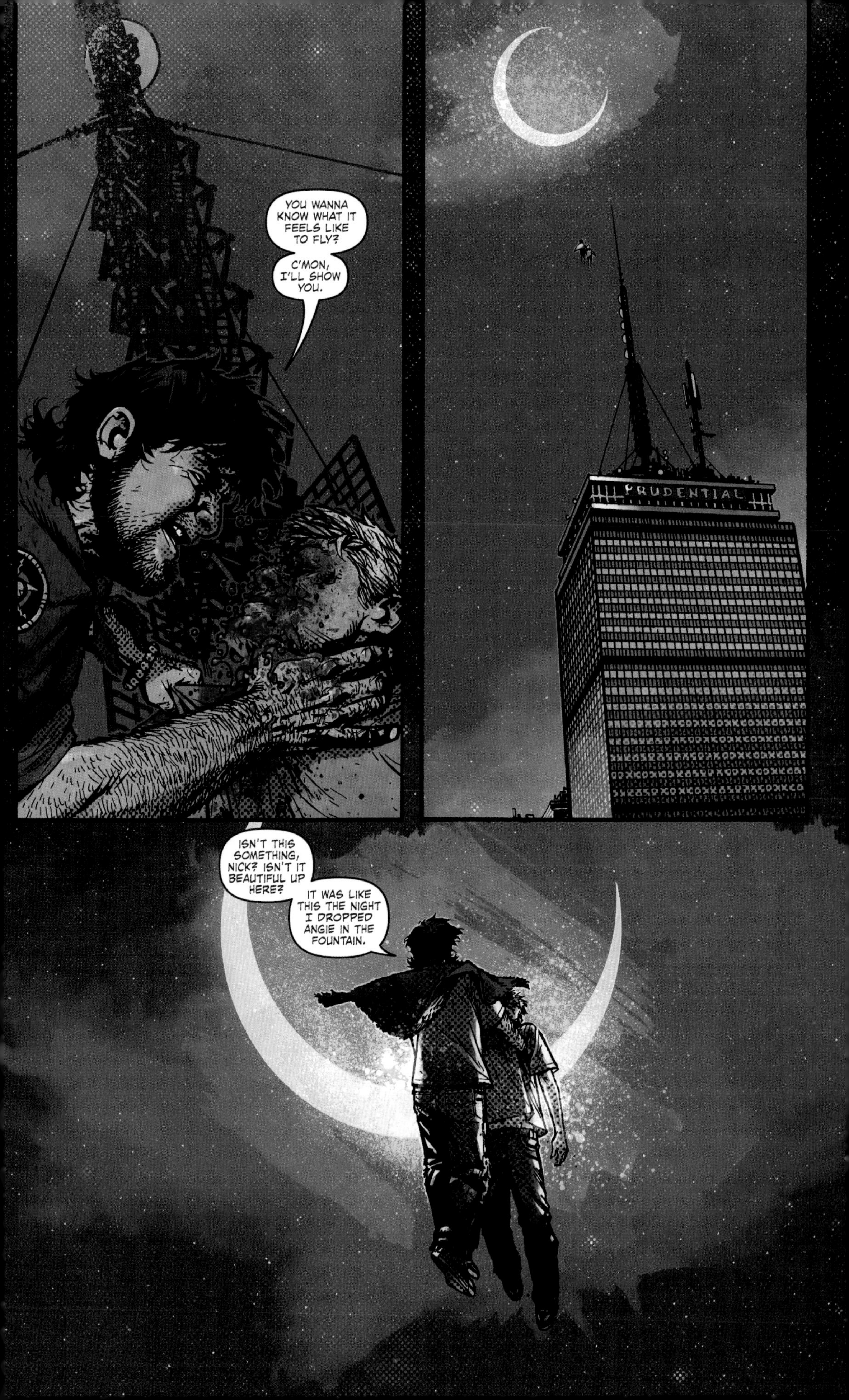
YOU WANNA KNOW WHAT IT FEELS LIKE TO FLY?
C'MON, I'LL SHOW YOU.
PRUDENTIAL
ISN'T THIS SOMETHING, NICK? ISN'T IT BEAUTIFUL UP HERE?
IT WAS LIKE THIS THE NIGHT I DROPPED ANGIE IN THE FOUNTAIN.

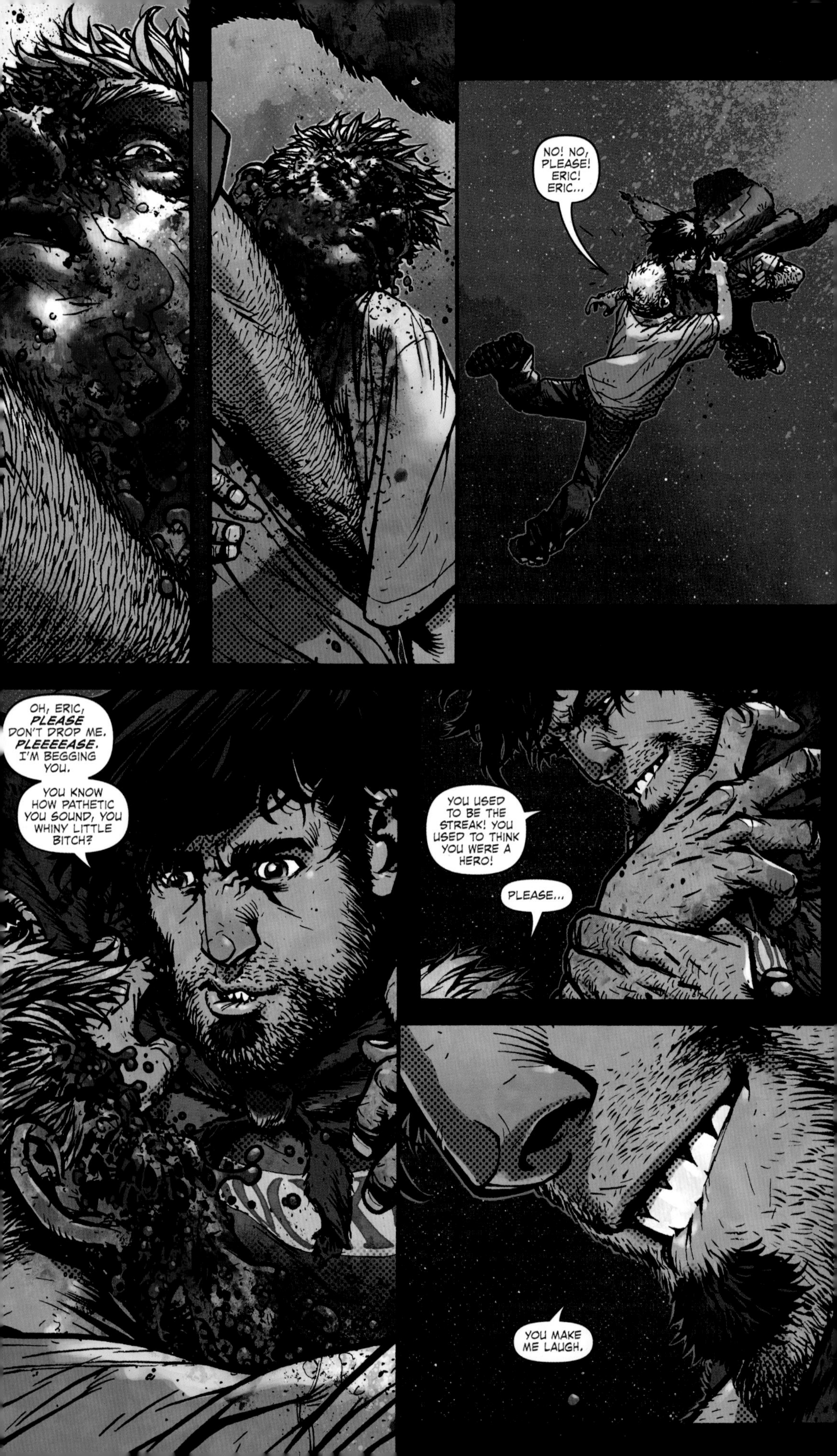
NO! NO, PLEASE! ERIC! ERIC...
OH, ERIC, PLEASE DON'T DROP ME. PLEEEEASE. I'M BEGGING YOU.
YOU KNOW HOW PATHETIC YOU SOUND, YOU WHINY LITTLE BITCH?
YOU USED TO BE THE STREAK! YOU USED TO THINK YOU WERE A HERO!
PLEASE...
YOU MAKE ME LAUGH.

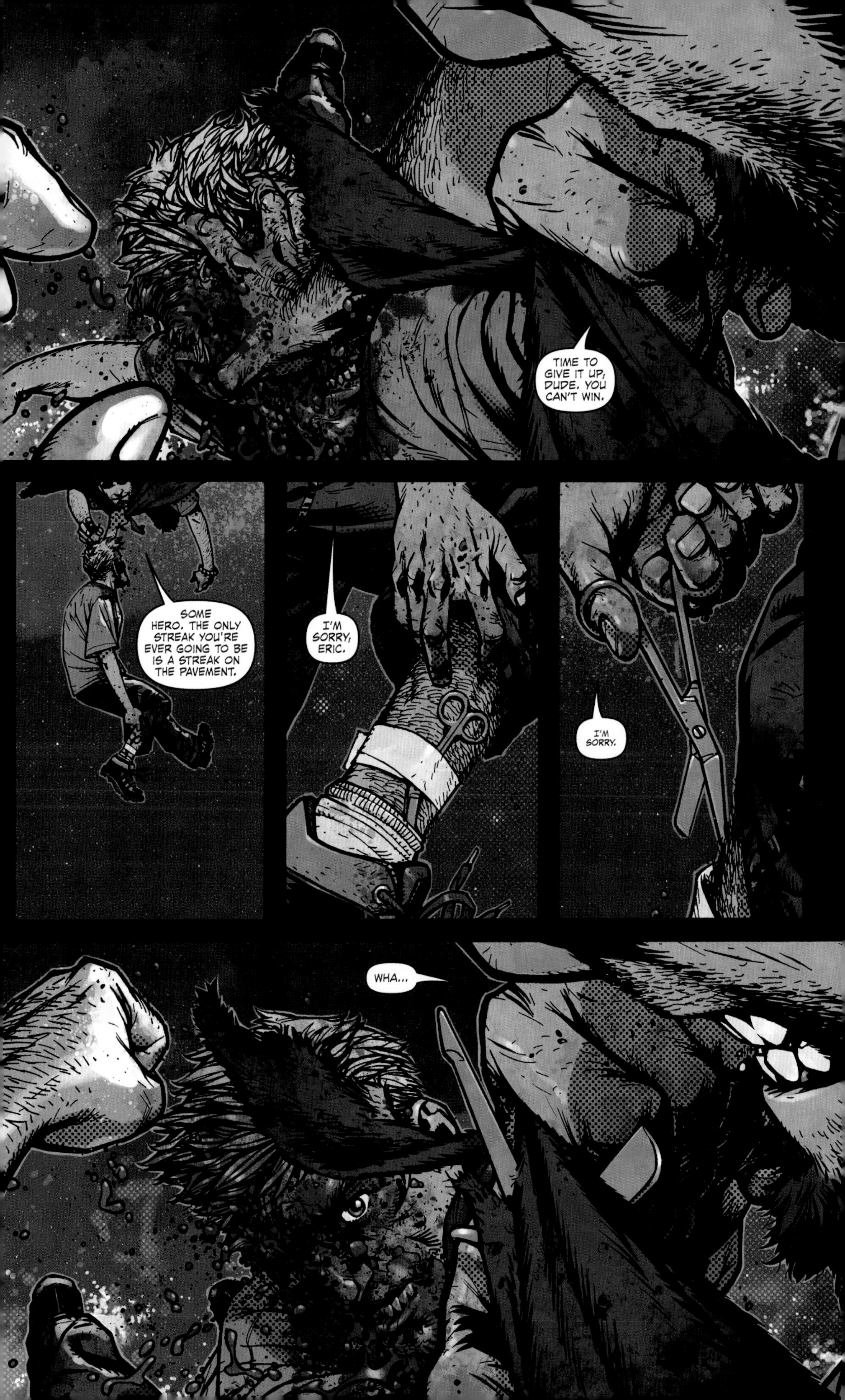
TIME TO GIVE IT UP, DUDE. YOU CAN'T WIN.
SOME HERO. THE ONLY STREAK YOU'RE EVER GOING TO BE IS A STREAK ON THE PAVEMENT.
I'M SORRY, ERIC.
I'M SORRY.
WHA...

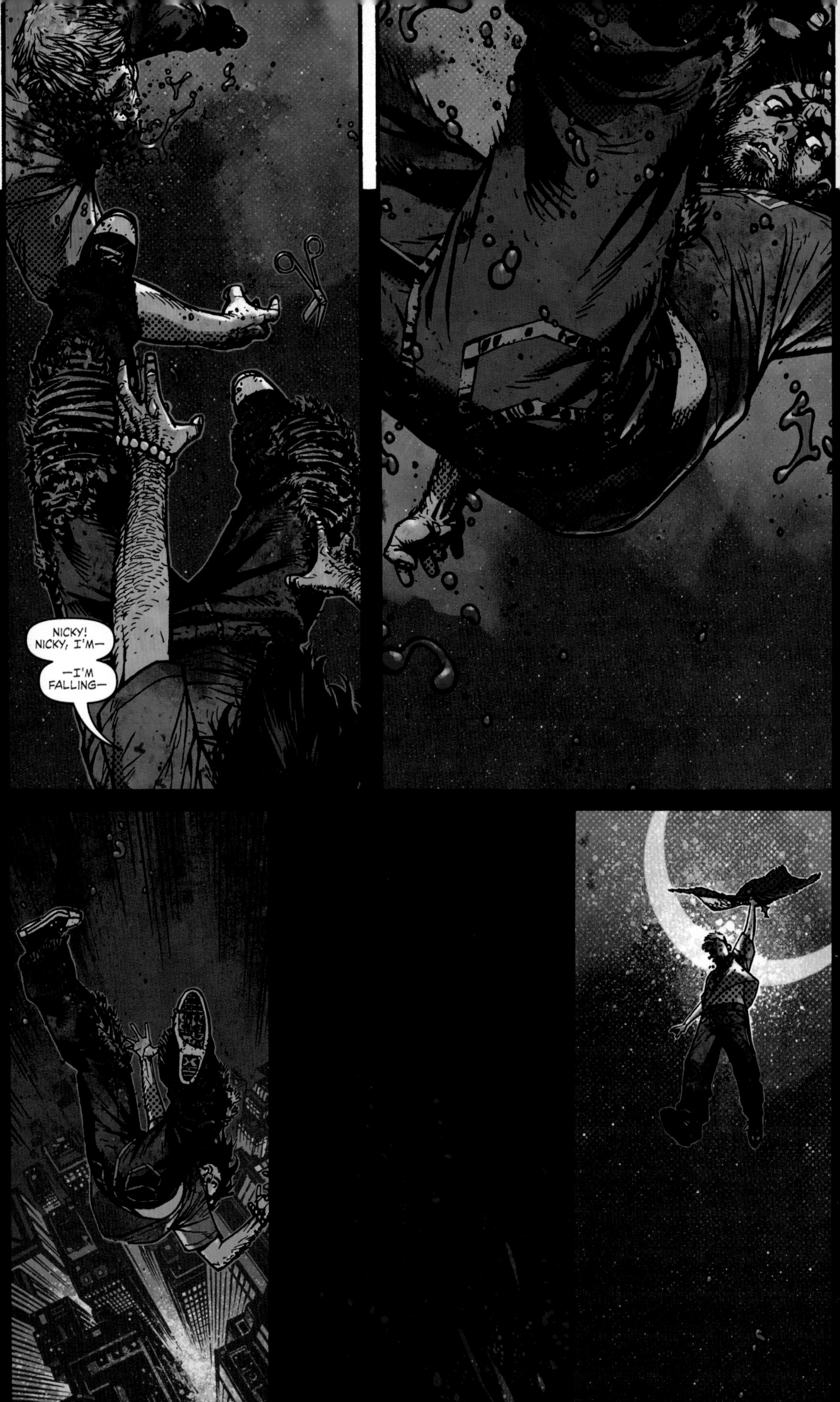
NICKY! NICKY, I'M—
—I'M FALLING—

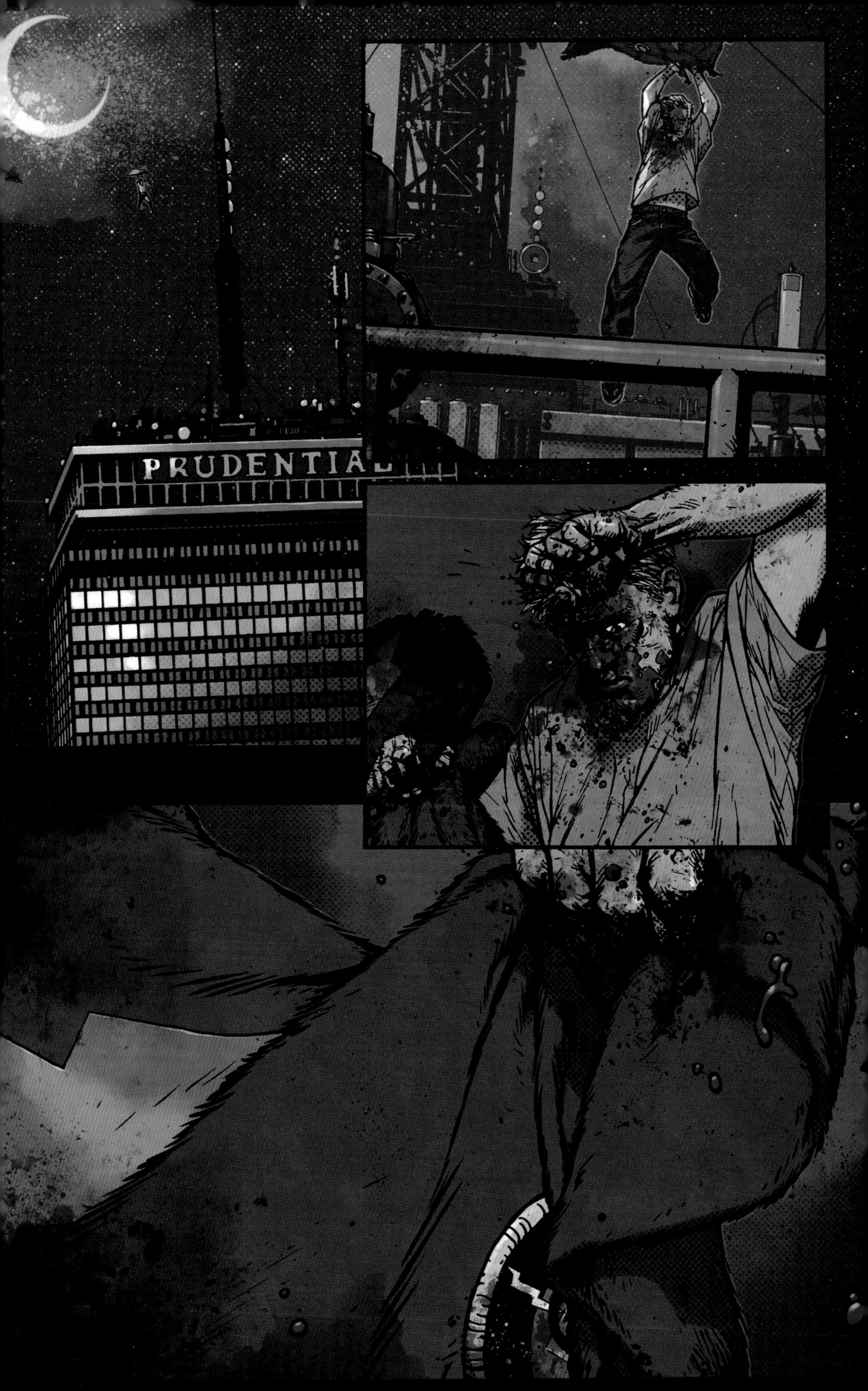
PRUDENTIA

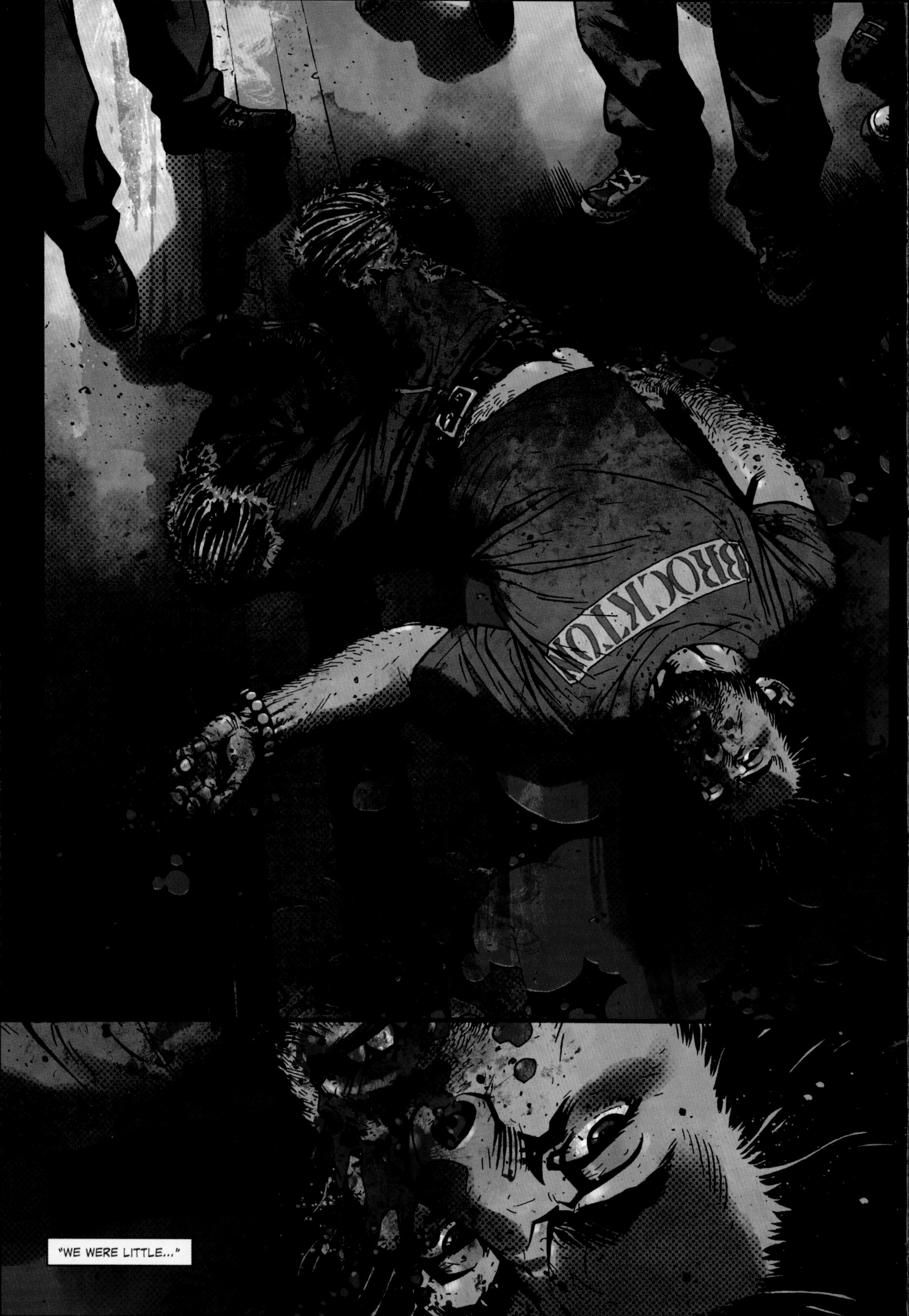
"WE WERE LITTLE..."

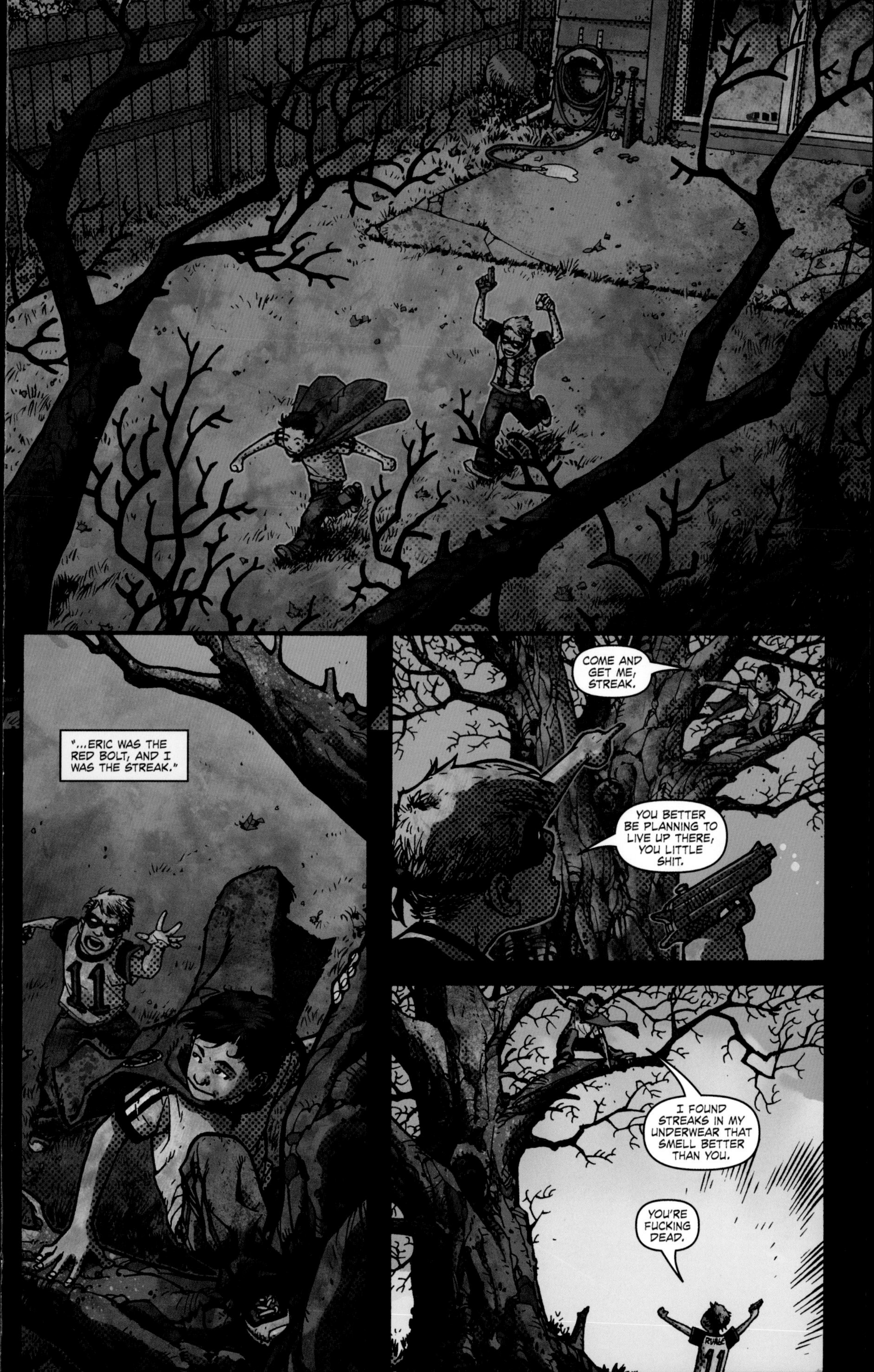
"...ERIC WAS THE RED BOLT, AND I WAS THE STREAK."
COME AND GET ME, STREAK.
YOU BETTER BE PLANNING TO LIVE UP THERE, YOU LITTLE SHIT.
I FOUND STREAKS IN MY UNDERWEAR THAT SMELL BETTER THAN YOU.
YOU'RE FUCKING DEAD.

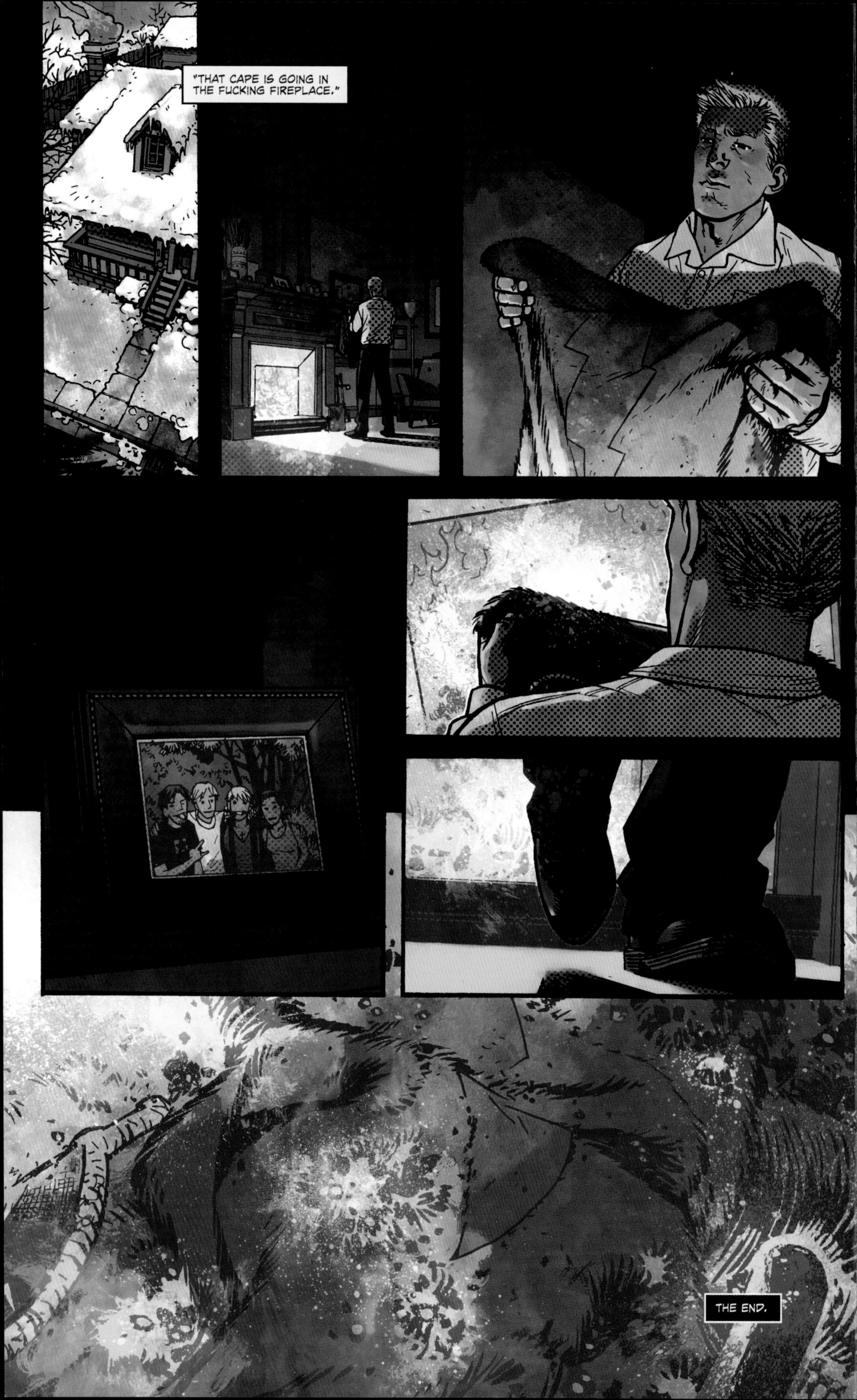

"THAT CAPE IS GOING IN THE FUCKING FIREPLACE."
THE END.

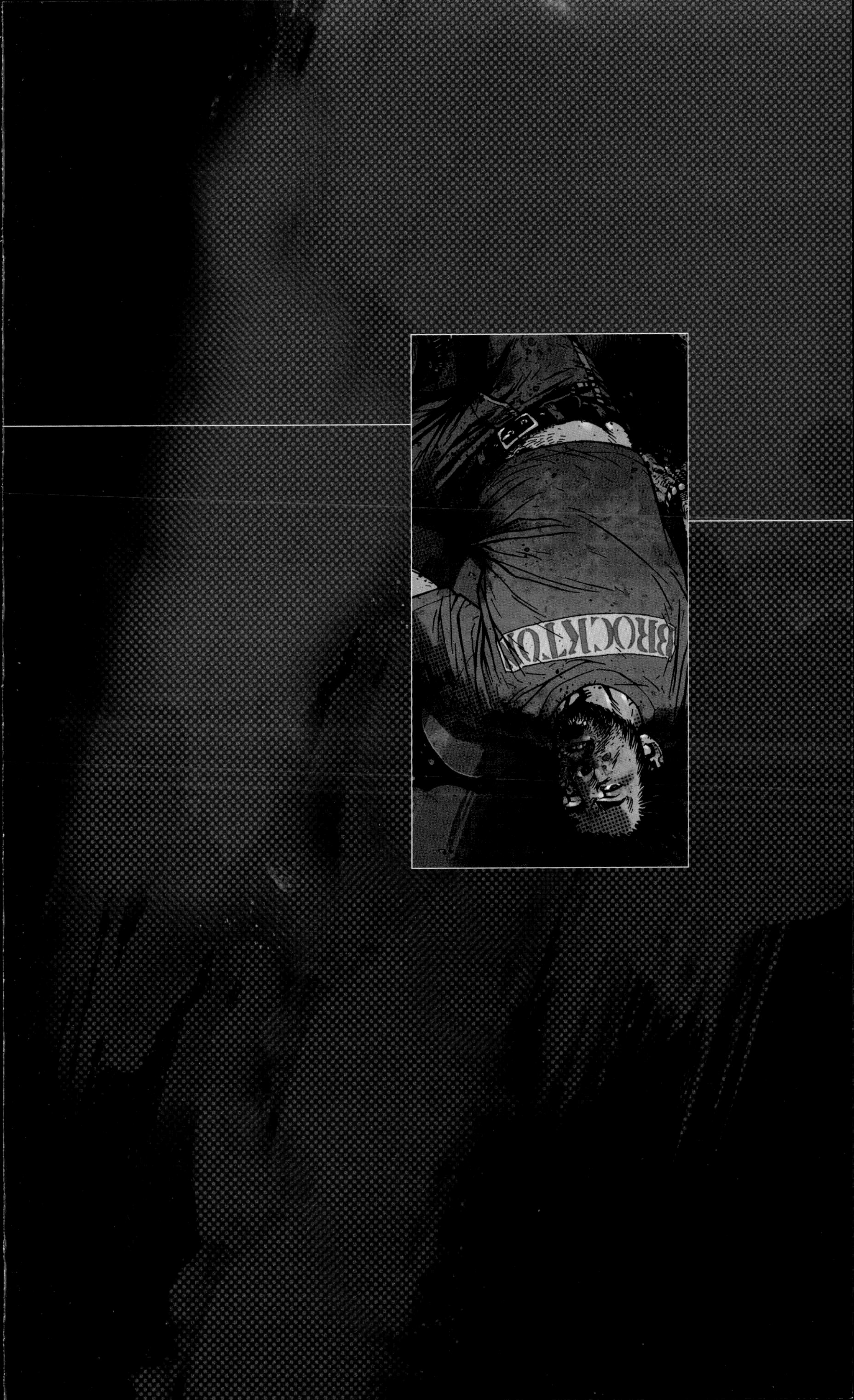
BROCKTON

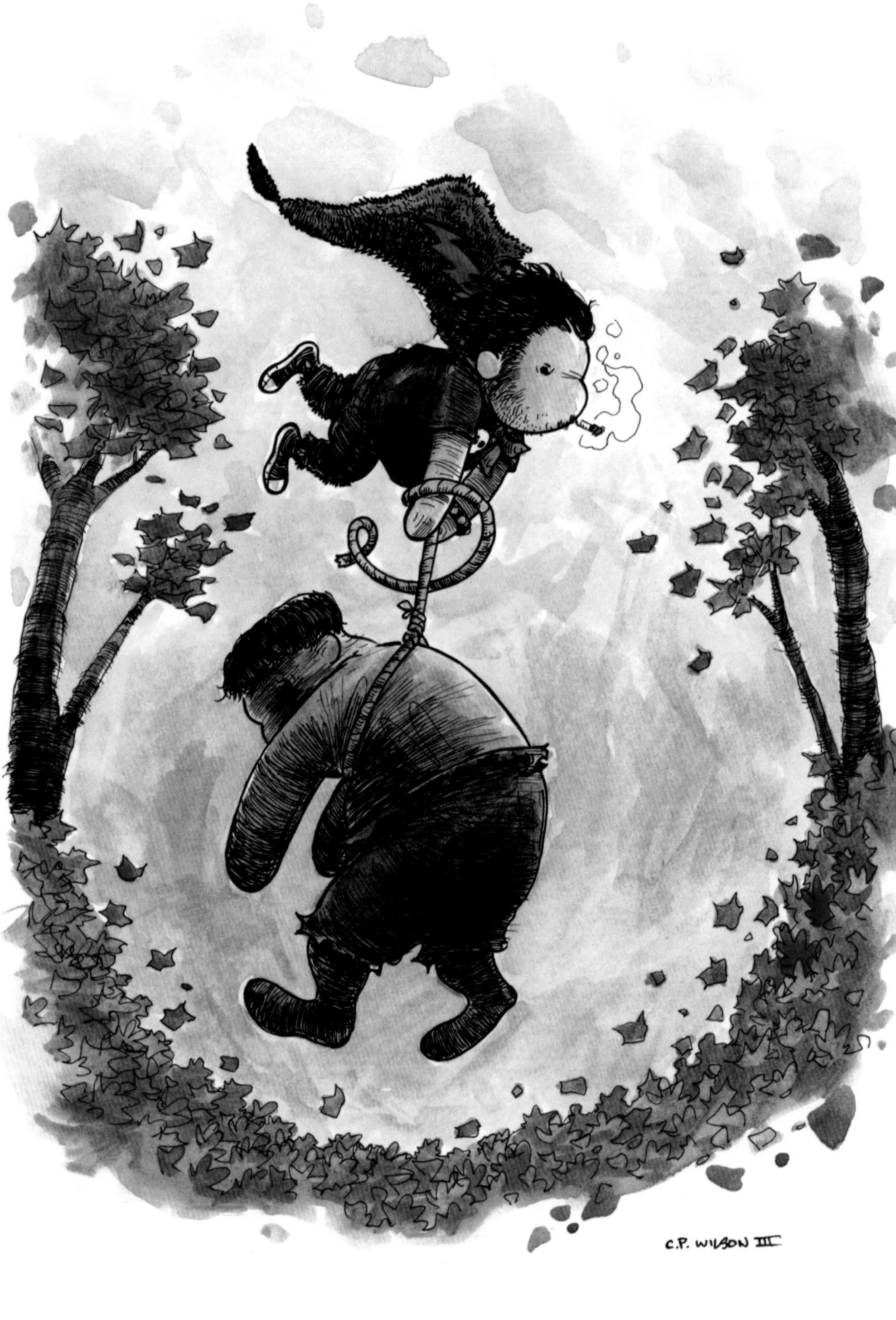
C.P. WILSON III

ART BY CHARLES PAUL WILSON III

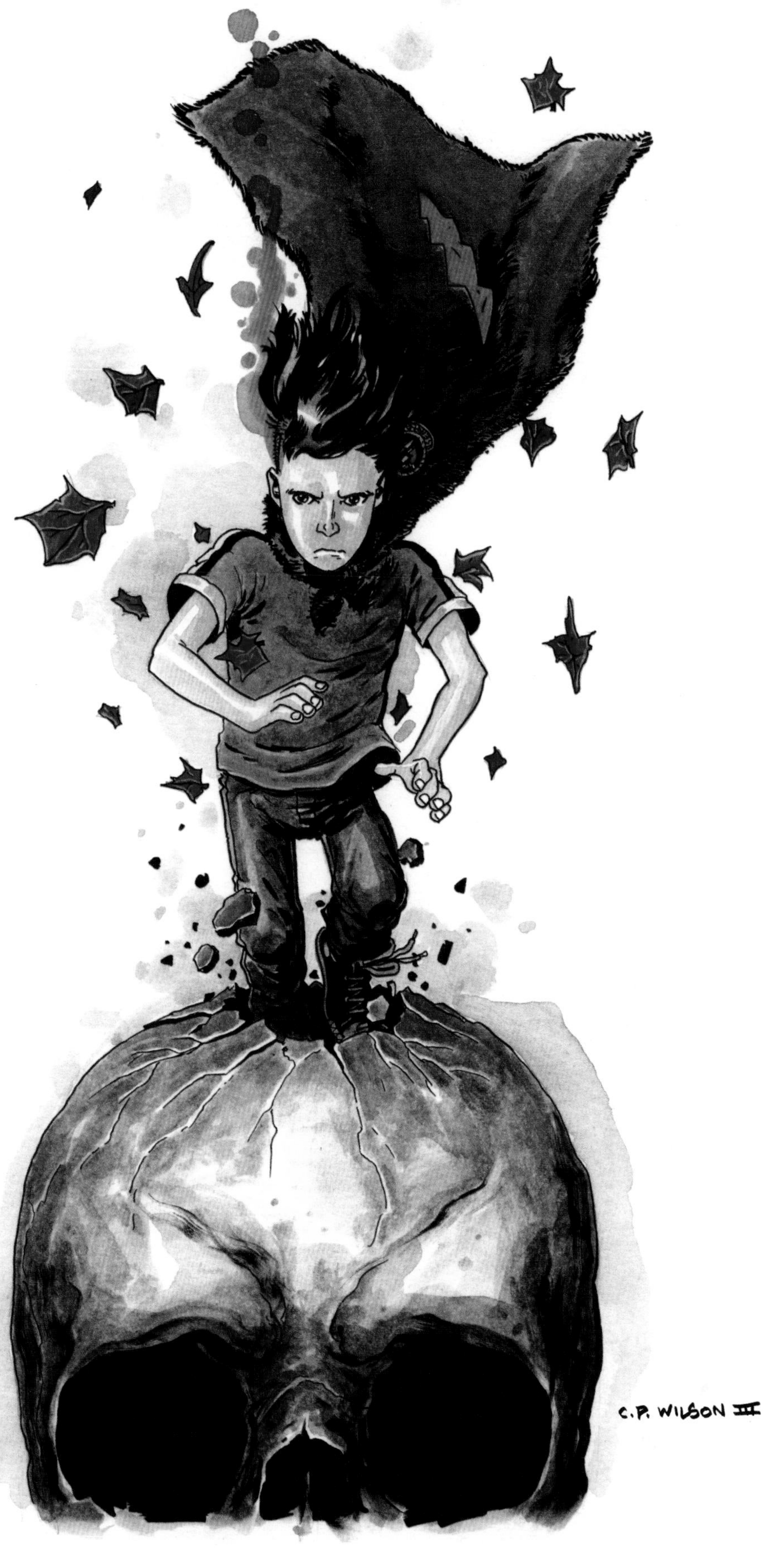
C.P. WILSON III

ART BY CHARLES PAUL WILSON III

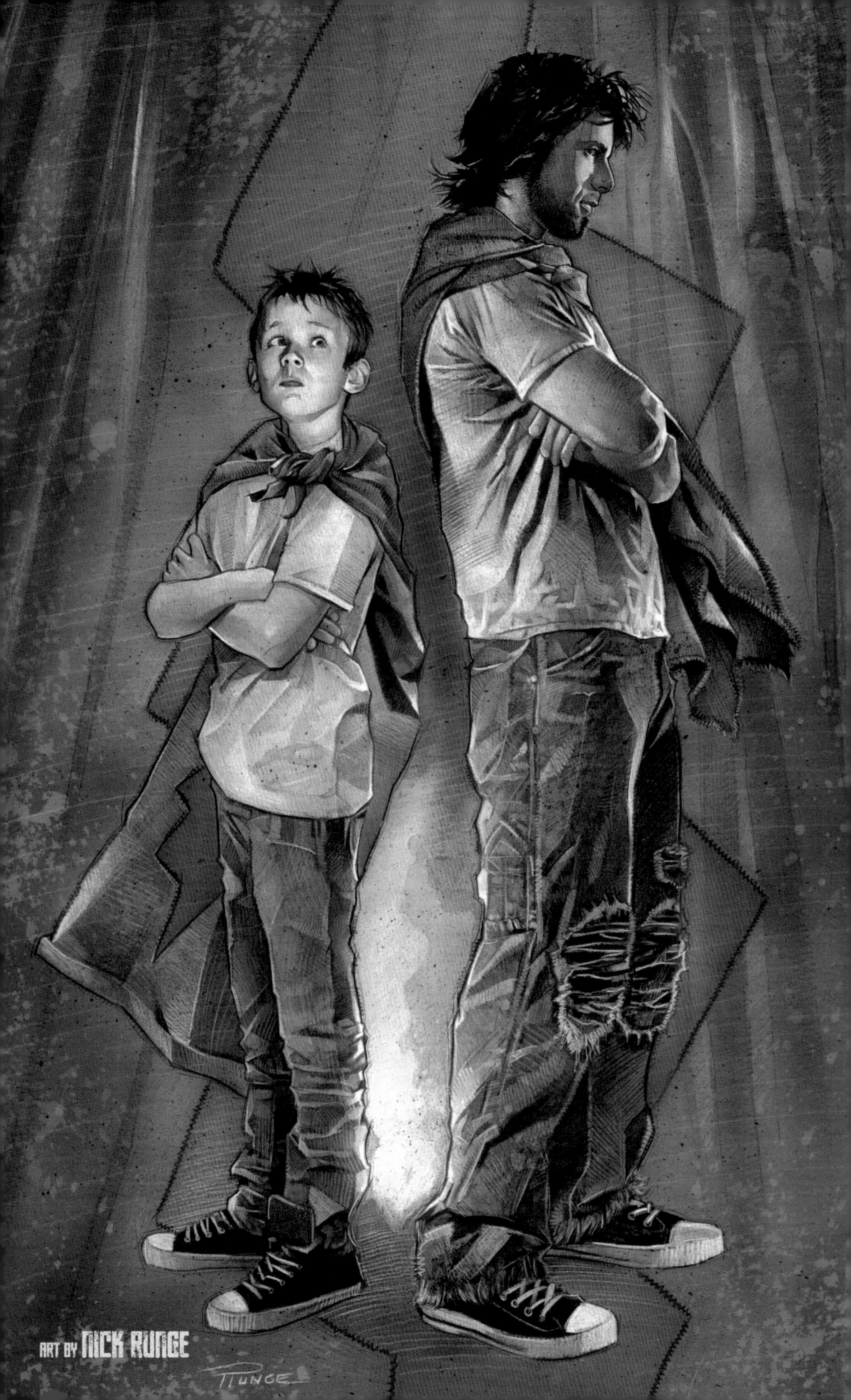
ART BY NICK RUNGE

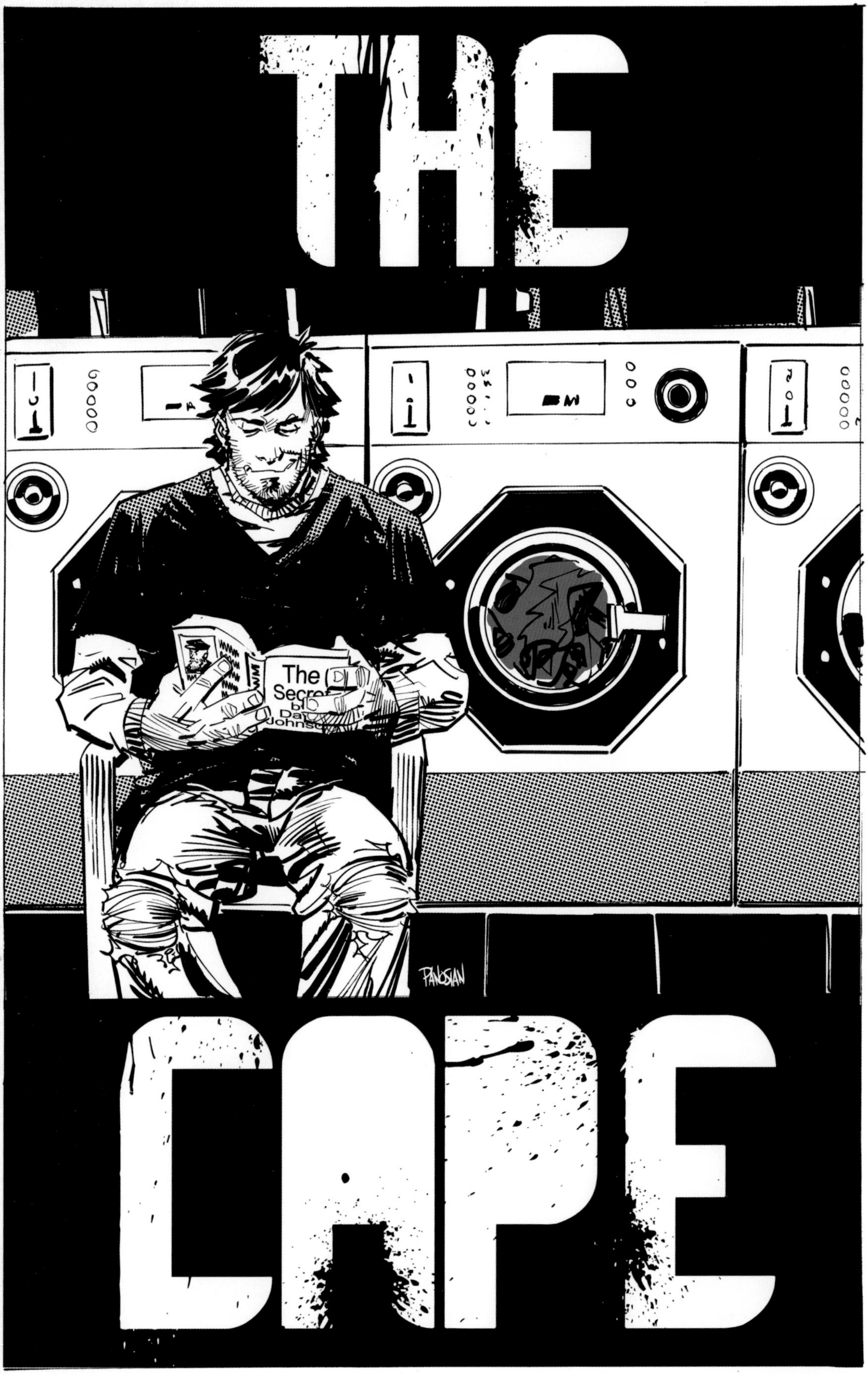
THE
CAPE
PANOSIAN

ART BY DAN PANOSIAN

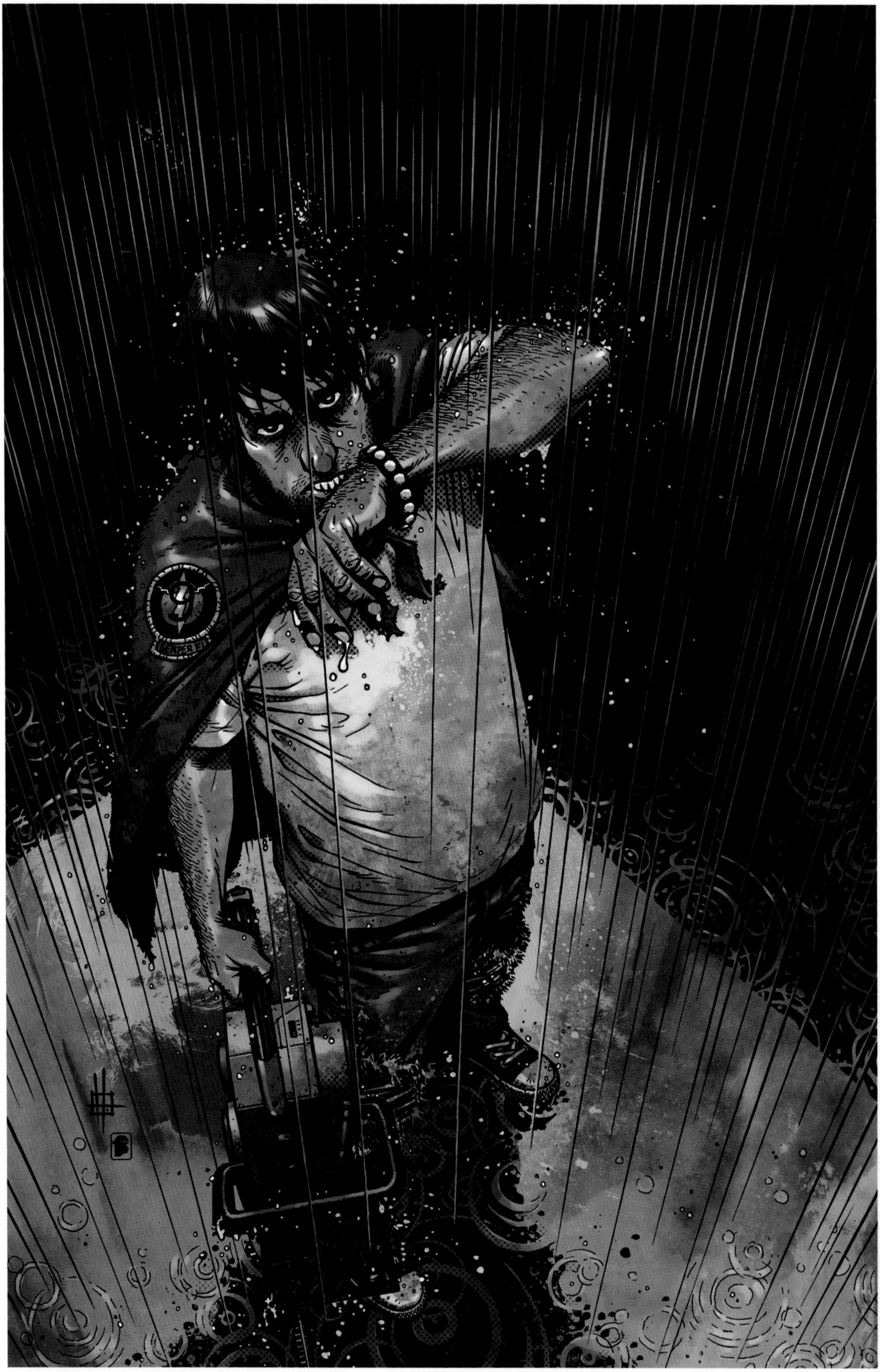

ART BY ZACH HOWARD
COLORS BY NELSON DANIEL

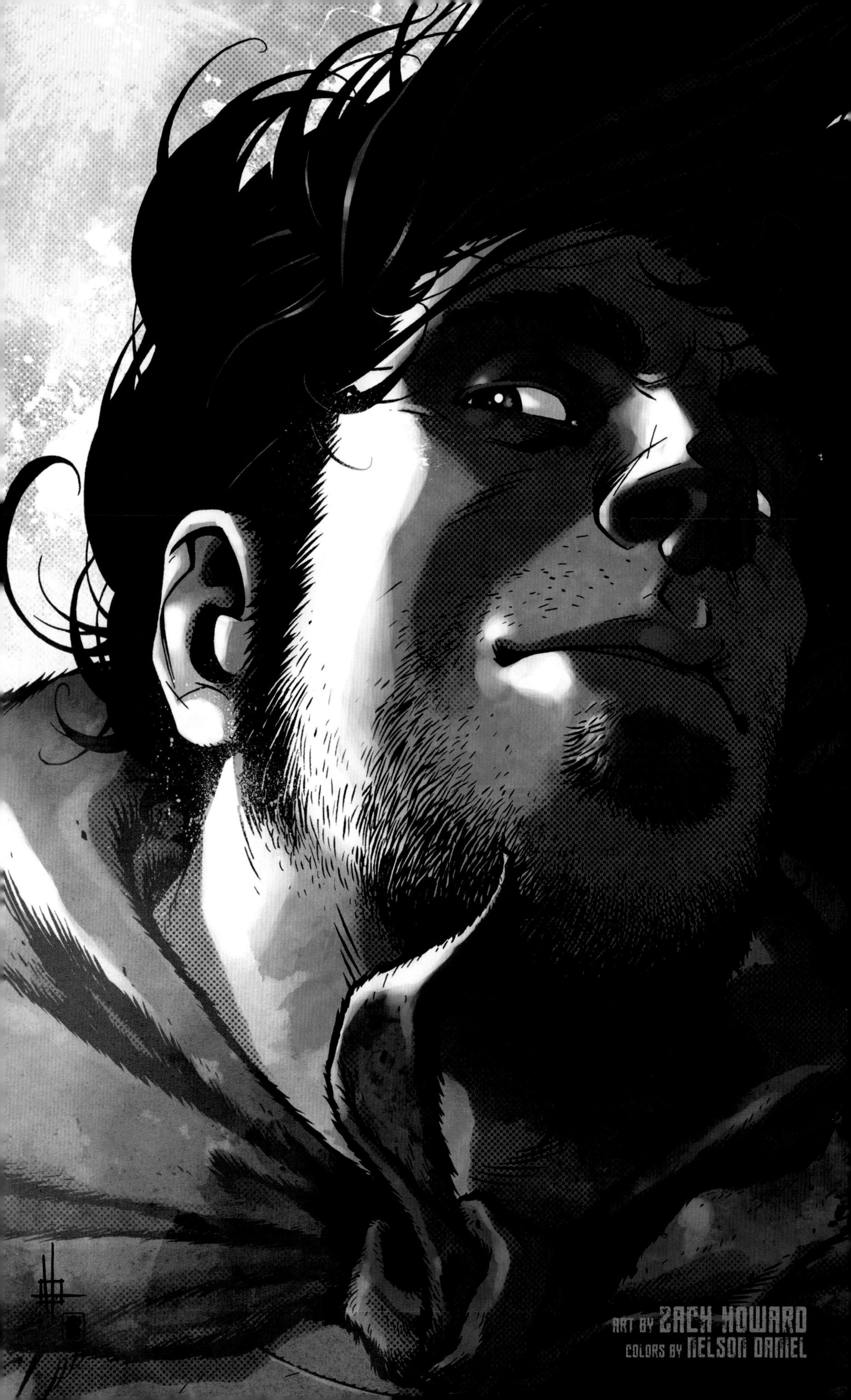
ART BY ZACH HOWARD
COLORS BY NELSON DANIEL

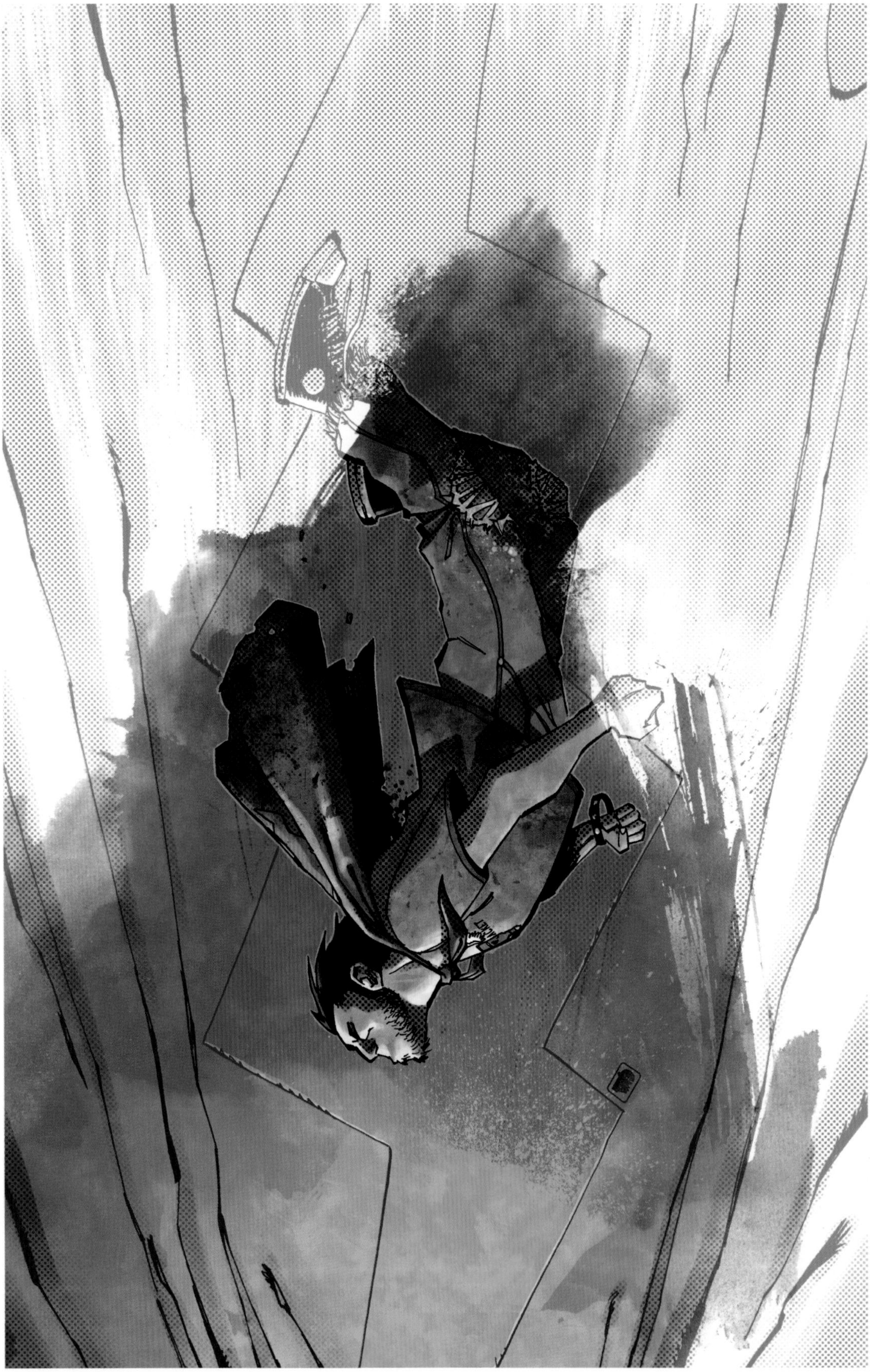

ART BY NELSON DANIEL

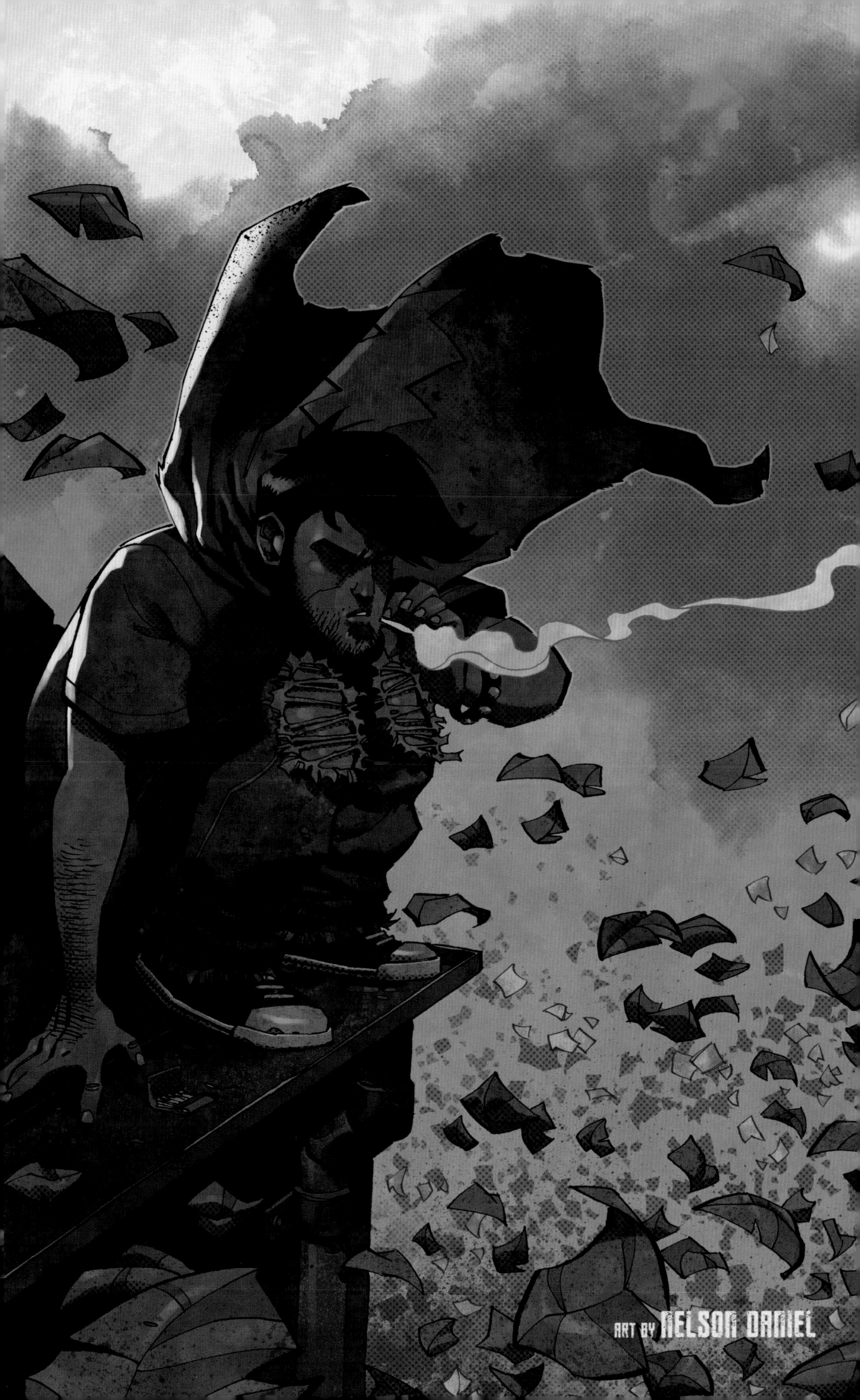
ART BY NELSON DANIEL

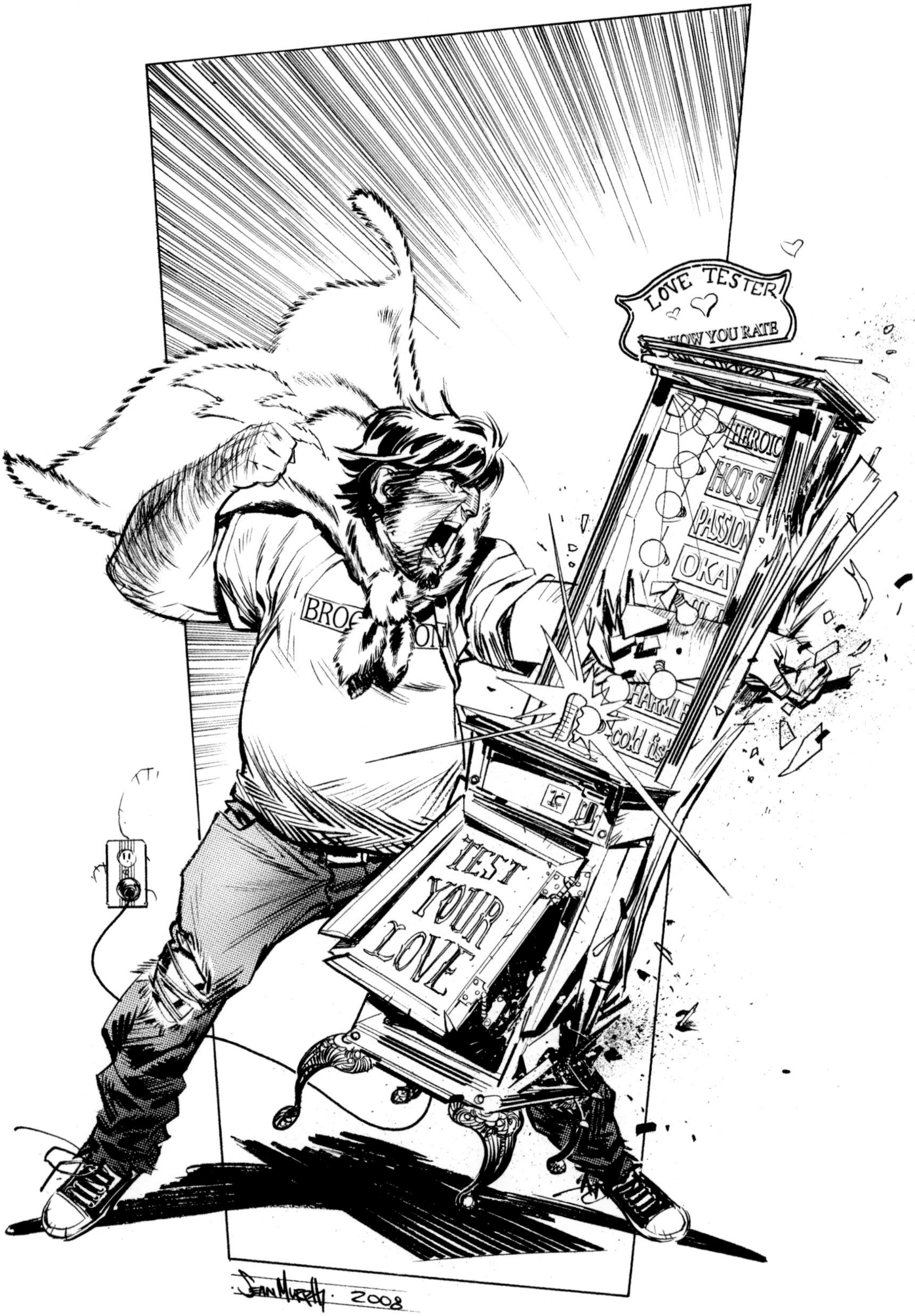
LOVE TESTER
HOW YOU RATE
HEROIC
PASSION
OKAY
TEST YOUR LOVE
SEAN MURPHY 2008

ART BY **SEAN MURPHY**

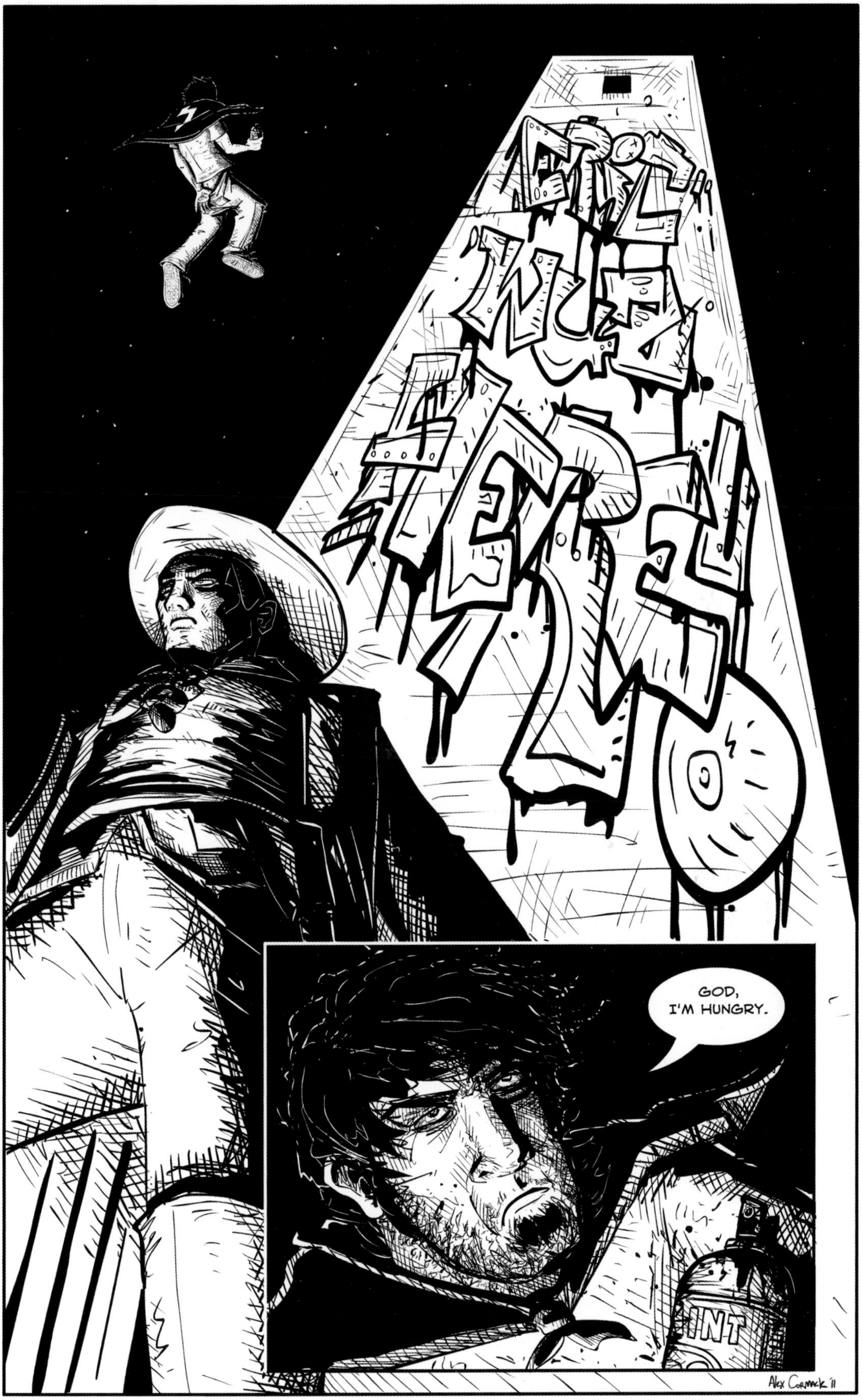
GOD, I'M HUNGRY.
Alex Cormack '11

ART BY ALEX CORMACK

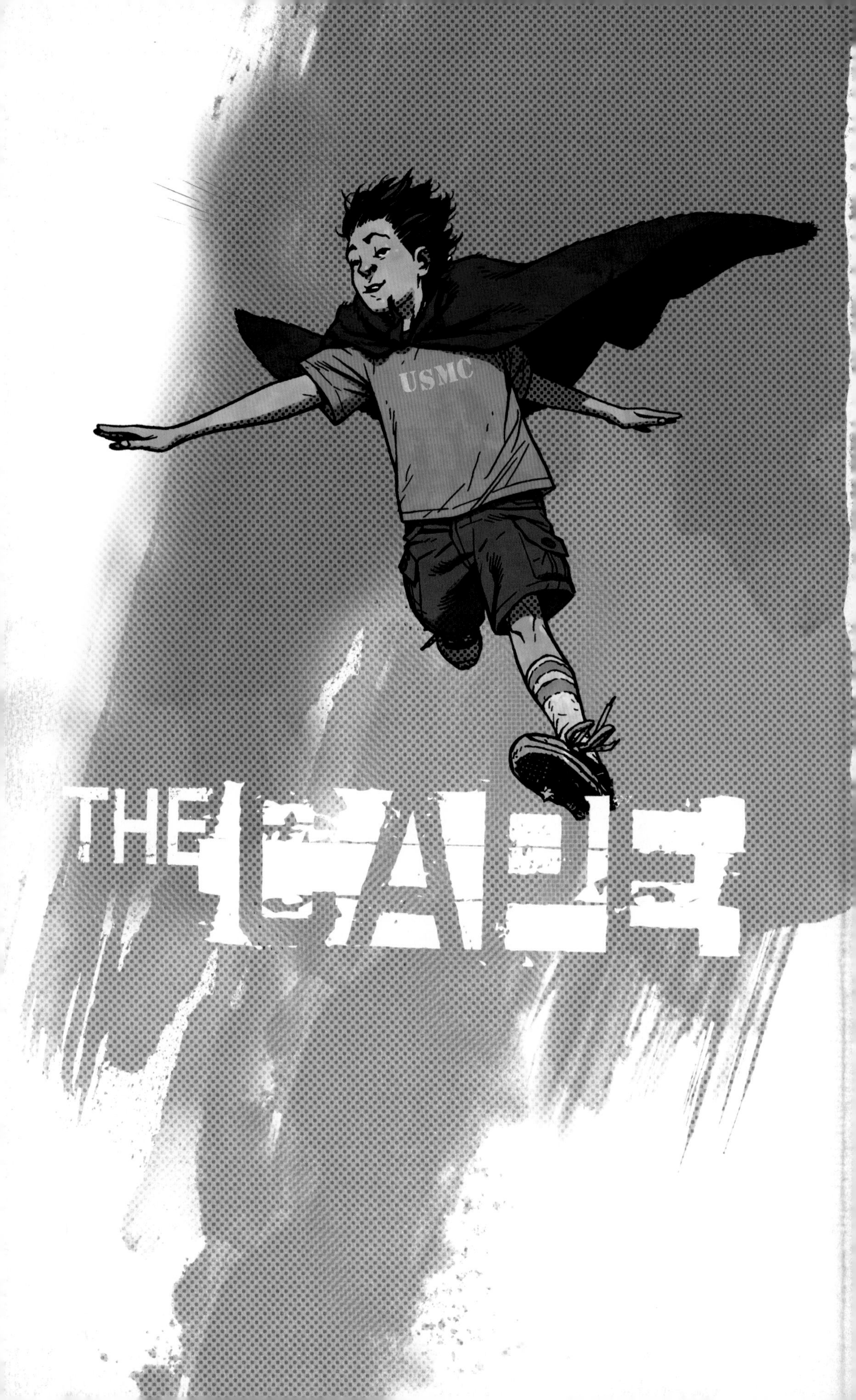
USMC
THE CAPE